O PLATA O PLOMO?

¿O Plata O Plomo?

¿O PLATA O PLOMO?

"SILVER OR LEAD?"

This is a true story, no matter how unbelievable.

JAMES KUYKENDALL

¿O Plata O Plomo?

Copyright © 2005 by JAMES KUYKENDALL.

Library of Congress Number: 2005905999

All rights reserved. No part of this book may be reproduced or transmitted in any form or by any means, electronic or mechanical, including photocopying, recording, or by any information storage and retrieval system, without permission in writing from the copyright owner.

This book was printed in the United States of America.

CONTENTS

Prologue 9
Chapter 1 Voices 12
Chapter 2 The City of Flowers 19
Chapter 3 Missing 36
Chapter 4 Combing the City 65
Chapter 5 Leyenda 77
Chapter 6 El Mareño 93
Chapter 7 Dragnet 108
Chapter 8 Lope de Vega 133
Chapter 9 The CIA Transcript and Juan Antonio Brito 146
Chapter 10 Innocents Abroad 160
Chapter 11 Trouble in the North 179
Chapter 12 Zacatecas Revisited 196
Chapter 13 Rafael Caro and the Rio Yaqui 227
Chapter 14 The Militant 237
Chapter 15 Operation Padrino 242
Chapter 16 Black, White and Gray/DFS, DEA and the CIA 257
Chapter 17 The Aftermath 270
Index 289

¿O Plata O Plomo?

"Ride toward the sound of the guns."
Jeb Stuart
Civil war general
Army of the south

"Ahora lo veran, cabrones!"
Santos Villareal-Molina
"El Soldado"
Mexican arms smuggler

James Kuykendall

This is a memoir, about one period of my life and about the people I shared that period with. Most of what is here I saw and heard, with my own eyes and ears. There is also hearsay, but it is relevant. This is not fiction but there are a few fictional names. Even though more than thirty years have passed since these events took place there are still people whose identity should be protected.

This story is from my point of view. Since this is a true story, the facts are just that. It has been told before and, undoubtedly, will be told again. My purpose was not to set the record straight but simply to tell it as I saw it, in my words. It is, unfortunately, a first person account.

This book is dedicated to Pete and Paulette, to Roger and Suzie, to Harvey and Alan, and especially, to the memories of Shaggy, Butch, Miriam, Susan, Capi and Kiki. To all the cool evenings and tension filled days. You were simply the best!

PROLOGUE

Taking one copy and a tape player, I found an empty room and put on the earphones; the sound came through; it was Kiki's voice; very weak and obviously in pain. The recording, or the copy, was of poor quality and the voices came through low in volume. I sat there, listening to the voice of my friend, six months after his death, and to the voices of his interrogators, who might also have been his executioners. The tapes were made just before he died and should contain clues to his death. There was no doubt they contained the motives for his abduction. "Copia 2" immediately preceded "copia 4" in content; it was also somewhat less intelligible.

The very first voice was that of a man, in Spanish, asking. "Let's see, where is the house?"

Then Kiki's reply, very weakly. "I think it's on Topacio."

Kiki explained to his captors how to find a house on Topacio Street in Guadalajara that belonged to a drug trafficker named Ernesto Fonseca. He directed them to turn left off of Mariano Otero Avenue at Manolo's Restaurant and onto Topacio Street, continuing past a traffic circle two blocks, to a house on the corner with a high wall around it.

It was just before Christmas of 1983, when the informant we called "Rodriguez" directed us to a house utilized by the Direcíon Federal de Seguridad (DFS) as a safe house. The informant explained that the house belonged to "Don Neto", (a popular nickname for the infamous drug trafficker, Ernesto Fonseca) and perhaps other drug traffickers as well. The DFS shared it with the traffickers. It was used when they were working together on a drug deal, and the DFS sometimes used it unilaterally to hide hostages they had kidnapped for ransom. Kiki and I picked "Rodriguez" up on an isolated street corner not far from the consulate, giving him a hat and sunglasses to wear and instructing him to slouch down in the rear seat of the car, before proceeding on, following the directions he gave us. At the corner of La Paz and Chapultepec, we turned right and drove several blocks before reaching the traffic circle at Ninos Heroes Avenue. We drove around the circle to the beginning of Mariano Otero Avenue and turned right. Then we traveled southwest on Mariano Otero, under the overpass at the Corona brewery, continuing on and around the traffic circle at the intersection of Lazaro Cardenas Boulevard, bearing to the right to drive on the lateral lane of Mariano Otero, following it to the new Manolo's restaurant, then turning left onto Topacio Street and continuing on around a smaller circle for another block to the corner of Cuarzo, there "Rodriguez" pointed out a very large and expensive house with entrances on both Topacio and Cuarzo. An eight-foot masonry wall surrounded the house and there was an antenna on the roof of the type used by ham radio operators.

"Rodriguez", himself a DFS agent, said. "That's the house, we stay there when we are on an operation and I've seen the city police chief there as well as the comandante of the Federal Judicial Police. And they all used cocaine. They also use the house for big parties; they bring women and a lot of cocaine to these parties. I'm sure they are going to have a party on New Year's Day."

On the tape Kiki continued to respond to the interrogators, giving them the locations of the houses we had learned of; a house belonging to another major trafficker, Juan Jose Quintero-Payan, in the exclusive Colinas de San Javier area; then the location of a small ranch belonging to yet another millionaire drug trafficker on the highway to Manzanillo, just past the Santa Anita golf club. And I remembered that ranch as well, where the traffickers had wild parties, drinking tequila and imported scotch, there were kilos of cocaine and pretty young whores for the guests; where they shot at the horses hooves with machine guns to make them dance.

The questions seem to skip rapidly and sometimes without continuity. The interrogator asked Kiki if he played golf at the Santa Anita club, and if he lived there. He was asked for the addresses of the DEA agents,

¿O Plata O Plomo?

the secretaries, about his DEA training. And question after question about what he knew and how he knew it. And who were our informants? And where did they live? And did he want to die?

CHAPTER 1

VOICES

Tuesday morning, April 16, 1985

Walter White, assistant agent-in-charge of the U.S. Drug Enforcement Administration's office in Mexico City, called from the Embassy. He sort of tested my temper before telling me the Central Intelligence Agency (CIA) had acquired information that the Mexican government possessed a tape recording of what appeared to be an interrogation of DEA agent Enrique "Kiki" Camarena. In the short note the CIA had passed to DEA mention was made of two men's names reportedly revealed to the interrogators. Kiki had named the men as informants, one name was "Jesus Ramirez", of course I knew who Jesus Ramirez was, or wasn't. Jesus Ramirez didn't exist. More correctly that wasn't his real name, it was a figment of my imagination. The real name of the man we called Jesus Ramirez was hidden in a secret file. I had given him the alias to protect his identity the first time we had met, but Kiki had known him in passing and only by his alias. It took a while for me to answer but I told Walter It seemed likely that the information was correct, no one outside our office could have known about Jesus Ramirez.

    That someone would have taped the interrogation I found unnerving and couldn't readily respond to Walter's other questions. After a few moments of strained silence he suggested that I travel to Mexico City to talk. There was always concern about the security of the telephones.

    I took the afternoon flight from Guadalajara on Aeromexico accompanying DEA Special Agent Bill Coonce, who was traveling to Mexico City to meet with the new Administrator of the Drug Enforcement

¿O Plata O Plomo?

Administration, John Lawn. Coonce had been assigned by headquarters to be in charge of what had been dubbed "Operation Leyenda", the investigation into the kidnapping, torture and murder of DEA Special Agent Enrique "Kiki" Camarena. John "Jack" Lawn, an FBI Special Agent, had recently assumed the position of Administrator of the Drug Enforcement Administration and was visiting Mexico City to discuss the investigation with the U.S. Ambassador and Mexican officials. I was, at the time, the Resident Agent in Charge of DEA in Guadalajara.

Upon my arrival at the DEA office in the U.S. Embassy late that afternoon, Walter White showed me the memorandum from the CIA. It didn't really contain much more information beyond that related on the telephone, but there were the names and information they had passed to DEA. Again I feared it must be true, in the note was the reference to an interrogator asking Kiki for the identity of informants and Kiki's response was that a man named Jesus Ramirez had helped us in the past.

Jesus Ramirez was someone I had met and hired as an informant before referring him to Agent Roger Knapp. He was also someone I liked. It was at "La Terraza", a small upstairs restaurant a block from the U.S. Consulate in Guadalajara where we met the first time. He had immediately captured my attention when he talked of some enormous marijuana plantations in northern Mexico. After our initial conversation he was instructed to call the office using the name of Jesus Ramirez and arrangements would be made to have an agent from the office meet with him somewhere to discuss the information at length. It was arranged for Roger to talk to him on the telephone when he called and meet with him thereafter. But Jesus Ramirez was not his real name, it was an alias, and it was the only name that Kiki knew for this man.

It was too late in the afternoon to meet with the CIA so we made an appointment for 8 AM on Wednesday.

James Kuykendall

At the meeting the CIA representative didn't have much to add to the information. According to them, the taped recording had allegedly been found in the house in Puerto Vallarta where the infamous drug trafficker Ernesto Fonseca had been arrested the previous week. The first person of authority in the Mexican Government to possess the tape was the head of the Jalisco state preventive police, Pablo Aleman-Diaz. It was that unit which had reportedly arrested Fonseca. The authorities in Mexico City now had the tape recording but, for reasons unknown to the CIA, were keeping its existence secret.

From the meeting with the CIA, Walter and I returned to the DEA offices or a meeting with Jack Lawn. Others at the meeting were, Senior Inspector Bill Coonce, Special Agent in Charge Edward Heath and Assistant Attorney General Stephen Trott. After I related my conclusions a discussion ensued to determine how to proceed. The decision was made to raise the subject to the Mexican Attorney General, Sergio Garcia, during the meeting with him that morning. At that meeting the Mexican Attorney General reportedly pled ignorance of the existence of the recording but promised to investigate. The meeting then continued briefly on other matters but was cut short by the Mexicans.

After Jack Lawn, Steve Trott and Ed Heath returned to the Embassy a call from the Attorney General's office confirmed the existence of the recording. The caller advised that Jack Lawn and his group could listen to a tape recording that afternoon. Again the three men journeyed to Attorney General Garcia's office and listened to what was almost certainly an interrogation of DEA Special Agent Enrique Camarena. The voice of Agent Camarena was weak and there were threats of bodily harm and death from the interrogators. The interrogators were obviously Mexican from their accents. The interrogation, conducted entirely in Spanish, appeared to be directed at discovering what information Kiki had about the activities of Guadalajara drug traffickers. Both Edward Heath and Steve Trott were fluent in Spanish and Heath was able to recognize Kiki's voice.

¿O Plata O Plomo?

The Attorney General refused to release the tape, or a copy, to the three U.S. officials, explaining that it would be too embarrassing for the Mexican Government to publicly admit its existence. Edward Heath was later allowed to listen to, not only one, but five cassette tape recordings. Two were recordings of the interrogation of Kiki; one was the recording of interrogations of an unknown man and, possibly, his wife; another was the recording of some DEA radio traffic in Guadalajara and the fifth was practically inaudible. The Mexican Government, however, remained steadfast in its refusal to turn over copies to the United States Government.

A couple of months later the CIA was able to obtain a transcript of the interrogation of Agent Camarena. When I visited DEA headquarters I was permitted to read it. There were the names I had heard before and many more, there was also a substantial amount of information about the investigations we had worked on and there were insistent questions by the interrogators of Kiki asking for more, asking for names of informants but also for the locations of the traffickers, as if they were themselves police looking for the traffickers.

The transcript covered forty-three pages and allegedly covered both sides of a tape recording. It was typed in question and answer form and very explicit as to the kind of language the interrogators had used in their questioning. Reference was made to complaints of discomfort from Special Agent Camarena and it was obvious from some of the comments written in the transcript that Kiki was tied, or bound, during the interrogation. He was asked about the type of automobiles the DEA office had in Guadalajara, he was asked about the homes and businesses the traffickers had in Guadalajara and he was asked for the residences of the agents and secretaries in the DEA office.

There was a line in the transcript that suggested the interrogation had taken place on the first day of Kiki's abduction.

James Kuykendall

The interrogator said. "You aren't going to be here just one day, it could be three or four days."

There were explicit questions from the interrogators about enforcement operations and there were searching questions in other areas where they obviously weren't well informed. They continued throughout with the charade that they were police, of some sort, interested in locating the major narcotics traffickers residing in Guadalajara, specifically Miguel Angel Felix-Gallardo and Rafael Caro-Quintero. They asked about other traffickers also; Juan Esparragoza-Moreno alias "El Azul" ("the blue one"), so named because he was so dark in complexion, and Javier Barba, a lawyer and ex-student activist turned drug trafficker. And they were especially interested in the identity of the informant who had been instrumental in helping us find and destroy a major marijuana growing operation in the Mexican state of Zacatecas.

At one point in the transcript Kiki related a story we had been told by an informant we called "Juan Garcia". The story contained an allegation that the Mexican Minister of Defense, General Juan Arrevalo-Gardoqui, was involved in the protection of large marijuana fields in that state. The interrogators were especially interested in this and asked several pointed questions about how to find "Juan Garcia".

Kiki didn't tell them the complete truth. He answered their questions, who wouldn't have under the circumstances, but he told them a false name and gave incorrect details about the case. He didn't know this information would lead the interrogators to another man they incorrectly identified as the "Juan Garcia" Kiki had named as the informant in the case.

The Guadalajara DEA office had not been involved in an enormous marijuana bust in the state of Chihuahua in November of 1984 but the interrogators apparently thought otherwise, as they asked question after question about the operation, and about the Mexican official, Miguel Aldana-Ibarra, who had led the raids on the marijuana storage center. They were just as insistent about the operations and whereabouts of the skinny drug millionaire, Miguel Angel Felix-Gallardo, and about several large cocaine seizures in Arizona, again believing that the Guadalajara DEA office had been instrumental in the seizures. They also had confidential information about a telephone wiretap of Miguel Felix's offices, which we had worked on with the Mexican Federal Judicial Police.

    The transcript haunted my thoughts through the following months and I often re-read it in my mind, always looking for the answer to the question, "How could anyone, no matter how brash, no matter how powerful, do anything so stupid as to abduct an agent of the United States Government, a Drug Enforcement Administration Special Agent on official business in Mexico, carrying credentials signed by the Mexican foreign ministry allowing him to live and work in that country?"

    The pressure was relentless on the Mexican government to turn over copies of the tapes to the U.S. and that persistence eventually paid off. After all, he was our man, we wanted justice and we weren't getting it. On August 28, 1985 Walter White finally received copies of the tapes from the Mexican government and sent them to me in Guadalajara, still sealed in the large envelope he had been given. I flew to Washington, D.C. the following day and on August 30 delivered them to the "Operation Leyenda" team. The envelope was unsealed and copies immediately made.

    There were five rather ordinary cassette tapes in the package I delivered to Washington, obviously not the original tapes either as they were each marked with the word "copia" and numbered 1 through 5.

    "Copia 1" was very short, radio traffic apparently overheard and recorded, from the DEA radio in Guadalajara on March 5 and 8. "Copia 2" and "copia 4" were the interrogations of Enrique Camarena; "Copia 2" was brief, the cassette was only half full and the interrogation was certainly picked up sometime after it began, in other words the interrogation began long before the recordings were started or, more likely, the cassette had been altered, or shortened, at some point.

James Kuykendall

One side of "Copia 3" contained the interrogation of a man known as Antonio Brito and that of his wife, or girlfriend, on the other.

"Copia 5" was almost unintelligible. It would be almost two years before it would be determined that it was another copy of "Copia 4".

The transcript previously obtained by the CIA was not represented on any of the tapes.

Several working copies of the original tapes were made and the "original" tapes were stored as evidence for use in any future legal proceedings, if indeed that ever came to pass. Numerous personnel, investigators, and analysts and probably even a few curiosity seekers within DEA studied the working copies. Somewhere within the interrogations lay the information as to the motive for the kidnappings and the identity of the mastermind or masterminds

CHAPTER 2
THE CITY OF FLOWERS

Guadalajara, Jalisco; February 1985

America's war on drugs began, again, on February 7, 1985. The chilling news that someone, most probably narcotics traffickers, had kidnapped a U.S. Drug Enforcement Administration Special Agent brought the U.S. news media to Guadalajara in force. Their perseverance over the next few weeks, in the face of their hotel rooms being mysteriously burglarized, managing editors back home wanting an end to the story and some heavy handed tactics by Mexican authorities, would eventually be the most significant part of the pressure on the Mexican government to take what action they did.

The Mexican government had never had to deal with a totally free press, and they did what they could to suppress it. Satellite transmission time was somehow not available when needed by the visiting press so the tapes were hand carried to the states to meet deadlines. In Mexico City, where several U.S. TV cable channels were available for rent, the nightly news broadcasts from the country to the north were replaced by local programming. With few notable exceptions, Mexican newspapers printed stories biased against the DEA with little mention of the powerful narcotics traffickers.

Nevertheless, the nightly news in the United States carried the running story of the failed attempts to locate Enrique Camarena, and of the conspicuous absence of the hundreds of arrogant drug traffickers who had previously inhabited the city and its clubs and restaurants. The anger and frustration felt by so many Americans over the loss of their soldier and the revelation of so much obvious corruption related to the narcotics traffic began to take seed and would eventually create a movement that even the president of the United States could not ignore. Eventually he and his wife belatedly jumped on the bandwagon, responding with their token "Just say no" campaign.

The "narco-journalists" really came into their own during this period as the networks and news publishers saw the public's interest in real life, real time drama. The drug problem and drug trafficking had been the subject of countless movies and books but the public was now convinced it was real. The bad guys were too often depicted as not so bad guys and given Robin Hood type personas. Now narcotics trafficking and the involvement of governments with the traffic was big news. For the narcotics trafficker in Mexico this was the end of anonymity.

What the U.S. news hawks found when they arrived in Guadalajara was violence and fear.

To the north the city is stopped from expansion by the deep canyon where the Rio Santiago flows. But it was growing in every other possible direction.

The city had changed through the years. Some of the old attractions were gone, the flower markets near the Aqua Azul park were missing, the Plaza de los Mariachis had deteriorated greatly and the traffic was something only a long time resident could manage, but the city still had its tree lined streets and sidewalk cafes, it's Mariachi music and blue eyed citizens, it's colonial beauty and native artisans and above all it's fantastic climate, the climate that had attracted so many Americans there to retire. There had been others attracted to the incomparable pleasures of living there also.

The city was experiencing rapid and ill-planned growth but Guadalajara remained one of the most beautiful cities in the world, and one of the most exciting. Guadalajara didn't display too much of the poverty that is present in any Latin American city, especially the large ones. The streets were clean, the people well dressed, smart restaurants and shops were everywhere and the automobiles were of fairly recent vintage. Quaint old hotels downtown vied with modern high rises on the west side of the city. Malls of every size were found throughout; there were theaters, clubs, museums, street magicians, quiet neighborhoods, and on and on. In short, a nice place to live.

The Mexican state of Jalisco is the birthplace of the famous mariachi bands and the city of Guadalajara is where they show them off. In restaurants, clubs, festivals, sidewalk cafes and at private fiestas their romantic spirit-lifting music fills the air and converts the most skeptical.

Mexican cowboys showed up everywhere in their high heeled boots and regional hats. The women are beautiful and wonderfully unsophisticated. People from the countryside were to be found on every street corner, some selling homemade wares and others simply gawking at the wonders of modern civilization. Guadalajara may not be Dallas or Los Angeles but rural Mexico in 1985 was a long way from the twentieth century.

Most of Guadalajara's suburbs were family farms and small villages a scant ten years earlier. The picturesque villages that still surrounded the city were being crowded out of existence but the people clung to the past as it disappeared around them. On any Sunday thousands of city weary people flocked to the small country towns to enjoy a Mexican rodeo, to visit a village fair, or just to relive the life they abandoned when they migrated from their own village.

The city grew, more people came, each with his own interest. Guadalajara in 1985 was a city of some two million people with few foreigners, but throughout Mexico the people were abandoning the rural countryside and moving to the cities in search of a less arduous way of life. Guadalajara principally attracted people from the west coast of Mexico and from the central highlands. One of the principal contributors to this migration was the state of Sinaloa, located along the eastern shore of the Sea of Cortez. The state directly south of Jalisco is Michoacan and many of its rural inhabitants also came to live in Guadalajara. The overcrowded capitol of Mexico also lost its share as the city dwellers came to Guadalajara to have a little space in which to move around and try to enjoy a better life in the city of the Tapatios. With this influx of people the city had to change, the wealthy spent their money on big homes in Providencia, Ciudad del Sol, Colinas de San Javier and other areas developed to meet the demands of the newly arrived migrants with money.

The Fiesta Americana and Hyatt Regency, modern skyscraper hotels complete with open atriums and glass walled elevators, had been finished. The foreign tourists, the majority of them from the United States, would enjoy Guadalajara's rustic charms in more luxury than ever. The travel agencies in the states were sending record numbers of tourists to Mexico in those days and it wasn't really cheap. The beaches at Puerto Vallarta and Manzanillo were also getting their share. Sales pitches and colorful brochures appealed to the travelers to get to know the "real" Mexico.

But there was a sub-culture in Guadalajara that the tourists in their search for the "real" Mexico didn't see. A powerful and wealthy group of neo-rich was gaining control behind the scenes. The money generated by the traffic in narcotics was having an inalterable effect on the country. There were billions to be made, and made fast, feeding the voracious appetites of the drug hungry Americans, and there was no shortage of men, and women, eager to share in this illegal bonanza. Guadalajara had become the site of the headquarters of the major drug traffickers in the western hemisphere.

A place known for tradition, beauty, an ideal climate and friendly people but with the legacy of the mordida (bribe) system from colonial Spain and France firmly entrenched. This wasn't new, just more sinister. There had been narcotics trafficking in Guadalajara for as long as there had been a market for narcotics and, in the sierra of Jalisco, marijuana and opium poppies have been cultivated for decades.

James Kuykendall

The king pin of Sinaloa's drug lords, Pedro Aviles, made his home in Guadalajara for a while but, preferring the more rural life style, returned to Culiacan as soon as he felt safe.

The notorious Texas drug trafficker and murderer, Fred Carrasco, made Guadalajara his base of operations for a few years and is credited with more than forty murders in the area before he was captured and returned to Texas. Carrasco received a life sentence in 1974 for attempting to kill a police officer. Subsequently he engineered an unsuccessful prison break in Huntsville, Texas in which he was killed along with several other prisoners and their innocent hostages in a bloody shootout with authorities.

The flower children of the sixties often made their way to the mountains of Jalisco to buy marijuana and retrace their steps to the U.S. border where the luck of the draw would assign them a U.S. Customs Inspector whose search, or lack of it, might send them to jail or let them sail through with their dope.

The Herrera heroin trafficking family of Durango financed opium poppy cultivations in the Jalisco highlands for the heroin markets of Chicago.

When the Mexican government began to put pressure on the traffickers in Sinaloa in the seventies they moved and the two most popular places they chose for relocation were Tijuana, Baja California and Guadalajara, Jalisco.

But really, who wouldn't have picked the city of Guadalajara? With a world renowned university, the unequalled climate, the local arts and music and all the things that make it a nice place to live, a nice place to raise a family. Even dope dealers have families. In fact they usually have several.

Narcotics traffickers have tremendous appetites for women, alcohol, music, gambling, guns, fighting roosters, fast cars and fast horses, big houses, ranches and cocaine, not necessarily in that order, or any order. That doesn't sound too different from the desires of many men in this world. But dope dealers stop at nothing to obtain the objects and sensations they crave so much, and the feelings and well-being of non-dope dealers and even other dope dealers are not of much concern to them. A narcotic trafficker wants something? The only thing limiting him is the weight of his money and degree of his influence. In Mexico money is more important than influence. Sometimes it's more important than life.

With the traffickers raking it in, a lot of people were not reluctant to be on the edges to pick up the chaff. And in any situation where wealth is flowing so freely, corruption and all its accompanying vices flourished.

Prostitution, drugs, gambling and murder were rampant in this paradise. Real estate sales soared, hotels and restaurants were built, official pockets were lined and prosperity was everywhere, in short everything that money, a lot of money, can buy was being bought. To this beautiful place they came, bringing with them their violence and vices, their contempt for other people's lives and their knowledge of the Mexican officials' weakness for the quick and easy road to riches.

When Luis Echeverria assumed the position of President of the Republic of Mexico in 1970 Mexico was still reeling from an uncharacteristic determination by the U.S. Government to do something about the runaway drug problem in the United States.

U.S. President Richard Nixon's administration had taken a bold and ambitious step toward this end with what was called "Operation Intercept", a unilateral plan to reduce the smuggling of drugs across the U.S./Mexican border. Along with whatever else they may be remembered for, the baby boomers had an enormous appetite for drugs and lived in the most permissive age yet experienced by the United States. Although many of the baby boomers would not survive the drug epidemic of the sixties, even the threat of painful death did not slow their drug consumption. They ingested and injected whatever each new drug guru prescribed. Since the United States government felt it had a duty to prevent its young citizens from killing themselves or becoming living vegetables it decided to do something about the problem. The users did not appear inclined to quit, so enforcement seemed to be the answer and the Nixon administration pushed enforcement like never before.

Mexico was the largest foreign source of supply for these drugs and when the Nixon administration began to try to attack the problem they decided the supply of drugs from Mexico should be shut off, if possible.

The border between the United States and Mexico is one of the world's most accessible. There are no raging rivers to cross, only the muddy Rio Grande. There are no towering snow-capped peaks, no chain link fences with machine-gun toting guards and the inspectors that staff the ports and bridges along that border spent much of their time looking for prohibited fruit and vegetables, and the good neighbor policy has always been the norm for visitors.

The administration's solution was to institute 100% inspection of people and vehicles at the ports and bridges and to increase the number of customs and immigration personnel working the river and land boundary between the ports. The operation was originally to run for sixty days before evaluation, with plans to continue if successful.

Secret though it was supposed to be, the word was out long before the plan was put into effect but no one could really believe the rumors that the U.S. government was going to block the border and when the target date arrived the public was caught by surprise. The lines of cars stretched for dozens of blocks in border cities such as Nuevo Laredo, Juarez and Tijuana as the Customs Inspectors performed minute inspections of each and every vehicle. It took hours to cross into the United States at almost every point along the border. Seizures of drugs were disappointingly low but the operation would be deemed a resounding success for another reason.

Within days the clamor from every sector doing business along the border or between the two countries began to be heard in Washington. American businessmen were losing millions as Mexican shoppers stopped braving the lines to cross to the states. Except for the people who were forced by necessity to cross back and forth, every day saw fewer crossers.

U.S. tourists were beginning to redevelop a taste for American beer as the three and four-hour wait to return to the U.S. was too big a price to pay for the visits to the Mexican shops and bars. Since there were more law enforcement types along the border, apprehensions of illegal aliens increased and their deportation taxed the always-delicate Mexican job market. Pressure was being put on the border economy and it was in trouble. Businessmen on both sides of the border were screaming for a stop to the inspections. After all, they weren't dope dealers, why should they suffer. The government should arrest drug traffickers and leave honest businessmen to conduct their honest business.

Meanwhile the dope smugglers waited to see how long Uncle Sam could fade the heat as the criticism mounted. For once Uncle Sam didn't bend so easily. For twenty-one long days and nights the cars overheated while inching forward in the traffic lanes as the Customs and Immigration inspectors really began to get into the spirit of searching. Tempers were short and tourists from both sides decided to explore their own back yards first.

Before the searches eased up the number of crossers had reduced to a trickle. Hundreds of Arrow shirts sat on shelves in exclusive men's stores, waiting for nonexistent Mexican buyers while U.S. shoppers paid a little more for beer and whiskey at home.

The smugglers desperately tried to get a few loads through and a few loads were seized. From a strictly arrest and seizure point of view the statistics were anything but impressive but the operation was a success and the real success came from pressure, pressure on the Mexican government, a government that can't take too much. Its position is too precarious.

The drug traffic, like the annual exodus of the unemployed illegals seeking jobs in the United States, was one of the safety valves that allowed the government to maintain its hold on power. Since many of the leaders of

James Kuykendall

the government weren't known for having any essential skills to fall back on if they lost their jobs, urgent action had to be taken.

Emergency consultations with Washington brought a new plan into effect. "Operation Cooperation" was born, a joint effort by the two countries to reduce the amount of drugs crossing from Mexico into the United States, a problem that the government of Mexico hadn't realized existed until the long lines began to form at the ports of entry. Instantly there was a slackening of the search process at the ports and the honest businessmen returned to hawking their wares.

But something had to be done or the hard won but meager gains would be lost. U.S. federal agents were sent into the drug producing areas of Mexico and, along with Mexican agents and soldiers, began search and destroy operations. At first this just involved flying around in small planes looking for fields and sending in ground forces, who, after long hikes into remote areas, would manually destroy the fields of marijuana and opium poppies. However, there were more fields than anyone had imagined and they were damn hard to find up in those rugged mountains.

Eventually a method was developed utilizing sophisticated aerial photography to locate the fields and helicopters to spray them with herblcides. Multi-lens cameras and experienced analysts found the fields and spray boom equipped helicopters destroyed them quite handily.

While this continued other agents were at work identifying the people behind this multi-million dollar business and, when they were identified, the pressure was on to do something about them. All the claims by the Mexican government that there was no official involvement in the narcotics traffic wouldn't hold water if the traffickers were allowed to continue their audacious life styles in public. Not surprisingly, the Mexican traffickers weren't cooperating with the program any better than the American dope fiends.

¿O Plata O Plomo?

Notwithstanding that the Nixon administration was in trouble and on the way out, the ball was rolling and President Echeverria sent the military into Culiacan, Sinaloa to rout the traffickers.

Culiacan is the drug capitol of Mexico. Corruption and violence are prevalent. Machine-gun toting young toughs are a part of the local scenery. Young girls are daily carried off to be raped and, later, returned unceremoniously without fear of prosecution. Family feuds result in dozens of deadly gunfights and executions annually; marijuana and opium plants grow on the western slopes of the Sierra Madre within sight of the city.

History has failed to document how the drug traffic began in Sinaloa or why so many people turned to the traffic for their way of life. Sinaloa is not an unpleasant place to live. It has a warm climate and is situated in a highly productive agricultural zone. The Sea of Cortez is at its front door and the Sierra Madre at its back porch. Assuredly there is poverty and illiteracy but less than in other similarly rural areas of Mexico. The Sinaloans are handsome and resourceful. Unfortunately a disproportionate number of them are involved in the trafficking of narcotic substances.

The Sinaloa drug trafficker has his life style. He swaggers through life with a bottle in one hand, a gun in the other and a woman under his arm. He discards the empty bottle for a full one and the familiar woman for a new one but hangs on to the gun in order to protect himself against his own kind.

When the Mexican military went into Culiacan in the mid-seventies, they went up against a proud and brutal people and they responded in kind. The Mexican Federal Judicial Police (MFJP), who accompanied them, also acted with brutality at times and a price would be extracted for that brutality in the years to come. These brutal tactics were successful, however, and the major traffickers bent under the pressure, at least for a while, relocating, principally to Tijuana or Guadalajara, and lowered their profile of violence. But their activities were only curtailed for a while and they would resurface, bolder, badder and better organized than ever, and they would run these organizations from Guadalajara, Jalisco, Mexico.

In the early seventies the U. S. federal law enforcement agencies suddenly discovered that marijuana was being produced in multi-ton quantities in Colombia and that several South American countries were producing hundreds of pounds of cocaine for the American market, effectively replacing Mexico as the number one supplier of drugs to the U.S. Also southeastern and southwestern Asian heroin began to appear in U.S. cities while Mexican heroin became relatively scarce.

Consequently the Drug Enforcement Administration transferred several hundred agents to south Florida to engage this problem. Since DEA had only about 1600 agents at the time, this left the U.S./Mexico border with only token defense. At the same time the Mexican Government appeared to be making inroads against the traffickers in their country so DEA removed many of its agents from that country and increased U.S. presence in South America and Asia.

U.S. Customs had suffered a loss in its drug enforcement authority because of the presidential reorganization in 1973 that bestowed all drug enforcement responsibilities and authority on the newly created Drug Enforcement Administration.

The result was apathy toward the potential resurgence of the problem in Mexico. One would think they would have known better. Obviously the Mexican drug traffickers were watching and waiting.

That is not to say there was no trafficking in Mexico during this time. Some of the more resourceful Mexican dope dealers had journeyed to South America to delve into the coke traffic, making the acquaintance of some enterprising fellows from there, resulting in relationships that would last for many very productive years.

In 1973 Ernesto Fonseca-Carrillo was arrested in Cuenca, Ecuador trying to take delivery of some 30 kilos of Ecuadorian cocaine, some of the highest quality nose candy in the world.

¿O Plata O Plomo?

Fonseca had arrived in Ecuador in a single engine Cessna aircraft piloted by Mauricio Rouselon, himself a veteran marijuana smuggling pilot, having flown pot out of Sinaloa and Sonora into California and Arizona. Accompanying Fonseca and Rouselon on the trip were a beautiful eighteen-year-old named Rosa Ester Valencia-Baez and Rosa's brother, Guadalupe. Rosa Ester was a native of the municipio (roughly translated as a county) of Badiraguato, Sinaloa, as was Fonseca. She was also his latest mistress. The buying trip ended in prison for Fonseca and Rosa Ester's brother. Several months passed before arrangements for Fonseca's release could be made. He was released after payment of a substantial bribe and returned to Mexico where he married Rosa Ester and began another family.

In the middle seventies quality marijuana was somewhat scarce in Mexico because the multi-lens camera equipped search planes and the herbicide spraying helicopters really did work very well.

Juvenal Gomez-Barrajas, a veteran drug trafficker from Jalisco, had a lot of marijuana clients in California who just couldn't break the habit and were complaining about the horrible weed they were being forced to smoke because of the successful eradication campaign. Gomez-Barrajas and a young man named Rene Verdugo made their mark in history by putting together the first large loads of marijuana to be smuggled from Colombia into Mexico by aircraft. Unfortunately for them, a couple of loads got busted by the Mexican army and put a temporary stop to their road to riches.

One of Sinaloa drug czar Pedro Aviles-Perez's bright young followers struck out on his own and tried his hand at the big time. Miguel Angel Felix-Gallardo financed a load of 138 kilograms of cocaine that was seized in Tijuana, Baja California in February of 1977, but that definitely was not his first foray into the field. The bust resulted in a warrant for his arrest, a warrant that was never served.

By 1978 the Mexican drug traffickers began in earnest to try the resolve of the U.S. Government. They found it lacking. Their time had come again. Mexico's re-emergence as a major drug-producing nation roughly began about January 1977 and flourished through December 1982. Not so coincidentally, so did the presidential tenure of Jose Luis Lopez-Portillo. Jose Luis Lopez-Portillo left office in January 1983, but the drug traffic was then so dominant that changes in administration could not affect it. Too many people had been compromised. The system was too dependent on the traffic.

During the presidential years of Luis Echeverria several major traffickers were imprisoned and remained in prison for long periods of time. The marijuana and opium poppy eradication effort was developed into an effective program through the use of the multi-lens camera search aircraft and the narcotics traffickers, more or less, lived a furtive, uncertain life.

In contrast, during the years Jose Luis Lopez-Portillo occupied the presidential chair, no major drug trafficker was imprisoned, (the minor ones that were arrested quickly bought their freedom), the expensive and effective multi-lens camera aircraft were hidden away, never to be seen again, and the traffickers crawled out from under their rocks. Unfortunately, one of those rocks must have been lying just outside Guadalajara.

Additionally, the U.S. Government was concerned with other U.S. interests in Mexico as American investors flooded Mexico with millions during the seventies and the Mexican oil discoveries increased dramatically. The Carter administration courted the Mexican government, attempting to acquire rights to its petroleum and alleviate the oil crisis. Even if DEA had bothered to analyze what was happening in Mexico, they would have been ignored.

When the Sinaloa traffickers arrived in Guadalajara they found a criminal underground already well connected with the local officials and ready to welcome them into the fold.

One of the most notorious crime bosses was Antonio Alcaraz-Ascencio. A close friend and compadre of the Director of the Jalisco State Judicial Police, Carlos Aceves-Fernandez, he operated several illegal gambling houses as well as the most active rooster-fighting establishment in Guadalajara. With his oversize ears, corpulent body and greasy complexion, he appeared as sleazy as he was.

Alcaraz made the out of town traffickers feel at home and introduced them to his friends. They were his kind of people and they had a lot of money. They could be expected to have a lot more if they could find a safe haven from which to operate. Antonio Alcaraz had been a busy entrepreneur in his life, becoming wealthy from a humble beginning by catering to the desires of the sporting element in the city and becoming heavily involved in the smuggling of American luxury products to the rich Tapatios.

In those days Mexican appliances, toys, electronics and clothes were of inferior quality and Mexicans would pay premium prices for smuggled U.S. merchandise. Mexico had some strict laws governing the importation of U.S. products and stiff duties for those items which could be imported. With a little grease on the appropriate palms, the merchandise slid into Guadalajara without a problem.

Another person of tremendous influence in the local underworld, and with whom the traffickers had an instant common interest, was a woman named
Maria Ester Camberos-Gomez. Ester Camberos owned almost all the houses of prostitution in Guadalajara and held much sway over the operation of those she didn't. An ex-prostitute herself, born in 1944, Ester Camberos was more commonly known as "la Comanche" for her past performances in Guadalajara's classier brothels as a beautiful exotic dancer dressed in her version of a Comanche Indian princess' costume, although an uncle claimed to have put the nickname for her fierce, defiant character. Either way, working her way up through the ranks from just another pretty young whore to the position of the supreme madam of Guadalajara's houses of

prostitution afforded her the opportunity to know just about anyone with any influence.

As another purveyor of goods and services to the sporting crowd, "la Comanche" was well acquainted with the rich and corrupt. Although prostitution wasn't exactly illegal, it was controlled, and those controls could become very strict if the right payments weren't made to the right people.

The problem with payoffs is that the person receiving the payoff becomes liable to the person making the payoff, and vice versa. Once you take the money (or service) from someone to permit them to commit an unauthorized act, you are subject to their denouncement, so you keep on taking and permitting.

And, once you've made that first payoff to commit the unauthorized act, you have to keep on paying to feed the greed of the person you helped corrupt.

Ester Camberos owned a house of prostitution named "La Comanche", another called "Guadalajara de Dia" and, in association with the then Governor of Jalisco, Flavio Romero de Velasco, in 1983 purchased the old Hotel La Giralda to convert into a nightclub and casino complex named "Aztlan". Ester Camberos had been the mistress of several politically powerful men and understood men and their vices very well. She became an employer of dangerous men as bodyguards for her whorehouses as well as an associate and procurer for the wealthy drug lords.

There were others, less powerful but still willing to assist the newcomers to feel at home, and there would be others later who, having watched the millions flow in, would also offer their services. Businessmen, politicians, police, student activists, bankers would all be a part of the service industries created to support the traffickers and their activities. Guadalajara accommodated itself to the traffickers.

It was the informant we called "Rodriguez" who one day in 1984 told us the story of the bold narcotics trafficker who strode, grinning, into the offices of the Federal Judicial Police in Guadalajara and confronted the man

¿O Plata O Plomo?

who had just transferred in as the new comandante. The trafficker knew he had the upper hand by virtue of his connections in the federal government in Mexico City. The comandante knew it too. The trafficker asked the Federal officer, "¿Que quieres, comandante, o plata o plomo?" (What do you want, comandante, silver or lead?) As usual, the comandante opted for job, and life, security.

Guadalajara is a beautiful city. Physically it is five thousand feet above sea level and located adjacent to a deep canyon, with hills on every horizon. The poor people live in the eastern section of the city, the rich in new developments principally west and south of the city center, and there is a highway loop (called the "periferico") encircling three quarters of the city. It is the second largest city in Mexico and is the capitol of the state of Jalisco.

It is also a state of mind. To think of Guadalajara, Jalisco is to conjure up images of rousing music, smiling maidens, laughing cowboys, rearing stallions, Tequila and fierce pride.

It was a hell of a place to do battle!

James Kuykendall

Marijuana is a weed; it has also had many uses. It is hemp, which is used to make ropes and hawsers. It was grown in the Mid-western portion of the United States by farmers contracted by the U.S. government to meet the war needs for rope. The seed is used to feed parakeets, (after it is sterilized). Marijuana can be grown almost anywhere there are three months of sunshine a year, but it's narcotic qualities won't be realized unless it is grown in a very warm or hot climate. Marijuana use was recorded in ancient Egypt. Just how, when and where it was introduced into Mexico is a matter of conjecture, but from Mexico it found it's way into the United States, brought initially by illegal migrant workers, then experimented with by a few movie actors, Bohemians and musicians in the early years and slowly spreading into U.S. society over three decades. By the nineteen sixties it had reached epidemic proportions. By the nineteen sixties the United States was addicted to marijuana.

Chapter 3
MISSING

It was not yet seven AM on February 8, 1985 when the telephone rang. Shaggy Wallace was on the phone, asking if I had any idea where Kiki might be. Kiki's wife had called him, concerned because Kiki had not come home the previous night. She also told Shaggy that Kiki had failed to show for a luncheon date the previous day but she had thought he was working and just couldn't make it, not an unusual thing for any policeman's wife. I made the same instant conclusion as Shaggy and Mika Camarena. It just wasn't like Kiki to get lost and we had all been acutely aware for some time that it was dangerous for us in Guadalajara.

Victor (Shaggy) Wallace had known Kiki for many years, working together as police officers in Calexico, California before they joined the federal government as narcotics investigators. Nicknamed for his unruly mane of hair, Shaggy was an extremely likeable man, tenacious in his profession and with a quiet sense of humor. Fearless, but cautious, he had deep feelings for Enrique Camarena. We recalled the events of the previous day between us and could think of no reason why Kiki would have failed to spend the night at home. We quickly made plans to look for him. Shaggy, typically cool and calm, said he would take his wife to stay with Mrs. Camarena while I began to call contacts and friends. After a few unproductive telephone calls to mutual friends, I dressed hurriedly and drove to the consulate.

It was still early and the streets were empty of traffic. The air in Guadalajara in February is cool with just a hint of humidity, the trees are richly foliaged and line both sides of the street on which the U.S. Consulate is located, blocking the sunlight and giving it a quiet, serene atmosphere.

¿O Plata O Plomo?

There was no traffic and there were no cars parked on the street as I approached the corner of Libertad and Progresso streets. There was a small restaurant on the corner in those days, it was called "Camelot" and we had received permission from the management to park our cars in the parking spaces alongside the restaurant because the parking lot behind the consulate had been closed to consulate employees since early January.

There, under the shadows of the trees and alone, parked where I had last seen it on the previous evening, was Kiki's vehicle. Before I parked my own vehicle I said a silent prayer that the day we all feared had not yet arrived.

The vehicle, a blue 1985 Ford pickup, should not have been there. Kiki was like a cowboy with his horse, he just didn't like to walk anywhere. He didn't like to ride with anyone else driving. Where others would take a taxi to government offices where parking was scarce, Kiki insisted on driving even if it meant time wasted in searching for parking. The unexplained presence of the truck without its driver was an ominous indication that something was indeed wrong. Parking near Kiki's truck I hesitantly approached the vehicle. It has been a long time now but I still remember how the pickup appeared that morning, keeping a lonely vigil for a man who would never return. The lack of dew under the vehicle indicated that it had not been disturbed during the night.

The door was unlocked and the alarm turned off. Kiki had delighted in designing that alarm with all the lights flashing and the horn honking when it was activated. The addition of five yellow clearance lights on the top of the cab helped it appear to be a Mexican made truck. And he always activated the alarm and locked the doors when he left the truck.

There was nothing of consequence inside the truck and I left it, almost running now in my urgency to find Kiki. There was a policeman standing at the corner near the consulate who answered that he had not seen anyone near the truck. It was fruitless to question him further since the

James Kuykendall

policemen assigned to guard the consulate at night spent most of their time sleeping huddled in blankets or serapes, the assignment not being too exciting but one sought by policemen as being more desirable than guarding banks in that violent era.

Fumbling with combinations and keys I made my way to the DEA offices in the consulate building, finding them empty. A quick glance at Kiki's desk confirmed my fears; yesterday's work was on his desk, something very uncharacteristic. After a call to Mrs. Camarena, who said she still had not heard from Kiki, the search began.

The other DEA personnel were summoned to the office while I called around to friends and associates, without success. The secretaries and agents arrived at the office with nothing positive to report but it really didn't take long to bring the agents in. Guadalajara was, at the time, the most important foreign office in North America but we were only four agents and Kiki had been in the process of being reassigned to San Diego, California with no replacement forthcoming. All of the obvious advantages of living in Guadalajara had dulled in the minds of prospective applicants after Roger Knapp's car was machine gunned in front of his house one morning and two visiting agents had been tailed around the airport by Miguel Angel Felix's thugs. Three agents who had been assigned to come to Guadalajara suddenly found major personal obstacles to their pending transfers and withdrew.

After the dreaded but necessary inquiries at the emergency medical services and hospitals proved negative I called the embassy in Mexico City to talk to my immediate supervisor, Assistant Special Agent-in-Charge Walter White. Walter was also a friend, and that friendship would be taxed seriously in the weeks to follow. Walter could sense the urgency in my voice as he asked all the questions that had to be asked.

"Yes." I answered him. "We have started to check with the hospitals and morgues, and we are starting to check with the police." (A frustrating task of breaking down bureaucratic barriers and dealing with inadequate records.) And, "No, there was no girl friend."

I told Walter that we would continue looking and call him back in an hour to make an official and formal report of the disappearance if we were unsuccessful. The hour passed but our furious efforts were without success and I reluctantly walked to the adjacent offices to report our fears to the Consul General, Richard Morefield. Mr. Morefield proved to be a man of great determination, compassion and courage who, from the moment he heard the news, committed his every resource to help find Kiki. Richard Morefield had been a hostage in the U.S. Embassy in Teheran, Iran for 444 days and didn't need to be told what family and friends go through when loved ones disappear. After listening, he told me that he would contact the Governor of the State of Jalisco, Enrique Alvarez del Castillo, and request his assistance should I deem it necessary. We put this off temporarily, still hoping we might find Kiki through the police or an office contact.

Shaggy Wallace had dropped his wife, Yolanda, at the Camarena home and was now in the office. Guadalajara agent Alan Bachelier and Fidel Sanchez, a young agent from New York temporarily assigned to the office, had gone to the office of the Mexican Federal Judicial Police (MFJP) to request their assistance. The secretaries were calling every conceivable police organization, medical facility, hotel or friend that we could think of. Still our efforts were fruitless and we were all trying hard to fight off the panic. Since we obviously needed help, official notification had to be given to the U.S. Government that an agent was missing. I called Walter White again and told him to advise the Agent in Charge, Edward Heath, that Kiki was missing and had almost certainly been kidnapped. He replied that Heath had been in the room when I had called earlier and had learned at that time of our conversation. I also told Walter that we had informed the Federal Judicial Police locally and requested their assistance. He tried to reassure me and hung up, on his way to report the kidnapping to Edward Heath.

James Kuykendall

Walter returned my call within minutes to say that Edward Heath would contact Manuel Ibarra-Herrera, the Director of the Federal Judicial Police, as well as inform the Ambassador and call DEA headquarters in Washington. Back in Guadalajara, things weren't so encouraging, Alan Bachelier learned that there were only three agents at the office of the Mexican Federal Judicial Police (MFJP) and that the office had been left in the care of an agent who appeared willing to help but lacked any authority. The comandante, Alberto Arteaga, and the bulk of the office had apparently gone to the state of Colima looking for the assassins of the Federal Judicial Police Comandante killed there the previous week. The agent did, however, contact the state judicial police who agreed to provide personnel to assist him. However, when he arrived at the offices of the Jalisco State Judicial Police to explain what was happening this assistance was withdrawn pending a formal request from a federal attorney. He hastened back to his offices and a federal attorney was finally located who drafted a letter to the Jalisco State Attorney General's office formally requesting their help. When this was delivered around noon the request was denied pending the filing of a formal missing persons complaint.

From the beginning we hadn't wanted to count on help from the state judicial police. The organization was inept and corrupt, and the director, Carlos Aceves Fernandez, associated openly with Ernesto Fonseca, Antonio Alcaraz and other major criminals and narcotics traffickers.

We weren't that anxious to continue trying to deal with the delaying and impeding tactics of the state judicial police or state attorney general's office so the consul general, Richard Morefield, tried to contact the governor of the state of Jalisco. Throughout that day and the next these calls were never returned and in fact the governor never contacted the consulate to offer his help or his concern or even acknowledge the incident. (Of course he had never been in the least reluctant to call in the past when he wanted a visa or favor for a friend).

¿O Plata O Plomo?

In the early afternoon a conversation between a major narcotics trafficker named Miguel Felix-Gallardo and one of his henchmen, Tomas Valles-Corral, was overheard on the radio scanner located in Shaggy's office, tuned to Felix's radio frequencies. Miguel Felix, using the call sign of M-1, was telling Tomas Valles-Corral (M-2) to meet him at the Chalet Gourmet restaurant (located on Avenida La Paz) and that "everybody" was going to be there. There was no one in the DEA office available to conduct surveillance on the restaurant.

We had begun to receive calls from DEA headquarters in Washington asking for information. We were told of their decision to send agents in for temporary duty to help us. Walter White called again from Mexico City to say that the MFJP director, Manuel Ibarra, was trying to contact Comandante Arteaga and Comandante Lorrabaquio in Colima and send them to Guadalajara. Walter said the MFJP agents were reportedly in the mountains somewhere and had no communications.

Time is critical in a kidnapping. The sooner action is taken the better are the chances of preventing a greater tragedy. For this reason we decided to try again with the state attorney general's office and the state judicial police. Consul General Morefield volunteered to accompany me to the office of the state attorney general to attempt to secure their cooperation, hoping his presence and position might lend some sense of importance to the request. We traveled to the Jalisco state offices on the Calzada Independencia in his chauffeur driven Jeep Wagoneer. At the offices of the Jalisco State Judicial Police we were seated and left to cool our heels. We had to complain loudly before anyone would even speak to us and fully an hour passed before a clerk took my statement and complaint. Then we were escorted to an inner office and again left waiting. The director of the state judicial police, Carlos Aceves Fernandez, who was visibly present in his office throughout this time, ignored us.

James Kuykendall

Again, after our repeated insistence, we were told that a group had been assigned to help us but it was the group supervisor's day off and they were trying to locate him. When asked why they couldn't assign someone who was on duty we were told that the director had himself personally assigned that group, headed by Victor Manuel Lopez-Razon, to investigate the disappearance.

While we were in the office, numerous unsuccessful attempts were made by telephone to locate the group supervisor. In the meantime Carlos Aceves-Fernandez, the director, had slipped out and was unavailable. The Consul General became angry and was attempting to get some action but suddenly there was no one of authority in evidence. We were being stonewalled and were about to leave when an acquaintance walked by and asked what was happening.

After hearing my story, Licenciado Rogelio Levy-Gallardo, a lawyer assigned to the homicide division of the state judicial police, told the clerks that he was an acquaintance of mine and asked to be assigned the case. He was told that the case had already been assigned. He said that he would help with his own group and promised to come over to the consulate right away to talk to me. By now dark was approaching and we hadn't really accomplished anything, so we returned to the jeep and were driven back to the consulate.

While we were at the offices of the state's attorney general I had placed a call to the Consulate reporting on our lack of progress and to check on any news there. During the conversation, agent Alan Bachelier told me that the family of Capitan Alfredo Zavala-Avelar had called to report that Captain Zavala had apparently been kidnapped during the previous afternoon on the highway between the Guadalajara airport and the city while he was returning from an out of town trip. Alfredo Zavala was a pilot for the Mexican Agriculture Department and helped us on those investigations that were in some way related to airplanes or the Guadalajara airport, which was utilized extensively by the major traffickers. Zavala was a valuable asset for our office, but he was also a close friend of everyone there. I told Alan that I was returning to the Consulate and that the state judicial police might be sending over some men to assist. Without much hope we returned to the Consulate to await the arrival of the state judicial police.

By the time we returned to the consulate the telephone lines between Washington and Guadalajara were buzzing with requests from DEA headquarters for information. Instructions were waiting for me to call Frank Monastero, then the ranking DEA special agent in the organization and the man in charge of actual day-to-day operations in DEA, and to call Walter White in Mexico City. I first placed the call to Walter White to check on the agents coming in from other parts of Mexico and to see when we could expect the Federal Judicial Police to take some action. Walter told me he was sending in every available DEA agent to help out and that the investigation had been assigned to Federal Judicial Police Comandante Armando Pavon-Reyes, who was also in the mountains of Colima and wouldn't arrive in Guadalajara until the following morning.

Walter told me that the DEA Agent in Charge, Edward Heath, was personally coming to Guadalajara but wouldn't arrive until the next morning because he was taking a train that left at 6:00 PM from Mexico City and didn't arrive in Guadalajara until 6:00AM the following morning. Edward Heath and his wife were traveling with a group of Shriners to their convention in Guadalajara, a trip he had planned some two months prior. The Guadalajara DEA office had made his reservations for his stay at the new, and very elegant, Hyatt Regency. I thanked him for the information about the reinforcements and told him I would be spending the night in the consulate. A call was placed to DEA headquarters to report on the lack of anything to report. Frank Monastero was on the line but he apparently had most of DEA's management in his office. Jack Lawn, then the Deputy Administrator, was in the room along with the head of the Cocaine

Investigations section, and others, talking and listening via a speakerphone. They anxiously listened to the little I had to report and they promised their full support. They said there were sixty agents volunteering to come to Guadalajara to help and they would send as many as they could, all with the ability to speak Spanish. They also said they would send communications equipment the next day on a DEA airplane. A small DEA office, such as the one in Guadalajara was forced to communicate via long distance commercial telephone, obviously not secure, or the state department's sophisticated communications system, which was secure but slow. In response to their question wondering when Edward Heath would arrive I believe I responded, "Whenever the train gets here". Their response to this was a long, long distance silence followed by the terse comment from Monastero, "Tell Ed to call me as soon as he gets there"!

Captain Zavala's son had related the circumstances of his father's abduction to Alan Bachelier just as a companion of his father had described them to him at the time of the abduction.

His father had piloted the aircraft belonging to the SARH (the Secretariat of Agriculture and Hydraulic Power) to the city of Durango on Wednesday, February 6, and spent the night, the purpose of the trip being to transport an official of the SARH on official business. He was to return to Guadalajara the following day.

On Friday morning Mrs. Zavala called the airport hangar where the SARH aircraft was kept and asked the mechanic if he had any news of her husband's arrival. The mechanic replied that Captain Zavala had arrived the previous afternoon about 5:00 PM and had left the airport en route to Guadalajara in an official car of the SARH accompanied by three unidentified men and a woman, Maricela Vega de Torres, one of the secretaries from the SARH office. Mrs. Zavala then telephoned another secretary in Guadalajara to ask if she had any knowledge of her husband's whereabouts. Mrs. Zavala finally located Maricela Vega de Torres at her home. Maricela told Mrs. Zavala that on the previous day she had driven to the airport in an official car of the SARH to pick up her husband who was on the plane with Captain Zavala who was returning from Durango where he had flown the government airplane to carry a SARH official to a meeting. When she arrived at the airport, the airplane was late and she waited for a while before the plane arrived. She then offered a ride home to Captain Zavala. They left the airport with her husband driving and Captain Zavala seated in the back seat of the car. When they had traveled a few kilometers on the highway to Guadalajara they were ordered off the road by two men driving a brown Ford LTD, about a 1975 model. The men, who were dressed in camouflage clothing and caps, were carrying sub-machine guns. The two men stopped the brown Ford in front of Maricela's car and walked back to the SARH vehicle, asking which of the occupants was Captain Zavala. After determining this, they removed Captain Zavala from the vehicle and placed him in their own car. One of the armed men then returned to remove the keys from the SARH vehicle before departing at a high rate of speed. Maricela Vega told Mrs. Zavala that they finally were able to stop a passing Federal Highway Patrol officer and told him about the incident.

As to why she had not informed Mrs. Zavala of the incident Thursday Maricela said she had told her boss who stated he would take care of everything. It was after his mother's conversation with Maricela that Captain Zavala's son called the DEA office to report the incident and ask if we had any idea what had happened.

DEA agents eventually interviewed Maricela Vega's husband, on February 21 and again on September 25, but were never able to talk to Maricela herself. She was pregnant at the time of Captain Zavala's abduction and her husband said she was too upset to talk to us.

When Maricela Vega's husband, Luis Alberto Torres-Sanchez, was interviewed he stated that he and a friend, Oscar Mendoza, were in Durango on business when he called his wife in Guadalajara and, during the course of their conversation, she told him that Captain Zavala was also in Durango in the government airplane and perhaps they could catch a ride to Guadalajara with him. Since Zavala was staying at the same hotel as Torres-Sanchez, the "Campo Mexico", they located him easily and he agreed to take them back the following day.

The following morning, February 7, they met for breakfast at the hotel with the agriculture auditor and Captain Zavala. Although they were to have left before noon their flight was delayed because of the auditor's business and they departed the Durango airport about 2:00 PM arriving at the Guadalajara airport about 4:00 PM. During the day Captain Zavala reported the delays via telephone to Maricela in the SARH office in Guadalajara.

Upon arriving in Guadalajara the aircraft stopped at the terminal for private aircraft and the auditor boarded a waiting automobile and left. Torres-Sanchez walked to the main terminal and located his wife while Captain Zavala taxied the airplane, with Mendoza as a passenger, to the SARH hangar. Torres-Sanchez drove the car his wife had brought to the hangar where Captain Zavala and Mendoza were waiting. They passed a, parked, brown Ford LTD with two men inside. Torres-Sanchez said that he thought at the time that the two men seemed to be some type of police officers.

After leaving the airport, with Torres-Sanchez driving, his wife Maricela in the front passenger seat and the two men seated in back with Captain Zavala behind the driver, they were ordered off the road, about two or three miles from the airport on the main highway to Guadalajara, by the two men in the brown Ford LTD. The Ford stopped in front of them and the two men exited carrying sub-machine guns. The passenger in the brown Ford approached their car brandishing his weapon while the driver stayed near the Ford. The passenger asked which one of them was Captain Zavala and he identified himself. According to Torres-Sanchez, Captain Zavala voluntarily accompanied the man back to the Ford where he was first placed in the front passenger's seat and then removed and placed in the left rear seat. The first man entered the car and then exited the car, returning to the SARH vehicle and removing the keys. The man then returned to the Ford and they left at a normal rate of speed. Torres-Sanchez said they remained at the site in their car until a Federal highway patrol officer stopped and they told him what had happened. He drove them toward town but did not see the brown Ford. They then returned to the airport and the policeman talked to a guard at the airport, who was never identified to DEA. He said that he also remembered having seen a brown Ford parked for some time under a tree, but couldn't describe the occupants. Torres-Sanchez went on to say that the two men who had taken Zavala were dressed in camouflage clothing with matching baseball type caps and that the brown Ford had no license plates.

Investigators from the Jalisco State Attorney General's office reportedly did interview Maricela Vega during the evening of February 8. During the interview Maricela said that she had been present when her supervisor, Carlos Manuel Castaños, had assigned Captain Zavala to fly an auditor to Durango on February 6. When she received a call from her husband, who was in Durango on business, she had told him that Captain Zavala was staying at the same hotel and that he might be able to return to Guadalajara with him.

On the morning of February 7, she had received a call from Captain Zavala telling her that they would be returning late, since the auditor was not finished with his business. She received a second call in the early afternoon from a SARH official in Durango advising her that the airplane had just left for Guadalajara and to send a car to pick up the people at the airport. Since Maricela knew that her husband was arriving with Captain Zavala she decided to go the airport personally to receive them. She stated that she had first sent the auditor's personal chauffeur to receive him. Maricela told her interviewers that Captain Zavala asked her for a ride to town and that the three of them got into the vehicle she had driven to the airport, an official SARH automobile. They left the airport with her husband driving and Captain

Zavala seated behind her husband. A few miles from the airport their vehicle was stopped by two men in a large brown Ford with no license plates. The two men, dressed in camouflage clothing, got out of the car brandishing submachine guns and ordered Captain Zavala to get out. They then took Zavala to their car and put him in the back seat. One of the men returned and asked her husband for the keys to their car, taking them before returning to the Ford where he sat next to Captain Zavala in the back seat. The Ford then departed toward Guadalajara at a normal rate of speed.

A passing taxi was flagged down and requested to call the police, which he apparently did. When a police officer arrived they told him of the incident and he went off in search of the brown Ford. They then stopped a passing motorist and asked that the motorist call a friend to come and help them with the car. The friend arrived, accompanied by a tow truck, and helped them get home. Maricela went on to say that she had then returned to her office, arriving at 6:00 PM and told her supervisor, Carlos Manuel Castaños, what had occurred. He told her not to worry about anything, that he was going to take care of everything. She went home and in the evening she received a telephone call from Castaños telling her not to get involved, that the men were obviously only interested in Zavala and that he (Castaños) would handle everything.

Captain Zavala had a government car at his home at the time of his abduction. The SARH didn't call to check on Zavala, the car, or the family until after the bodies were found, almost a month later. Carlos Manuel Castaños could not be located for an interview. A newspaper article in March related that he had resigned his post as head of the SARH in Guadalajara and had returned to his hometown of Caborca, Sonora.

The obvious discrepancies between Maricela's story and her husband's recollection have never been resolved, Maricela Vega was never interviewed by a DEA agent, refusing to meet for one reason or another.

With the details in mind of Capitan Zavala's kidnapping, it was more certain than ever that Kiki had also been kidnapped and that the only possible suspects were drug traffickers or their associates, the DFS (Directorate of Federal Security).

The question was which drug trafficker? There were literally hundreds in the area, and, more importantly, how the hell were we going to find him.

It was still daylight on the 8th when the agent from the Federal Judicial Police came to the office to inform us that he had talked to his director in Mexico City by telephone and had been told that agents were coming from Mexico City and that Comandante Arteaga and First Comandante Pavon were coming from Colima with men to assist in the search. This agent then asked me what case Kiki had been working on so he could concentrate on those particular traffickers. I told him, as I would tell the agents who continued to come over the next week, that the entire office was working on the same thing, we were concentrating on the "family". (Considering our number it's questionable how much concentration we were putting on anything.) The agent went back to his office not convinced that I was telling him the truth.

About then the Consul General's secretary, staying late in her office to help in any way she could, called me to the telephone to talk to Mr. Morefield who had departed the consulate for his residence upon our return from the State Attorney General's office. Mr. Morefield told me that when he returned to his house, driven by his chauffeur, he had eaten his dinner alone in the dining room while the chauffeur had eaten in the kitchen, accompanied by Mr. Morefield's son, Bill.

As often happens when people get together around servants, or people they think of as servants, we had ignored the chauffeur. Mr. Morefield and I had been conversing in English during our drive from the Consulate to the AG's office and back, the chauffeur didn't understand anything we were talking about and, as a discreet employee of the United States government, hadn't asked questions of those people we saw at the

James Kuykendall

State Judicial Police office. Consequently, when he sat down to eat with Bill Morefield, the chauffer had no idea that Kiki had been kidnapped. Bill brought up the matter during dinner and the chauffeur said that he might have seen something the day before that was related to the disappearance. Bill listened to his account of the previous day's experience and immediately summoned his father. Mr. Morefield heard the story and called me. He asked if I would like for the chauffeur to come back to the consulate to tell me the story. I agreed that the information might be important and the chauffeur returned within a half hour.

Meanwhile I called my acquaintance at the State Judicial Police, Rogelio Levy-Gallardo inquiring as to why he hadn't come over to help as promised. He appeared reluctant to talk as if he was being overheard but when I told him there might be a witness he said he would be right over with his men. He was as good as his word and arrived immediately after the chauffeur. Right behind him came the man who had been assigned the case by the director of the state judicial police, the same man who could not be found earlier, Victor Manuel Lopez-Razon, a group supervisor in the homicide section of the state judicial police, a young man about 32 years old, medium height, stocky build. He was obviously aware that he was arriving late, carrying a worried look on his face. He was unaccompanied but said that his men were on their way. My acquaintance, Rogelio Levy-Gallardo, had arrived with several agents and another lawyer. Together we listened to the story of the chauffeur's observations of the previous day.

Mr. Morefield's chauffeur, Gilberto Villanueva-Moreno, was a Mexican citizen employee of the United States State Department. He had previously been a driver at the Embassy in Mexico City and had only recently been transferred to Guadalajara. He was a slightly built man about five feet six inches in height and in his middle thirties. He had black wavy hair and a thin face. He was quiet, polite, honest, intelligent and strong. He never wavered in his account of what he had seen, even under the antagonistic questioning he would be submitted to later by the MFJP. I don't believe it was because of loyalty to his employer as much as strength of his own convictions.

According to him he had left the consulate about 2:15 the previous afternoon to walk to a cheap restaurant for lunch, he told us his salary didn't permit him to eat near the consulate. He was walking west on the north side of Libertad Street, across the street from the Camelot restaurant. He had already passed the restaurant and was about mid-way down the block when he noticed movement behind him and to his left. Glancing back he saw what he remembered as two men forcing a third man into the back seat of a small square-shaped, four door, beige colored, car, maybe a Volkswagen Caribe or Renault. He also caught a glimpse of a handgun stuck inside the waistband of one of the men. One of the two men doing the pushing entered the car behind the man being arrested (because that's what he thought it was, some sort of police action). The other man ran around the car to enter the driver's door and the car departed the area very fast. The chauffeur thought no more about it and continued on about his business.

The chauffeur later gave descriptions of the two men he saw to a police artist who sketched composite drawings of the two alleged kidnappers. The chauffeur said that the man being taken away had his head down and he couldn't see his face. The chauffeur who, at that time, had been in the consulate only a week had never met Enrique Camarena.

Afterward DEA headquarters sent a hypnotist to interview the chauffeur and another man. Under hypnosis the chauffeur repeated the story almost verbatim.

Unfortunately the FBI agent who had accompanied the hypnotist to Guadalajara later lost the taped interview of the chauffeur.

We all walked over to the corner where the Camelot restaurant was located and examined Kiki's truck and the area surrounding it. The Mexican agents interviewed the waitress at the restaurant but she said she hadn't been there the afternoon before. The streets were deserted and the group from the state police left to make plans as to what they would do. The rest of us waited, each in our own way, but the loss was already gnawing away inside and the anger was growing. Dopers are scumbags that we, as cops, must fight with limited resources and rules with which we didn't agree, but they had committed the unforgivable sin of touching one of ours.

Mrs. Camarena, affectionately known as "Mika" by friends and family, began the long and frustrating wait for news and results, having to trust others to find her husband. Throughout the search she displayed tremendous inner strength and more confidence in us than we had in ourselves.

She told Victor Wallace that the previous day she and Kiki had made plans to meet for lunch at Mimi's Chinese restaurant on Ave. Lopez Mateos about two miles from the consulate. She had called him at the office during the morning of the 7th, since they had not talked at home before he left for the consulate. They mutually agreed to meet at 2:00 PM. When Kiki didn't arrive by 3 she called the office and was told that Kiki had left to meet her for lunch. She waited a little longer and, deciding he was not coming, she returned home. She believed that he was probably working on something. Later Mika said that she and Kiki had planned to eat alone and that no one else knew of their plans. She was aware that Kiki hadn't come home before she retired for the night but he often returned late. However he had never stayed away overnight without advising her. The next morning, when he still hadn't come home, she called Shaggy to inquire. She still remembered the obvious warning from the traffickers when they had fired upon Roger Knapp's government car, disregarding the lives of the Knapp children.

Reconstructing Kiki's activities over the two or three days preceding his disappearance, nothing of particular consequence comes to the mind of anyone to set Monday, February 4, apart from any other day. The office was open and we were doing our customary jobs.

Tuesday, February 5, was a Mexican holiday, the anniversary of the Mexican constitution, and the consulate was closed, including the DEA offices. Kiki spent the day with his family, attending a movie together in the afternoon.

Wednesday, February 6, the office was again open. Kiki met a friend of his near the consulate and the two drove to an upholstery shop to pick me up. I left an automobile there to have new seat covers installed. The three of us, in Kiki's pickup, drove to a used auto parts shop where we looked at a used motor Kiki was interested in buying for an old Mustang convertible he was planning to restore. He was not satisfied with the motor so we returned to the consulate and Kiki's friend departed in his own automobile.

Kiki and I climbed the stairs to our second floor offices and remained there until about 5:00 PM when we went to "La Troje" restaurant on the Avenida Americas to meet with some friends. We spent the evening listening to the music, watching the show and enjoying the company of a large group of close friends. Some of those friends were talented in their own right and they sang to the accompaniment of the mariachi groups who performed there. Most of the men in the group had been friends of the agents in the office for a long time.

About midnight, one of those friends and I accompanied Kiki to his house to taste a new Tequila he had acquired. The friend and I left in a taxi soon after.

Thursday, February 7, 1985, the day of Kiki's disappearance, was a typically beautiful day in Guadalajara. Kiki arrived at the Camelot Restaurant about 9 AM and parked his Ford pickup in the small area off of Libertad Street beside the vehicle of Shaggy Wallace, who had arrived earlier. Because of the loss of the parking lot directly behind the consulate on January 1, the DEA contingent had negotiated with the owner to park at the restaurant during the day. We often spent time after work on the veranda of the restaurant, drinking cold Estrella beer, enjoying the cool evenings and talking about drug cases. The area had space for four vehicles and all spaces were now occupied. When I arrived some twenty to thirty minutes later

James Kuykendall

driving a brown Jeep Cherokee I parked in the small space directly behind Kiki's pickup, but parallel to the street, blocking the pickup from leaving.

The morning was taken up between Kiki's preparations for his upcoming transfer and meetings with informants. At about 11 AM he walked, alone, the two and one half blocks to a branch of Banamex, located at the corner of Chapultepec Avenue and Avenue Vallarta to exchange money, and returned to the consulate.

About 1:00 PM, Kiki, Alan Bachelier and I met with an informant, his wife and young son on the outdoor balcony of the Camelot restaurant, remaining there about twenty minutes before returning to our respective desks.

Sometime after two o'clock Kiki hurried out of the office alone, shouting to the secretaries. "I was supposed to meet my wife for lunch at 2 o'clock, if she calls tell her I'm on my way." Those were the last friendly faces he saw in his life.

At 2:30 PM Fidel Sanchez and I left the consulate and I drove the brown Jeep Cherokee along the sidewalk and off the curb to turn onto Progresso Street. Kiki's truck was still parked beside the restaurant but could now be moved.

Fidel and I left in search of a mansion being built by Rafael Caro-Quintero, a very recent piece of information. We found the mansion, all three floors of it, at least fifty-thousand square feet, Inside a twelve-foot high, walled enclosure of forty-three acres in size. Rafael Caro had bought the land for two million U.S dollars, surprising the seller by pulling the cash out of the trunk of his car right after his inspection of the site. Afterwards Fidel and I ate tacos at an outdoor restaurant before returning to the consulate.

At 2:45 PM Alan and Shaggy met with a contact at the Camelot restaurant. Kiki's truck was still there.

About 4:30 PM Shaggy, Fidel and myself left the consulate in Shaggy's car for a meeting with an informant at the Sheraton hotel

¿O Plata O Plomo?

concerning an attempt to meet with some crooks undercover who had 150 kilos of cocaine to sell. We returned to the consulate about 6:00 PM. The blue Ford pickup was still parked in front of the restaurant.

As close as we all were and as much as we enjoyed each other's company, the reason we weren't concerned was because Kiki was being transferred soon and we thought, or at least I did, that he was with his wife and some friends having a long lunch and toasting their departure. Kiki had not told anyone where he was going to meet his wife for lunch and we all assumed it was somewhere nearby where he would have walked to meet Mika.

Returning to the events of February 8th, the first DEA reinforcements began to arrive at the consulate during the late evening, coming from various parts of Mexico. Most of us bedded down in the DEA offices as best we could, awaiting the arrival of the Federal Judicial Police, without whom we had no authority to operate in their country.

Very early the next morning we received word that most of the Mex-Feds had arrived during the night and had checked into the Lafayette hotel to get some rest.

Edward Heath arrived at the DEA office about 8:30 AM, looking fresh in a neatly pressed black suit and asked what had happened during the night. I filled him in and told him that DEA headquarters wanted to hear from him. He made a private call to Washington and then suggested that we go to the offices of the Federal Judicial Police and see what their plans were.

The offices of the Mexican Federal Judicial Police, who we usually referred to as the Mex-Feds, were packed with agents, all heavily armed and appearing to have come ready for action, the man placed in charge, Comandante Armando Pavon, hadn't showed up yet, the word being that he had arrived in Guadalajara about 3 AM and was still at the hotel.

About 9:30 AM Comandante Armando Pavon-Reyes walked into the offices where we were waiting. He was followed, or accompanied, by the largest group of judicial police comandantes ever assembled for anything except pictures. The comandante in charge of the Jalisco office, Alberto Arteaga, was also there but his grade was secondary to that of Pavon's and Pavon had been placed in charge of the investigation by Director Manuel Ibarra.

One of the men accompanying Pavon was a lawyer named Sergio Saavedra, said to be one of Director Ibarra's legal counselors and trusted friends; he was loudly proclaiming that he was ready to get something done. The scene was rapidly approaching bedlam by now, the limited space crammed with over one hundred Federal Judicial Police agents, DEA agents, and attorneys from the office of the Mexican Attorney General.

The MFJP informed us that they were taking over the investigation, as the kidnapping of a foreign official was a Federal offense. This was fine with us, since we had not heard another word from the state judicial police, However, as it turned out, they were wrong about the referenced offense, it wasn't true, and there was no such law.

The first order of the day, according to Pavon, was to find transportation for the mass of agents he had brought with him and for those that had arrived from Mexico City by bus and airplane.

A group of people, including Comandante Pavon, Comandante Arteaga, Comandante Silvio Brussolo, Sergio Saavedra, Mario Cueva-Cerpa of the Mexican Attorney General's office, Edward Heath, veteran DEA agent Charlie Lugo and myself headed for the offices of the Jalisco State Judicial Police to try to borrow vehicles for the search.

We were herded into the office of the director, Carlos Aceves-Fernandez, who gave us a thirty-minute speech on the reasons why he couldn't participate or assist. No amount of pleading or cajoling could make him change his mind so we returned to the offices of the MFJP. While everyone was shouting and arguing about what to do next, Pavon placed a call to Director Ibarra to apprise him of the situation and ask for instructions.

¿O Plata O Plomo?

It was my observation that anything he did was always preceded and followed by a call to Director Manuel Ibarra. Ibarra was calling the shots; Pavon made no decisions without consulting him. This led to many heated arguments between Pavon and Saavedra, who constantly shouted that he wanted to take some heavy action against the traffickers.

From the beginning we expected the Mex-Feds to act as they always did. To step in and start picking up people involved in the traffic and interrogate them, in order to find out where the major traffickers were hiding out and who might know something about Kiki's abduction. The Mexican police methods of interrogation were brutal but effective. If the person being interrogated knew anything he would give it up. We knew the MFJP didn't like us but we never doubted they would use their very effective tactics to find Kiki. After all, no one could be allowed to get away with something like this. Much to our surprise, the MFJP had developed an overnight respect for human rights. Their response was that they had no arrest or search warrants.

I'm sure no one there had ever seen a search warrant. Since there were no vehicles available for the MFJP some DEA agents rented automobiles, utilizing their personal credit cards, for the Mex-Feds to use. We rented three that morning and while waiting for the rental cars to be brought to the office, the word came from the DEA office that a radio conversation between Miguel Felix and his office had been overheard on the scanner in which he had requested a large sum of money be brought to the airport because he was leaving town right away. This information was furnished to Pavon and he decided to go to the airport to try and intercept Felix's private plane. Maybe the information about the money influenced him.

Comandante Armando Pavon, Comandante Silvio Brusolo and others were waiting for the rental cars in the front yard of the MFJP headquarters, a large converted house on the corners of Ave. La Union and Ave. La Paz. Kiki

James Kuykendall

Camarena had always referred to this place as the cave of Ali Baba and the forty thieves. When the cars arrived they quickly mounted them for the trip to the airport. I provided Pavon with the descriptions and registration numbers of the airplanes that we knew Miguel Felix had at his disposal and Pavon left in the rental cars loaded with Federal agents armed to the teeth. I screamed at several DEA agents who were standing in the yard to climb in the cars and go with the Mex-Feds. (Many of the agents who came to help had never worked in Mexico and didn't comprehend how deep the corruption was.)

Three DEA agents actually climbed into the cars for the trip, DEA Special Agent John Brown was already at the Guadalajara airport, having taken our Jeep Cherokee and two Mexican agents to meet the DEA aircraft arriving from the United States with personnel and equipment to assist in the search.

Just before the group headed by Pavon arrived at the airport, a Federal Judicial Police agent assigned to guard the Mexican government airplanes at the hangar of the Attorney General, spotted some men armed with shoulder weapons and advised Pavon's approaching team, by radio, of his observations. The armed men were obviously associated with a Falcon jet aircraft that was taxiing out of a hangar adjacent to the hangar utilized by Miguel Felix to store his aircraft. The Falcon jet had to pass directly by the Attorney General's hangar to reach the runways. Pavon's group exited their vehicles and approached the unidentified, armed men, whose number had now grown to about twelve, having been augmented by men coming from inside the hangar. The Federal Judicial Police group numbered about twenty. The unidentified men were all armed with shoulder weapons, principally M-16s (U.S. military full automatic assault rifles) and AK-47s (Russian full automatic assault rifles) and handguns. The Federal Judicial Police were similarly armed but they outnumbered the other force.

The two groups confronted each other almost within the shadows of the Falcon jet. Pavon shouted "cortan cartuchos" (load your weapons). Both forces leveled their weapons at the other and for a few tense moments it looked like a blood bath was about to ensue. Pavon ordered the other group to drop their weapons but they would not comply. It is unclear just how the situation was defused but there were certainly men in the other group that Pavon knew, Pavon had been a member of the DFS, as had Sergio Saavedra and at least one other member of the Mexican government contingency. On the side of the group confronting them was at least one person very well known to many of them; Rogelio Munoz-Rios was an ex-comandante of the Federal Judicial Police and had been the comandante of the DFS in Jalisco until suffering a heart attack and a subsequent quadruple by-pass at a clinic in Houston, Texas. Afterward he had become one of the DFS agents assigned to guard the traffickers, principally Rafael Caro-Quintero. Munoz-Rios was in his late fifties, well liked in spite of his reputation for ruthlessness and had, in fact, been in my office at the consulate in Guadalajara. He had known several DEA agents well, including Kiki Camarena, for several years.

However it happened, Pavon approached Rogelio Munoz and another, younger man standing beside him and began a conversation.

Without any doubt, this was the first time that an American narcotics agent ever saw Rafael Caro-Quintero, and knew it. The four DEA agents who were present at the airport later described the man with Rogelio Munoz as being in his late twenties to early thirties, about six feet tall, slim but muscular, wearing expensive, western style, dark clothing with cowboy boots. He was bare headed with long black hair and a thick mustache and much gold jewelry on his wrists, fingers and around his neck (necklaces and chains made more visible as he had his collar open down his chest). He had a wide grin on his face and was carrying an AK-47 with a seventy-five round drum magazine. He was obviously in charge and, just as obviously, didn't give a damn whether they shot it out or not. He kept glancing at the group behind Pavon with a menacing grin while they talked.

James Kuykendall

Pavon was given what appeared to be some sort of credential by the two men, which he examined. Then he left the group and, still carrying the credentials, walked alone to the Attorney General's hangar where he climbed the stairs to the office and made a phone call, observed through the windows, by the people below. He returned to talk to Rogelio Munoz and the unidentified man in dark clothing, returning their credentials. Pavon and the young man then walked to the other side of the Falcon jet for a few minutes for a private conversation. Afterward they rejoined the group and Pavon embraced the young man and Rogelio Munoz, and shook hands with most of the rest, as did several others of the Mex-Feds.

Pavon, Saavedra and a couple of other Mex-Feds entered the Falcon jet for a few minutes and observed a young woman in a passenger seat and the pilot readying the jet for takeoff. There was no co-pilot.

The man in dark clothing and others of his group entered the aircraft and it started to taxi away toward the distant runways with the passenger door still open. The man in dark clothing appeared in the doorway and held aloft a bottle of champagne or brandy, before drinking directly from the bottle and shouting in Spanish, "good bye children, the next time bring better toys." The men left behind climbed into two vehicles near the hangar and departed the airport.

The DEA agents remembered that one of the vehicles was a late model, white, Ford station wagon.

The DEA agents there that day were shocked and spellbound as they watched this most outrageous scene unfold before their very eyes. It was the very essence of how influential and brazen the traffickers had become. When the DEA agents pressed Pavon for an explanation, he said that the people on the Falcon jet were DFS agents and Jalisco state judicial police.

One of the DEA agents at the airport transmitted the message over the radio that a jet aircraft with registration no. XB-ZRB was departing the airport with several armed people aboard. He gave a brief account of what had transpired. I was, at that time, in the DEA office at the consulate and heard the radio transmission. I responded by radio, telling the agent that the numbers were those of an aircraft suspected to belong to Rafael Caro-Quintero. Edward Heath was apparently listening to a DEA radio we had installed at the offices of the Federal Judicial Police and immediately demanded to know why the aircraft had not been detained. There was no response from the radio.

Later, Armando Pavon was asked why he had allowed Rafael Caro-Quintero to depart the airport in the jet aircraft. He replied that he did not personally know Rafael Caro-Quintero and that the man, later known to be Rafael, identified himself to Pavon as Pedro Sanchez and presented DFS credentials in that name. Pavon also said that there had been DEA agents at the airport and they hadn't told him that the man was Rafael Caro-Quintero.

The agents at the airport did not know Rafael Caro-Quintero, in fact no DEA agent had ever knowingly seen him, nor did we possess a photo of him.

Undoubtedly, had one of the agents permanently assigned to the Guadalajara office been present at the airport, events would have been different. A shoot-out might have occurred, as we did know the airplane and knew it to be an airplane that had been provided to Rafael Caro by a respected Guadalajara resident and businessman.

Edward Heath did not know the tail numbers on the trafficker's aircraft, could not be expected to know them, it was not his job to know the minute details of every investigation in Mexico.

Later that afternoon, one of the men who had been in Pavon's group at the airport, sought out Edward Heath and told him that Rafael Caro-Quintero had been the man at the airport and that he had promised Comandante Pavon seventy million pesos to let his party proceed on its way. According to Heath's source this money was to be paid the following day by Rogelio Munoz, through the source, to Pavon.

Heath's source is the only person who ever reported this alleged bribe. Later the Mexican government charged Pavon with accepting this alleged bribe and produced evidence in the form of a check written by Rafael Caro-Quintero against him. But that evidence was false because that check had actually been written to the comandante of the Federal Judicial Police in Saltillo as payment for protection against seizure of several marijuana fields in the state of Coahuila. Further, the check was dated weeks before the alleged bribe at the airport.

When we eventually obtained the telephone toll records for the telephone at the Attorney General's hangar office, we found evidence of a call to the office of the Federal Judicial Police in Mexico City on that day. We could not obtain records of local calls and there were no other long distance calls from that number on that day.

After the Falcon jet took off, the MFJP examined the flight records at the airport but said they were unsuccessful in finding any evidence that Miguel Felix had left the Guadalajara airport that day, either in a private jet or commercially.

Later in the afternoon the group returned to the MFJP offices, after conducting a fruitless search of the hangars at the airport. By now the size of the MFJP contingent had swelled to about 130 agents and the DEA personnel numbered some thirty or so.

The Camarena home was put under heavy guard and a recorder was installed on the telephone to tape any ransom demands or threats that might be received. Other informants were contacted to be certain that other people who had helped us had not been the targets of the kidnappers, as had happened with Alfredo Zavala. As far as we were able to determine, there had been no other kidnapping.

In the early evening Federal Judicial Police agents, accompanied by DEA observers, established surveillance on several residences and businesses known to be owned or utilized by the traffickers or their associates.

¿O Plata O Plomo?

It was February 9, 1985 and throughout DEA there was but one thought in mind. Find Kiki Camarena.

The Special Agent in Charge in San Diego, California had rented quarters in a luxury hotel for a vacation weekend with his wife. He canceled the reservation and spent most of the night at his office, personally supervising the search for information in the Mexican traffickers' favorite playground.

Agents everywhere frantically tried to help. And officers from every police agency in the United States lent their assistance when able and certainly their sympathy.

Mika Camarena and her children huddled and waited. Several DEA agents waited with her while MFJP agents guarded the outside of the Camarena home.

In the period following Kiki's disappearance, there was much uncertainty concerning the safety of Kiki's family. A suggestion was made to move then to the states while the search was being conducted. Mika refused to without her husband, but did agree to allow her boys to leave if Yolanda Wallace, Shaggy's wife, would accompany them. The decision was then made to evacuate Yolanda, her twelve year old daughter, Lisa, and Kiki's three sons to San Diego. DEA agents and heavily armed federales escorted them to one of DEA's aircraft to the flight to California. They would never return to Guadalajara.

James Kuykendall

Kiki Camarena

Chapter 4
COMBING THE CITY

DEA Agent Alan Bachelier was with the group of MFJP agents on surveillance at the house of a woman named Leticia Corona-Santander, located on Mimbela Street, the evening of February 9. Leticia was the private secretary of Tomas Valles-Corral, Miguel Felix's administrative manager of his hotels and contact with money laundering bankers throughout the world. She had actually traveled with Tomas Valles to Spain and France on missions for Felix-Gallardo, but we knew that she had also been associated with Miguel Felix for several years and was well acquainted with the affairs of Felix and his band of international dope dealers.

Some of the Mex-Feds had been assigned to watch the businesses and houses of people we suspected of association with the major traffickers.

When he saw someone through the window that looked like Leticia, Alan took the bull by the horns and went in after her. A reluctant MFJP supervisor accompanying Alan could not allow the U.S. agent to arrest the woman alone and went in with him.

After she was taken to the Mex-Feds office, Leticia was not reluctant to talk, telling her interviewers everything about her job with the hotels but denying that she knew anything about narcotics trafficking.

Leticia was an unlikely looking participant in the drug traffic. Not the femme fatale type at all, she was in her late thirties, rather plain looking and wore horn-rimmed glasses. She said that she had not seen Tomas Valles since the morning of February 7, when she had been told that the offices where she worked were to be closed and that she should look for new office space. She gave us the location of Felix's personal offices, at 2838 Quebrada

¿O Plata O Plomo?

St. and said that she had closed the offices, as ordered, on February 7. She stated she knew Miguel Felix was a narcotics trafficker and owned the hotels but said that everyone in Guadalajara knew that and, besides, she worked for Tomas Valles, not Miguel Felix. She also gave us the location of Miguel Felix's home at 445 Mixcoatl St.

Comandante Pavon promptly called MFJP Director Ibarra with the news that we had Leticia Corona in custody and what she had told him about the Felix organization. Pavon told us that the Director's instructions were to release Leticia Corona so she could relay a message to Miguel Felix that he had 24 hours to return Enrique Camarena or there would be no regard for the civil rights of the traffickers and that the MFJP would "make them pay for what they had done".

Leticia Corona said she had no idea how to locate Miguel Felix but she would try. In spite of protests from the DEA agents present she was released.

Two of Miguel Felix's motels, both located on one of Guadalajara's main thoroughfares, Avenida Lopez Mateos, were searched that night. At the Motel "Las Americas" there appeared to be only legitimate guests and employees, the employees stating they had not seen Miguel Felix or Tomas Valles since February 7. At the "Suites Real" the employees gave the same response but two Americans, who were found in the motel, were in possession of firearms and had documents with them indicating they were well acquainted with Felix's banker, German Harper and the hotel manager, Tomas Valles. The two men, Albert J. Alvin and Henry Donalson, were taken into custody and questioned, but professed to know nothing about the kidnapping. The two men were questioned by the MFJP outside the presence of the DEA agents and, when they were returned to the office where the DEA agents were waiting, had their hair wet as if they had been subjected to some version of the MFJP's "water" method of extracting confessions. However, they still insisted they were innocent of any wrongdoing and were only tourists. Had they been truly subjected to the MFJP interrogations they would have confessed to anything, even if innocent, including their associations with Miguel Felix and his group, something which future investigations would eventually prove to be the case. Donalson was a documented narcotics trafficker, utilizing several aliases.

The office of Tomas Valles-Corral, which we had unsuccessfully sought for months and which Leticia Corona had finally pointed out, was entered on February 10. Inside, the officers found a modern cellular telephone in a briefcase, (just how it was made to function in a country that had no cellular service at the time we never knew.) There was a local newspaper dated February 7, 1985 and business records and receipts for the hotels and other businesses. There were also many business cards, which by them told a revealing story. As we already knew, Tomas Valles background was in banking, and that had been his primary role for Miguel Felix. Since he had moved up to manager of the various enterprises, he had been more or less replaced in this role by German Harper, but the business cards bespoke of his earlier role as banker and money launderer.

Of particular note were the following:
(1) Multibanco Comermex
Francisco Javier Santos-Santos; gerente [manager]
Plaza del Sol
Ave. Plaza del Sol y Lopez Mateos
Guadalajara, Jalisco
Tels. 22-55-69, 22-53-44
*Note, this was the bank where Miguel Felix-Gallardo's associate, German Harper, had an office and paid the bills and the expenses of the IPS (Investigaciones Politicos y Sociales) an agency of the Mexican government controlled by the traffickers, which was located behind the Fiesta Americana Hotel. From this office Harper also paid for the installation of radios for Ernesto Fonseca and Rafael Caro, and from here expense money was sent to the marijuana plantations in northern Mexico.

¿O Plata O Plomo?

(2) Motor Hotel de las Americas
Ave. Lopez Mateos Sur #2400
tels. 31-44-15 y 31-52-76
Guadalajara, Jal. Mexico
Tomas Valles-Corral
Director general
Hotel Suites del Real
Ave. Lopez Mateos Sur. #5045
tels. 31-41-31 y 31-40-75
Guadalajara, Jal. Mexico
(3) Mervin D. Grant, P.C.
Beus, Gilbert, Ware and Morrill
Attorneys at Law
Suite 1000 United Bank Tower
3300 North Central Ave.
Phoenix, Arizona
*Note, Mervin Grant represented Mardoqueo Alfaro-Margarina in his deposition regarding the $6,500,000.00 seized in El Paso, Texas and personally removed over $2,000,000.00 from Tesoro Savings and Loan in Laredo, Texas. This money had been flown from Guadalajara in Felix-Gallardo's private airplanes and deposited into accounts by his henchmen.
(4) Viajes Pacifico
Issac Kattan
Gerente General [general manager]
Calle 12 No.3-06, Edif. Zaccour
Ap, Aereo 6231
Telegrafo "VIP"
Cali, Colombia
*Note, Colombian trafficker involved in money laundering, operated the VIP Travel Agency and ran an unauthorized money exchange business between

Cali and Miami in late seventies, arrested in Miami, Florida in possession of multi-kilo load of high quality cocaine, convicted and doing time.
(5) Transportes Fluviales del Amazonas Ltd.
Bogota, Colombia
Vicente Rivera Gonzales
Carrera 4. No. 18-50 of.150E
Bogota, S.E.
*Note, the captain of a boat plying the waters of the Colombian Amazon rivers.

Most of the other business cards were from bankers and banks, in Mexico, the United States and Canada.

A mansion belonging to Rafael Caro-Quintero and occupying half of a city block in a fashionable area of Guadalajara was entered on February 11. The house, located at the corner of Xochitl and Cuahtemoc, in Ciudad del Sol, was unoccupied except for a caretaker who claimed that he knew nothing. At least that is what the MFJP told the DEA agents.

Inside one closet in the master bedroom was a cold storage vault full of expensive furs and over fifty pairs of expensive cowboy boots made of various exotic animal skins. The home had been professionally decorated with furniture from the finest stores in Guadalajara and top of the line appliances from the United States. The grounds and swimming pool were immaculately maintained and several late model automobiles were stored inside the garage or parked on the driveway, which ran though the grounds from side street to side street. Some of the vehicles had license plates from Jalisco; others had tags from Tamaulipas. A ten-foot high wall surrounded the entire residence.

A startling discovery was made on February 11 when the MFJP, accompanied by DEA agents, entered the residence of Miguel Angel Felix-Gallardo at no. 445 Mixcoatl, in Ciudad del Sol. Present in the house was Maria Elvira Murillo de Felix, the wife of Miguel Felix, and her maid. Maria Elvira de Felix told the MFJP officers that Miguel Felix had left the house on

¿O Plata O Plomo?

February 9, taking with him their two small children. She claimed that she did not know where he had gone or how to locate him. She said she knew nothing about the kidnapping or about Miguel Felix's drug business. Maria Elvira Murillo de Felix was from Sinaloa, the daughter of a drug trafficker and her brothers were also all in the business.

On a shelf inside the house one of the Mexican officers found a leather purse of the type carried by men a few years ago. The purse, or bag, contained personal documents of Miguel Angel Felix-Gallardo, including some credit cards and a laminated immigration permit to visit the United States as a tourist. It was issued at Hidalgo, Texas in January of 1982 in the name of Miguel Angel Felix-Gallardo, in spite of the fact that Miguel Angel Felix-Gallardo had been of record with the DEA since 1977 and was considered a major international trafficker. But, in those days, the various U.S. enforcement agencies didn't share information and Immigration didn't have access to the data. The U.S. State Department, which issued visas to visit the United States, refused to put DEA's information about suspected traffickers into their lookout system unless DEA would turn over total access so they could evaluate the information. Since neither agency would bend, the information was not available for consideration when visas were issued. When the bag was opened a photograph fell to the floor, DEA Agent Tony Ayala picked it up and looked at it. The photo depicted three men inside a building and facing the camera. Tony recognized one of the men in the photograph as Enrique Camarena; he did not know the other two. A small plaque above a doorway in the picture bore the words "Policia Judicial Federal".

Once again Comandante Armando Pavon-Reyes made his telephone call to Director Manuel Ibarra. Afterwards he informed the MFJP and DEA agents that Director Ibarra had advised him not to take Maria Elvira de Felix into custody, but rather to tell her to take the message to her husband that Director Ibarra was imposing a twenty-four hour deadline for the return of

Enrique Camarena or he would begin to wreak terrible vengeance on the traffickers. The MFJP left Mrs. Miguel Angel Felix-Gallardo in her luxurious home and returned to their offices.

I was summoned to look at the picture and was able to identify one of the men in the photo as a Federal Agent named Roberto Valdez who had worked at the MFJP office the previous year, but had been transferred to Nuevo Laredo. It happened that Valdez was, in fact, in Guadalajara at that time on the special detail to look for Kiki and he was interviewed regarding the photograph. He stated that he believed DEA Agent Butch Sears had taken the picture. He stated that he had no idea how Felix-Gallardo had obtained a print. The other man in the photo was a state judicial police agent formerly assigned to work with the Mex-Feds. Butch Sears was interviewed in El Paso and said that he had not been the photographer.

Another possible photographer was a MFJP agent who had lived rent-free for several years at Miguel Felix's "Motor Hotel Las Americas" and provided security for the trafficker. Juan Gilberto Hernandez had been the errand boy for each new comandante due to his connections with the underworld. But he had also maintained an acquaintanceship with the DEA office. If the comandante needed a visa for his girlfriend or family, Juan Gilberto usually brought the passports over. We passed that information on to the Mex-Feds, as if they didn't know!

Tony Ayala said there were other photographs inside the house, pictures of men at functions and parties, and men in uniform sitting with men in civilian clothes. But Pavon-Reyes' men quickly gathered these up, watchful that the U.S. agents did not slip away with one.

Kiki's truck was stilled parked at the restaurant. Since the kidnappers had the keys, we thought they just might return for the truck. We waited without luck. A fingerprint expert arrived from the states and meticulously dusted the truck, inside and out, for prints. We then put the truck into operation since we needed vehicles.

¿O Plata O Plomo?

The Mex-Feds and even the DEA agents kept pushing for the names of the traffickers we were working on in the office. This was a common practice of the MFJP agents, acquiring information from DEA about a trafficker and then using it to extract extortion. It didn't matter with Kiki missing, finding him was all that did matter; there was no tomorrow.

I wrote out a list of every possible suspect, most of the people, but not all, were members of the "family". That list would add substantially to the drama in years to come.

Just a few days after the raids on Miguel Felix's hotels we were informed that an "amparo" (roughly the equivalent of a legal restraining order in the United States) had been issued by a Mexican federal judge prohibiting the MFJP from conducting any investigation relative to Enrique Camarena's disappearance against the people listed in the "amparo". The listed people were:

[1] Luis Ernesto Casillas-Zavala
[2] Sotero Gastelum-Ruiz
[3] Miguel Angel Walls-Plasencia (one of Miguel Felix's pilots)
[4] Julio Cesar Castillo-Beas
[5] Manuel Garcia-Garcia
[6] Marta Sanchez Espana de Walls (wife of Miguel Walls)
[7] Albert J. Alvin and Henry Donalson (the two U.S. citizens arrested in the Suites Real)
[8] Astolfo Perez-Contreras
[9] Miguel Felix-Gallardo
[10] Ernesto Fonseca-Carrillo
[11] Maria Elvira Murillo de Felix
[12] Tomas Valles-Corral
[13] Juan Manuel Jimenez-Lopez
[14] Saul Pena-Quiroz
[15] Esteban Manzano-Holquin

James Kuykendall

It was unclear just what the MFJP intended to do about the amparo. Legally they could not investigate these people, but some were already in custody and others were definitely suspects. There were people named in the amparo whom we had never heard of before. However, we didn't spend too much time then trying to determine what their relation was to the traffickers as we had another priority. Apparently, some were people who had helped Miguel Felix launder money by lending him their name. The others we never investigated further.

We continued to make raids on the houses and ranches of the traffickers. A luxurious ranch on the highway to La Barca, Jalisco belonging to Rafael Caro-Quintero was entered. The MFJP enlisted the aid of the federal highway patrol, an obvious indication of their apprehension toward entering the property of such an influential trafficker. The house was a very U.S. style, one story ranch house with many stables full of fine horses. The fields were well cared for and horses and cattle grazed on both sides of the nearby highway.

The Mex-Feds talked to the foreman who was not too unwilling to cooperate. He said that the MFJP had raided the ranch in early January looking for Rafael Caro-Quintero and the Cosio girl. The foreman stated that he had been treated badly on that occasion. The MFJP agents apologized for their fellow officer's behavior on that earlier visit and asked the foreman where Rafael Caro was hiding this time. The foreman said he did not know but Rafael Caro had been at the ranch about one week earlier and had stated he was going away again because "things were going to be very bad this time." The foreman suggested that we talk to Rafael's business manager, Jorge Leon Keschner, who had an office on Lazaro Cardenas Boulevard. The Mex-Feds never got around to that.

Following orders, one of the DEA agents busily walked around the grounds, snapping photographs until he was confronted by several of the Mexican agents, demanding to know why he was taking their pictures. Another tense standoff took place when we declined to turn over the pictures but we didn't take any more, either. On the way back to the MFJP offices in Guadalajara we pushed the MFJP to canvass the area around the village of Lopez Cotilla, where the veterinarian had been threatened on the 12th. The entourage stopped alongside the periferico and Pavon made lame excuses for half an hour before saying that they were not going to search anymore that day. The team was comprised of at least 100 men that day and we were parked less than half a mile from where the vet had seen the black Gran Marquis on February 7.

A large and well-equipped ranch near Tototlan was located and searched and a ranch with a large house near Mazatepec, and a weekend retreat just south of the Santa Anita Golf Club. This retreat, called "Villa Guadalupe", was comprised of about 25 acres. It contained a large home, a swimming pool, a private shooting range, a private zoo and a horse race track with stables. The caretaker stated he worked for Emilio Quintero-Payan.

"Give me another location, come on, talk!" The interrogator demanded.

"We haven't exactly located this one, but there is a ranch just past the Santa Anita club. We were afraid to get too close, but some bricklayers were hired to work there and they told a friend of Mr. Kuykendall's about it. Just past the golf club to the right." Kiki answered.

"You found that one?" The interrogator asked.

"No, for the same reason, I am unarmed, that is why I am afraid."

A home belonging to Ernesto Fonseca was also searched. This house, located on Apaches street, had closed circuit television cameras monitoring the approaches and, inside the house, was another cold storage vault for furs, but this one was empty. Under a bed the agents found two fully automatic weapons, either left behind in haste, or maybe there were just too many to carry. Reports were received that a body had been mysteriously buried in the municipal cemetery at the village of Yahualica, Jalisco. This story was checked out with negative results. Information came from the states that Kiki was being held in an abandoned mine near Monterrey. Anonymous letters maintained that he and Captain Zavala had been taken to Colombia, or Panama, or Ecuador. We followed up on every lead, frustratingly, without success.

The Mexican agents were also feeling the frustration and were becoming angry. Stories were circulating that Kiki had been taking money from the traffickers. We also heard that the Mexican agents believed that Kiki had not been kidnapped but that the "gringos" had fabricated the event in order to force the Mexican government to enter the traffickers' homes in Guadalajara. Several of the MFJP agents said they thought Kiki was vacationing in Florida.

These frustrations almost led to outright fights between the DEA agents and the Mex-Feds. DEA Agent Tony Ayala and a Mex-Fed, with the unlikely name of Frank Miller, faced off in the front yard of the MFJP office, hands hovering over their firearms, but suspicions lingered.

We continued to receive anonymous letters with information concerning the alleged whereabouts of the missing men or denouncing corrupt officials. Information was received that a body had been discovered on a hill south of the city. When the body was examined it appeared that almost all of the bones in the cadaver were broken. There was also no evidence that a vehicle had driven anywhere near the area where the body was. Several men looked skyward, remembering the stories of traffickers, reluctant to talk, shoved out of airplanes and helicopters. We never discovered the identity of that deceased individual either.

An anonymous letter, received on February 20, directed us to investigate an "Hacienda" near "Puente Grande". The letter read "the kidnappers of your agent are people paid for by Ernesto Fonseca, Miguel Gallardo, Rafael Caro-Quintero, Manuel Salcido alias el Cochiloco, his brother "the crooked mouth", Juan Manuel Esparragoza alias "el azulito" and Antonio Alcaraz. According to the letter, they took him to the hacienda that belongs to Fonseca, which is located passing the Puente Grande (the big bridge) on the right hand side called "La Providencia". There they have cocaine located behind one of the paintings in the principle sitting room and below the bed made of wood in a drawer beneath the rug attached to the wall beside the large easy chair. Our supervisors, Carlos Aceves-Fernandez and Locheo are their people. They receive money and drugs from them. Also the following people know of this matter, Francisco Valdez and Jose Maria Carlos-Ochoa and Jorge Salazar."

The hacienda "La Providencia" was located near the village of Puente Grande and the MFJP raided it on February 22. No kidnapped agent was found nor was there cocaine concealed behind the painting on the wall. What was discovered was a fully operational cocaine laboratory capable of producing hundreds of pounds of cocaine hydrochloride on a monthly basis. One hundred kilos of cocaine was seized at the site along with 200 kilos of lidocaine, a substance used to "cut" the cocaine before marketing. A portable radio seized at the lab site was equipped with the frequencies of the Federal Judicial Police. There was no one at the hacienda but a pot of beans boiling on a gas stove indicated that the occupants had hastily departed only minutes before the raid. Among the documents discovered were several which linked the ranch to Miguel Felix.

From the Dept. of Agriculture, a permit to transport mangos from Culiacan to Mexico City, the transporter: Rodolfo Sanchez-Duarte of Culiacan, the consignee: Leopoldo Sanchez-Celis with an address of San Jeronimo #20, Col. San Jeronimo, Mexico D.F. *Leopoldo Sanchez-Celis was an ex-governor of Sinaloa and a major associate of Miguel Felix-Gallardo. Miguel Felix had been his chauffeur and bodyguard when he was governor, the relationship had blossomed. Sanchez-Celis was the "padrino" at Miguel Felix's wedding and Miguel Felix had repaid the favor by being the padrino at the wedding of Sanchez-Celis' son, Rogelio, in Culiacan in 1984.

James Kuykendall

A federal registration form was found, authorizing a private radio telephone network in the name of Rosario Valenzuela-Diaz at Ave. Universidad #8, Col. Domingo Silvas, Mexico DF. *Our past investigations had revealed that several houses known to belong to Miguel Felix were registered in the name of Rosario Valenzuela-Diaz, as well as telephone and utility services.

CHAPTER 5
"LEYENDA"

Almost immediately upon receiving the report from Mexico, DEA headquarters tasked its organization worldwide for information concerning the kidnapping, advising its agents to query sources and other agencies for any leads. But information had already started to filter in before this formal call to arms was issued. On Feb. 8 from San Diego, California came the news that a veteran informant had picked up something interesting. A man named Rafael Muñoz, calling from Tijuana, Baja California, had held a telephone conversation with Manuel Salcido "El Cochiloco" on Wednesday evening, Feb. 6.

Salcido was in Guadalajara when the conversation took place. The man from Tijuana had said "We did not do anything yesterday (Feb. 5) because "la leyenda" was with his wife and family". Salcido became very angry and advised that he did not care who he was with, "la leyenda" was to be done away with and if anyone retaliated for his disappearance, they would be dealt with in the same manner. According to the information Muñoz was associated with an individual named Octavio Alcaraz-Muñoz, a Mexican army intelligence officer. Also, a man named Samuel was somehow involved in the conversation. The informant did not know if the conversation concerned Kiki. On the day he received the information there was nothing to relate it to, he hadn't known of the kidnapping.

We asked several times that the informant be tasked to find out more. Nothing came of the requests. We were eventually told that the agent who handled the informant had suffered a nervous breakdown. There was no explanation as to why another agent could not talk to the informant. Did DEA think the information was credible? Kiki had taken his wife and children to the movies on Feb. 5, 1985, the day the man in the telephone conversation had referred to when he said "la leyenda" had been with his family. A Mexican holiday, the consulate was closed, he had a day off from the job!

The investigation into the kidnapping would eventually be labeled "Operation Leyenda" (leyenda is Spanish for legend). But no one pursued this information until 1988.

Finally, in July of 1988, over three years after the information was received, the informant was interviewed. He was visibly shaken and reluctant to talk. Was he truthful? The DEA had sworn by him on numerous occasions and he was considered the last word in DEA headquarters on the operations of the major traffickers in Mexico. The Guadalajara DEA office, and others, had been told to step aside when their interests clashed with what this informant was doing. And, of course, what reason did he have to lie?

The informant said that he had no notes but that he remembered the conversation and the parties to the conversation. How had he obtained the information? He simply would not answer that. Was the information reliable? "Without question" he answered. Why had he not provided more information since it was so important at the time? "He wasn't asked," he said. In explaining the conversation the informant said that he had been working on a large trafficking organization at the time. In the course of his investigation he had identified a paramilitary group assisting the traffickers. A man named Rafael Muñoz was in charge of some sort of intelligence gathering operation headquartered in an office in downtown Tijuana. He had several men working for him, at least 10. The group had sophisticated radio equipment, was well trained in surveillance and even had telephone intercept capabilities. One of the group, a man named Octavio Alcaraz-Muñoz, was somehow connected with the Mexican military and talked like a military officer, that is he used language usually encountered in the military. Rafael Muñoz was not a DFS agent, the informant thought, but he communicated with two DFS comandantes, Daniel Acuña and Rafael Chao, on a regular basis. He also had some type of relationship with Francisco "Paco" Tejeda-Jaramillo, another trafficker with DFS credentials. The group also worked for a well-known trafficker named Jesus Labra and the infamous Arrellano-Felix brothers from Tijuana.

The surveillance group, according to the informant, also conducted regular operations in the United States, following people at the direction of the traffickers and DFS based in Tijuana. The informant wasn't sure, but thought they might have even kidnapped people pursuant to those directions. The group appeared to act autonomously while in the field.

Muñoz was paid by the traffickers, including all the office expenses, but took many of his orders from a Mexican army general who lived or worked in Rosarito. The informant said that perhaps the general had a weekend home there. The informant stated that the original information as received in Guadalajara on Feb. 8, 1985 had been sent incorrectly. The conversation actually took place between Rafael Muñoz in Tijuana and Ernesto Fonseca in Guadalajara, not Manuel Salcido as had been reported. Someone named "Samuel" had also taken part in the conversation and, by his accent, was believed to be from Sinaloa. Apparently, Muñoz had sent some of his people to Guadalajara and, during the period the conversation took place, they, working with others, were actively engaged in a surveillance of someone they referred to as "la leyenda". The informant repeated that he was never asked to pursue his investigation into the activities of Rafael Muñoz in February of 1985.

Rafael Muñoz was described as about 35 years of age, 5 feet 6 inches tall, wavy black hair, mustache, usually wore sunglasses and drove a Mustang or Camaro. His offices were but a few blocks from those of the mayor of Tijuana. Several times on the interrogation tapes the inquisitors

James Kuykendall

angrily told Kiki that he must give them directions to the places he told them about. They said, "We are not from here." The voice of one of the interrogators has an accent not unlike that of someone raised on the U.S./Mexico border. MFJP Comandante Brussolo described the speaker's voice as like that of "Art Rodriguez," one of the DEA agents temporarily in Guadalajara to help in the search. Art was a native Texan, raised on the border.

The offices described by the informant could never be located and Rafael Muñoz could never be identified but the three DFS Comandantes, Acuña, Chao and Tejeda were well documented. The information was too coincidental to be incorrect but the informant was still holding back, even so long after the fact.

From the first day that the alarm went out about Kiki's disappearance, we began to receive messages through official channels on information and rumors gleaned from informants, criminal contacts and concerned citizens trying to help. Before the search was over there were literally thousands of such messages. We received telephone calls and commercial telegrams, letters, and notes dropped on the doorsteps of the consulate. DEA and the Mexican officials both received anonymous information. All had to be followed up on for the simple reason that, at the time, there were no clues, no witnesses. Some were heartening, others depressing. In their anxiety to help, agents accepted any plausible theory, even psychics were not ignored and their dreams were studied and investigated whenever possible. Police agencies in the U.S, both state and federal, passed on what they heard. Some of these many, many leads held more promise than others.

On February 13, a message was passed from the United States concerning a telephone call received by a man working for another federal law enforcement agency. This man reportedly had received a telephone call on the previous day from a man he knew as William Wayne Collins. Collins had called from Guadalajara, Mexico and he was noticeably upset because, according to the information, Collins had been standing less than 100 feet from the site where the DEA agent had been kidnapped. According to Collins, he had recognized two of the men as being members of the Tomas Morlett drug trafficking organization. Collins had not realized he was watching the kidnapping of a U.S drug agent until he read a newspaper a few days later since the kidnapping did not make the local press for a few days. The message further explained that both the source reporting the call and Collins had known Tomas Morlett previously. The caller had stated that Morlett was a Mexican of French Algerian descent, that he was the head of the Mexican DFS, that he was heavily involved in drug trafficking of both Mexican and South American drugs and that he was fully capable of kidnapping a DEA agent. A subsequent interview with the source of information in the United States revealed that Morlett had previously been active in the Monterrey, Nuevo Leon and Torreon, Coahuila areas of Mexico, as a DFS Comandante providing protection for drug traffickers and large marijuana growers. Morlett allegedly owned two "Longhorn" Lear jets, red in color, with black tigers painted on the tails. He had also been in charge of the protection of the Shah of Iran during the time the Shah was residing in Acapulco after being ousted from Iran. Reportedly, Morlett was recommended by the CIA for that assignment, which greatly enhanced his political influence. Morlett was described as being about 48 years of age, athletic in appearance, 5'10" inches tall, always well dressed, sometimes with a neatly trimmed mustache or beard, usually wearing contact lenses, with a penchant for heavy jewelry, a frequent user of cocaine and marijuana, and with a medium olive complexion and "European" features. He also, reportedly, always had women around. An investigation was set in motion to identify and locate William Wayne Collins. We also queried everyone concerning Tomas Morlett, whom we had never heard of before. Neither probe accomplished much. William Wayne Collins just could not be positively identified. If he had been a mere 100 feet from the site of the kidnapping he might have been visiting the consulate but he hadn't signed in as a visitor or recipient of any of the consulate's services, at least not under that name. No one with that name had a criminal record in the United States. Tomas Morlett did exist, was a DFS commandant, but there was not much more readily available on him.

The caller also provided the name of a man in prison in the United States who had once been deeply involved with Morlett in the drug traffic in Mexico. The incarcerated man was interviewed and confirmed the caller's information concerning Morlett. He was a very important figure in the DFS, a major drug trafficker and dangerous, as well as extremely cruel. DEA had no record of Tomas Morlett.

Another development of interest, but apparently unrelated at the time, occurred on Feb. 13. The Guadalajara office was contacted by the MFJP to interview a man who had presented himself to the state judicial police to register a complaint that he had been threatened. The state judicial police had referred him to the Mex-Feds and they called us. DEA Special Agent Joe Gonzales conducted the interview of the small, concerned man. Eduardo Fabian del Valle-Lopez stated that he was a self-employed veterinarian but, as he did not earn much from his profession, he also operated a small second hand store in the village of Lopez Cotilla on the southern outskirts of Guadalajara. Del Valle-Lopez told DEA Agent Joe Gonzalez what he had experienced.

His store, a one-room affair in an adobe building, is located on a narrow, cobblestone street in the dusty village of Lopez Cotilla. The village is located just outside the "periferico" (loop) encircling the city of Guadalajara. He was standing on the narrow cement sidewalk outside his store on February 7 at about 3:00 PM when two cars drove past from east to west. The vehicles were moving as rapidly as they could negotiate the uneven surface of the street. As the vehicles passed directly in front of him on the one lane street, he was able to view the occupants. The leading automobile was a late model Ford Gran Marquis, black in color, four doors with a half vinyl top. Five men, two in front and three in the rear, occupied it. The two men seated on the outside, in the rear seat, were beating the man in the center with what appeared to be iron pipes or clubs. Del Valle was able to give a description, not too detailed, of the men in the Ford. He did, however, remember that the car had license plates from a state other than Jalisco, perhaps the state of Tamaulipas, containing the numbers 978 or 6. He couldn't remember the other number or the letters. The second car, following the first by no more than a meter, was a white Volkswagen Caribe, (the equivalent of a U.S. made VW Rabbit) two-door, occupied by three men. The Caribe had Jalisco license plates. Del Valle gave an incomplete tag number of JBT177.

  Del Valle didn't mention the incident to anyone, even though he was deeply disturbed by what he had seen. On February 12 at about 6 :00 PM he was inside his little store alone when three men arrived in a light blue pickup truck. He couldn't remember the make but it had license plates from the United States. Again he couldn't remember from what state. The three men entered the store and confronted him, one man, the tallest of the three, standing in front of the other two and doing most of the talking. This man told Del Valle that he knew his name, the names of his wife and children and that he knew where he lived and where his children attended school. The stranger went on to say that if he told anyone about what he had witnessed in front of his store, he and his family would suffer. There was no doubt in Del Valle's mind what event the men were referring to or what they intended to do. Del Valle described the leader of the three men as being about 50 years of age, 1.80 meters (5'10") tall, 90 kilograms (198 lbs.) in weight, straight black hair, dark complexion, square face, well-trimmed mustache, with an accent in his speech as if he were from Sonora or some other northern Mexican State. He was carrying a large automatic pistol, with wooden grips, tucked into the waistband of his pants. He was wearing black cowboy boots with pointed toes and a gold watch with a brown leather strap. The second man, and the only other one who spoke, was short, about

James Kuykendall

1.63 (5'3") meters tall, 100 kilograms (220 lbs.) in weight, had Negroid features, kinky black hair, a wide nose, double chins and was wearing a brown leather jacket, designer jeans and slip on shoes. He appeared to be about 35 to 40 years of age and had a South American accent. The third individual, who stayed in the background, was about 30 to 35 years of age, 1.70 (5'6") meters tall, 70 kilograms (154 lbs.) in weight with light brown hair combed forward and to the side, a large forehead, protruding lower lip and no mustache. He was wearing a white wristwatch on his left wrist. Although Mr. Del Valle had not reported the happenings of February 7 to anyone, his fear for his family convinced him that he needed protection and he presented himself at the office of the Jalisco State Judicial Police on February 13 to ask for assistance. Mr. Del Valle gave the descriptions of the three who had visited him, to a police artist who drew composite pictures for the investigators. Upon seeing the composite drawings, Comandante Pavon said that John Doe #1, the man who had done all the talking, resembled Tomas Morlett and that Morlett was perfectly capable of committing the kidnapping.

Eventually, both Eduardo Del Valle and Gilberto Villanueva, the Consul General's chauffeur, consented to and were subjected to an interview under hypnosis and their recollections were essentially the same as their original statements. Six days after the kidnapping occurred and five days after we had become aware of it, everyone was working night and day, feverishly trying to find something to lead us to Kiki. There were no clues. There had been no ransom calls, no claims by any group that they had him, no informant had come forward with something positive. Yes, each rumor was being checked out, every anonymous call and letter was being treated as fact, each and every one of the messages received from the United States advising us to look here or there or somewhere was followed up. But most disconcerting of all was the growing realization that DEA's much-acclaimed network of informants knew nothing!

¿O Plata O Plomo?

Not a hint, not a boast, no gossip, nothing. We found the traffickers' homes, their businesses, their ranches, their paramours, their bankers, but we couldn't find where they had Kiki. In fact we didn't really know who had Kiki. After those first few days I became frustrated with the lack of positive action by the Mexican authorities and broke a cardinal rule. Employees at the level of office agent-in-charge were not permitted to talk to the press without clearance but the press was there, and clamoring for information. I gave them addresses and names and they produced news stories. The Mexican government fumed. The obvious affluence of the trafficker's lifestyles, their impunity from law enforcement, their enormous wealth in the midst of poverty, were the things the reporters found and reported. The news people received no cooperation from the Mexican government but they continued to dig and publish or televise and their efforts eventually help to force the Mexican government to take positive steps to halt the bad publicity. When Kiki was kidnapped many U.S. officials really believed that the Mexican government would take immediate, strong, action against the traffickers, of course these same U.S. officials had never read the reports available to them on the collusion between the traffickers and the government. When no action was forthcoming, the disillusioned U.S. officials issued strong criticisms against the Mexican government's lack of response. Mexican officials then made strong statements against the U.S. and DEA. One such statement, especially distasteful, was made by Jesus Sam-Lopez, the official in the Mexican Attorney General's office in charge of the eradication campaign. Sam-Lopez publicly said that the U. S. was making too big a fuss about one agent, when the Mexican government lost many officers and soldiers every year in the war against drugs. Of course one of the reasons we were unable to get more immediate response on February 8 was because the MFJP agents in Guadalajara were searching the mountains of Colima for the killer of one of their own. The Mexicans always reacted immediately and firmly when one of their officers was attacked. Although we asked no more than that, we didn't get it.

In spite of the problems there was much of which to be proud, DEA had said "to hell with the budget" and committed everything to the search. The organization was small, not well known and ill equipped in 1985 but it sent what it had and scrounged what it could from other sources.

The agents who arrived for temporary duty were the cream of the crop; they came to work and work they did. Some of the MFJP agents had friends in DEA and some of them had known Kiki personally and these men tried as well. Consul General Richard Morefield and the staff, and employees of the consulate, quietly and unselfishly stepped back and supported the DEA personnel who flooded their building and unsettled their lives.

But the real tears of gratitude and pride were for the friends we had made in Guadalajara and throughout Mexico. Knowing full well that DEA agents were not much in favor by their government at that time and that there might even be some danger in associating with us, they came, to offer their services, their help, their strength and their knowledge. Without the U.S. passport to shield them, without DEA's warriors to fight for them, with little or no resources, motivated by friendship and common decency, these people were the strongest of all.

DEA's Administrator, Francis "Bud" Mullins, came to Guadalajara to see firsthand what was happening. The MFJP stopped everything to set up security, insuring that nothing would happen to the DEA chief. One entire MFJP group was taken off the search and assigned to protect him. Mr. Mullins, a senior FBI agent as well as DEA's administrator, was totally confused with the Mexican investigation and Mexico. He was also unhappy with the DEA's efforts in Guadalajara. Having spent his law enforcement career in the United States operating with the authority and reputation endowed by a FBI badge, he was not able to comprehend how anyone could accomplish anything working without authority, depending entirely on his wits to survive and function. Administrator Mullins asked to be issued a pistol to carry for his personal protection. The office had no pistol to issue, we were not in the U.S. with a big supply room. Besides, we had no authority to carry weapons in Mexico. One of the agents loaned him a .38 revolver, which is all he would carry, as that was the FBI issue. He then all but demanded a holster, stating that he could not carry a pistol without a holster. Luckily, one of the agents had an old one stashed somewhere. After two days of frustration he traveled to Mexico City.

In Mexico City he met with the Director of the Mexican Federal Judicial Police, Manuel Ibarra, and with Ambassador Gavin and others before returning to Washington, D.C, but not before he and the Ambassador made some scathing news releases.

Some people in Washington applied a little more pressure than others. William Von Raab, the commissioner of U.S. Customs, received a call from the Administrator of DEA, upon his return from Mexico, asking if he could do anything to help. Von Raab consulted with his staff and a few old hands remembered "Operation Intercept" from the seventies and how effective it had been in making people realize a problem existed. The commissioner of Customs gave the order to initiate 100 percent inspections at all ports and airports receiving travelers from Mexico. In addition, small ports without the staffing necessary for full security were shut down and the inspectors reassigned to help at the larger ports. The Mexican government cried foul, but now they were not alone as the U.S. businessmen also raised their voices in protest. Politics and business should be kept separate, they said, look for your agent but don't bother us; we aren't drug traffickers. Von Raab withstood the storm for seven days before the order came from upstairs to cease and desist. Patriotism wanes when profits fall. But that effort by U.S. Customs really upset the Mexican people and they put a lot of pressure on their government to end it.

During the time that Customs was conducting its 100 percent inspection of persons and vehicles coming from Mexico an automobile was searched at the port of Hidalgo, Texas, and the driver, a female, became indignant at the delay. She told the inspector that there was no reason to be conducting the searches and that they weren't going to find the agent Camarena because he was at the bottom of Lake Chapala. The inspector didn't like her remark and referred her for questioning by Customs agents. They referred the matter to a customs investigator in Laredo with prior experience in Mexico and who had become a friend of Kiki. He felt the information should be passed on. When the irate traveler was identified as the daughter of Tomas Morlett, already a suspect in the investigation, DEA agents were called in to interview her. The subject told the agents that her father, Tomas Morlett, while visiting his brother in Mexicali, had made the statement that "Camarena had been killed and his body dumped in Lake Chapala". Morlett's daughter said that she thought her father had direct knowledge concerning Camarena's abduction but that he would be untruthful if interviewed. She told the agents that Tomas Morlett lived with his current wife in Mexico City at Leonardo De Vinci #98 and that his telephone number was 598-2176.

Too much coincidence, everyone thought. We checked again. Morlett existed. He was a DFS co-coordinator, the DFS had two red Lear jets with black Tigers painted on the fuselage, and Morlett had been in charge of the Shah's security in Acapulco.

A photo of Morlett was obtained and the word was put out to look for and detain him. Sometimes the unbelievable happens. DEA agents stationed in Calexico, California, found him and secured the assistance of a MFJP comandante to help them. On Feb. 23 Tomas Morlett arrived at the Tijuana airport from Mexico City and was met by DFS agents who speeded his trip through the airport. Morlett left the airport in a gray Chrysler LeBaron accompanied by several people and with several bodyguards in attendance. He was lost temporarily but the group looking for him learned he had traveled to Mexicali. Further information indicated that he would be traveling to La Paz by automobile so surveillance was established on the highway to Tijuana. The Chrysler LeBaron was stopped. Tomas Morlett was inside, along with two other men and two women. He was extremely indignant and threatened the MFJP Comandante with reprisals. Morlett demanded that the comandante not make public his DFS credentials.

The other two men were identified as Eduardo Ramirez-Ortiz and Enrique Gonzalez-Aguilar. Although they carried credentials identifying them as security agents for the Mexican national pawnshop, they were obviously Morlett's bodyguards. One woman was Morlett's wife, the other Ramirez's girlfriend. Three handguns were found in the car, one lying on the seat and one each on the persons of Ramirez and Gonzalez. Significantly, one of the pistols was a .45 caliber semi-automatic with wooden grips.

Tomas Morlett-Borquez was paraded before television cameras and asked if he had any knowledge of the whereabouts of DEA Special Agent Enrique Camarena. He answered by looking away from the camera and stating that he knew nothing. Surprisingly, he did say that he had been to Guadalajara, staying at the Hotel Plaza del Sol on Feb. 13 and 14. Morlett said that he had been sent to help in the investigation. The three men were put aboard a Mexican government airplane and sent to Mexico City, allegedly to be interrogated. They were soon released and dropped out of sight for a while.

When Morlett was detained he was sporting a beard two to three weeks old, wearing eyeglasses and his feet were clad in black cowboy boots with pointed toes.

Hotel registration records for the Hotel Plaza del Sol were obtained and show that Tomas Morlett was registered in rooms 2130 and 2131, but on Feb. 11 and 12. The hotel records indicate that he arrived from Mexico City.

Tomas Morlett-Borquez was born Jan. 8, 1937 in Mexicali, Baja California, Mexico, the same city where Enrique Camarena-Salazar was born roughly ten years later.

James Kuykendall

Tomas Morlett was arrested in California in 1960 for auto theft and deported to Mexico after serving time in Lompoc penitentiary. He was again expelled to Mexico from Texas for the same offense, trafficking in stolen automobiles. At the time of his second arrest he was carrying credentials identifying him as an agent of the Direccíon Federal de Seguridad. The first conviction should have prevented him from re-entering the United States. But agents of the DFS enjoyed some unusual privileges, sometimes to the dismay of auto owners in the U.S.

When FBI Agent Bob Montoya was working on the stolen car investigation in southern California, which would lead to the indictment of the Director of the DFS, Miguel Angel Nazar-Haro, and the dismissal of the United States Attorney William Kennedy, the head of the Registro Federal de Automoviles was one Tomas Morlett. That was the agency charged with preventing the entry of illegal automobiles into Mexico and with the issuance of permits for automobiles to legally enter Mexico. All the stolen cars entering Mexico as a result of the activities of this massive auto theft ring had permits issued by Morlett.

On the 26th of January in 1987 Tomas Morlett met his death in Matamoros, Mexico, gunned down in the street in front of the infamous restaurant/bar Piedras Negras. Another man, Saul Hernandez, met his fate at the same time. Hernandez was a well-known trafficker from that area. Conflicting stories from the authorities cloud what actually happened. The first version was that the two men were gunned down from a passing Ford Gran Marquis, but the bullet impacts on the opposite wall indicate that the shots came from the direction of the door of the bar. Also, Hernandez reportedly had large bruises on his face, from severe blows. After his death it was learned that Morlett had been a recent, frequent, visitor to the area of the lower Rio Grande valley of Texas, and had been seen in the company of an FBI agent several times, something that had not escaped the local press. Once again Morlett had somehow obtained travel documents to enter the United States, in spite of his extensive criminal record.

¿O Plata O Plomo?

When Morlett was murdered in Matamoros he was wearing contact lenses and was clean-shaven.

In Laredo one day, a federal agent with some artistic skills drew a beard and eyeglasses on the composite drawing made at the veterinarian Del Valles' instructions. Tomas Morlett-Borquez stared back from the paper. The image was identical to the picture of Morlett taken after his arrest on the Tijuana highway. Why should the U.S. Central Intelligence Agency want to guard information about a dead, car thieving, dope dealing, murdering, ex-comandant of a now defunct secret police? In 1989 the freedom of information request was summarily dealt with. No!

From Spain came another lead, passed through DEA headquarters. A wiretap that the Spanish police had placed on some important Colombian cocaine traffickers in Madrid was being closely monitored because of the ties the traffickers had with Guadalajara traffickers, most notably Miguel Felix-Gallardo. The operation, coordinated out of Mexico City, but with most of the activity in Guadalajara, had been ongoing for more than a year.

DEA headquarters said that a female in Madrid had called Juan Ramon Mata-Ballesteros, inquiring about his health. Through a simple code they discussed Kiki's kidnapping with Mata-Ballesteros stating he had not been involved. Mata-Ballesteros was a Honduran citizen who had married into a major Colombian cocaine trafficking family but had proven himself to be more ambitious than they. He had established a very profitable arrangement with Miguel Felix. Felix provided the transportation from South America, though Mexico, to the southwestern United States. Mata provided the cocaine through his Colombian connections. The millions in profits were returned to Guadalajara by various means, sometimes on the same aircraft. Mata invested his share in Spain and Colombia. Felix opted for investments in Mexico and the United States. The Spanish police provided a telephone number in Guadalajara where Mata was staying. The telephone number was registered to the Plaza del Sol Hotel on Avenida Lopez Mateos.

James Kuykendall

The information was provided to Comandante Pavon-Reyes and his agents, without revealing our source, and a plan was formulated to place the hotel under surveillance and to have two DEA agents register in a nearby room in the hotel until we were sure that Mata, or some other important trafficker, was actually in the room. Some DEA agents checked into the hotel and other units set up surveillance around the area. There was some activity on the floor where Mata was suspecting of staying. Then, suddenly, all was quiet. The agents on surveillance failed to see the occupants of the room leave the hotel. The next morning, DEA agents interviewed the manager of the hotel who told them that someone named Fernando Garcia from Veracruz had registered into room number 836 at the hotel on February 9, 1985, then he had rented the adjoining rooms, numbers 835 and 837 on February 11, checking out of all three rooms on February 12 at approximately 9:00 PM, which was just about the time the DEA agents were checking in. Not having a photo to show the manager, the agents could not positively identify the occupant of the room as Juan Mata but the sudden and mysterious departure led us, once more, to question the integrity of our counterparts. If Mata had been in the room, he felt secure until we shared the information with the Mex-Feds.

The Spaniards continued to prove their worth. DEA's administrator, Bud Mullins, personally called Walter White at the embassy with the news that an individual in Madrid had called Juan Ramon Mata at a private residence in Mexico City, and held a short conversation with him concerning his health. The gist of the conversation, again in a simple code, was that Mata had barely escaped capture in Guadalajara. Mullins told Walter to contact the director of the MFJP, Manuel Ibarra, and request his personal attention to the matter of arresting Mata. Director Ibarra welcomed Walter's information. He then sat on the case for two days, explaining that he was watching the house to make sure that Mata was there.

Frustrated with Ibarra's lack of action, Walter sent DEA agents to watch the house. The U.S. agents saw a black Ford Gran Marquis drive up to

¿O Plata O Plomo?

the house and a man run out and jump into the car, which sped away. Now that secrecy was no longer an issue, the MFJP agents, accompanied by Walter White and other DEA agents, entered the house and found the wife of Juan Mata's brother, who admitted Juan Ramon had been in the house. Director Ibarra explained his actions by saying his men had to be careful as the traffickers were very dangerous.

Chapter 6

"El Mareño"

The early evening of Thursday, February 28 found several DEA agents in the offices of the Federal Judicial Police talking with Comandante Pavon and several other Mexican agents. Pavon produced an anonymous letter that he said had been received by the Jalisco state attorney general, and forwarded to his office. He allowed us to read the letter and then replaced it in his desk. The letter alleged that a certain Manuel Bravo-Cervantes and his sons had kidnapped Kiki because they mistook him for a state police officer named "Guillen" whom they had been paid to abduct and who was allegedly blackmailing two Guadalajara narcotics traffickers named Luis and Rogelio Sanchez. The letter alleged that Manuel Bravo-Cervantes had offered to take care of "Guillen" for five hundred thousand pesos and that Manuel Bravo had sent his three sons to kidnap the police officer. Somehow the three brothers took Kiki by mistake and when they informed their father he told them to take Kiki to their farm located at La Angostura, about five miles east of Vista Hermosa, Michoacan. The writer further explained that the last time Enrique Camarena was seen alive he was tied and blindfolded in a small room at the Bravo farm and if Enrique Camarena was not found alive at the "rancho" of the Bravo family, his body would be found buried in the fruit tree orchard behind the house. The letter also alleged that Mr. Bravo was a murderer and was in someway related to "Cochiloco's" band of drug traffickers.

The letter was accompanied by the envelope, in which it had been received. The envelope and four pages of the letter were date stamped by

¿O Plata O Plomo?

the Jalisco attorney general's office. Amazingly, the envelope bore a return address of "Adan Vega, 1807 Wilcox St., Los Angeles, CA 90060". The postmark read Industry CA, 1:00 PM, 23 Feb. The envelope was addressed to Procuraduria de Justicia Edo Jalisco, Dom Conocido, Guadalajara Jalisco Mexico (Jalisco State Attorney General, General Delivery, Guadalajara).

Pavon said that he wanted to raid the ranch and we insisted on accompanying him and his people, to which he agreed. Plans were made to depart Guadalajara about 9:00 AM on Saturday for the trip to the farm, which was located in the neighboring state of Michoacan but near the town of La Barca, Jalisco. The raid did not take place immediately as there were other leads to run down.

Saturday morning about 7:30 AM I was en route to the consulate when I heard Alan Bachelier calling for Edward Heath on the radio and advising him that the MFJP had hit the ranch in Michoacan and were met with heavy resistance. They were sending reinforcements. When asked how he knew this Alan replied that the comandante had received a message from the site but he did know how it had been transmitted.

Heath and Tony Ayala raced to the Feds office along with two or three other DEA agents but Ayala alone accompanied the Mexican agents to what is now known as "El Mareño ranch". They arrived sometime after Pavon and the reinforcements. As two sets of eyes are always better than one, it would have been in our best interests to have had more than one observer that day.

Pavon told the DEA agents that he had sent a force of men to the ranch very early that morning to conduct surveillance and observe the activities around the house but that they had been under orders to take no action until he arrived with his men and the DEA observers.

Throughout the day we received updated accounts of what had occurred. We were told that five members of the Bravo family had supposedly waged a lengthy gunfight with the MFJP and all were killed, while one Mexican agent lost his life. When Tony Ayala returned to Guadalajara in the late afternoon we got a preview of the MFJP's version of the events as he told us of the bravery of the Mexican agents and that even the mother, a woman of some sixty years of age, had fought it out before she died in a hail of gunfire. He also told us that since the house had been specially constructed as a sort of fort, it was hard to understand how they were able to gain entrance. The Mex-Feds also told him they had arrested five other people as they arrived at the house, attempting to help those inside. Two of those were the wives of Hugo and Manuel Bravo (two of the dead men). The two women were allegedly bringing ammunition to their husbands. The other three people arrested were state police from Michoacan.

At a subsequent press conference the Mex-Feds produced an impressive array of automatic weapons and a kilo of cocaine, which they claimed to have confiscated in the house. After much urging the MFJP gave us serial numbers from the weapons so we could check with U.S. authorities and arms dealers to determine if the weapons had been stolen or to whom they had been sold. Without exception the serial numbers they provided were phony. Do I even have to say that we later saw many of those weapons once again in the hands of the Mexican agents from whom they had been borrowed for the press photos?

Later, when it became apparent that something was amiss, Pavon admitted that they had planted the cocaine to strengthen their case against the Bravo family for shooting at them.

The truth about the incident at the "Mareño Ranch" was not readily apparent and in our efforts to find Kiki and Capi we pushed for a search of the orchards and grounds of the ranch to follow up on the other information in the letter. The MFJP agreed to the search but it was delayed for four days due to the funeral of the young Mexican federal agent who died during the massacre. The bullet riddled and bloodstained home and outbuildings of the small farm were visited by many curiosity seekers, public officials and the foreign media during that time.

¿O Plata O Plomo?

The search finally took place on March 5. DEA Agents Shaggy Wallace and Bobby Hernandez, accompanied by some 75 Federal and Jalisco State police, drove to the ranch to conduct the operation. Federal Judicial Police Comandantes Espino and Cano headed the Mexican effort and they contracted 25 local campesinos to dig in search of the bodies, which we had all concluded would be found.

About 3:00 PM the campesinos began half-heartedly looking for the bodies of the missing U.S. agent and Captain Zavala, obviously still angry and confused about the violence that had taken the lives of the Bravo family.

Around 4:00 PM the Governor of the state of Michoacan, Cuauhtemoc Cardenas, made a short, angry visit to the site, becoming more irate upon learning that the police were at the ranch without his knowledge. Cardenas later made strong protests to the Federal government, demanding an investigation, an investigation that did not take place for several months.

The search was called off about 5:00 PM, without positive results. In addition to the campesinos with shovels, the police officers walked over the entire ranch without finding anything of consequence. The DEA agents drove slowly back to Guadalajara, again empty-handed.

That evening I caught a flight to Mexico City, having been summoned to help write a paper for the Ambassador on corruption in the Mexican government, a report I did not help complete. I spent the night at the Maria Isabel Hotel, adjacent to the American Embassy.

Up early the next morning and watching the news on the television I was startled to hear that the bodies of Enrique Camarena and Alfredo Zavala had been found the previous evening at the "El Mareño" ranch in the state of Michoacan. The reporter continued by stating that a peasant farmer had discovered the bodies near the area that had been searched the previous day.

What had actually happened at the Bravo ranch?

James Kuykendall

Very early on the morning of March 2nd Pavon had dispatched Second Comandante Alfonso Velasquez and some twelve agents to the "Mareño" ranch to check out the information in the letter without the bothersome presence of the American agents. Alfonso Velasquez was well known for his brutality, even among the Mexican Federal Judicial Police who have no aversion to applying electrical shock to prisoners or to administering mineral water through the nostrils during interrogations or engaging in any number of tongue loosening techniques. When Comandante Velasquez arrived at the small farm it was still very early, no later than 5:00 AM. He was met by a couple of his agents who had spent the night in the area conducting surveillance.

Present in the house were the patriarch, Manuel Bravo-Cervantes, his wife, Celia Segura de Bravo, their son Rigoberto and two 12 year old grandsons, cousins, each the child of two married sons, both of whom lived in the town of Zamora, Michoacan, about a 45 minute drive by auto. The sixty-five year old father of the family and his sixty year old wife were asleep in the upstairs bedroom of the typical cinder block and concrete building they called home while the two grandchildren and their unmarried son, Rigoberto, were all sleeping downstairs in a section of the building which was separated from the upper section by a sort of breeze way. It was this room that the Mex-Feds entered first by breaking the lock on the door to enter and grabbing Rigoberto and the two children.

Rigoberto, awakened from a deep sleep, didn't know who the men were and shouted at his father that "they" were attacking the house. The federal agents removed the two young boys from the house but remained in the bedroom, using it as a vantage point against the rest of the house. Manuel Bravo-Cervantes was a crusty sort of man who didn't take much bullying. He reportedly had killed two men in arguments and had even, at one time, been a minor local politician. When he was awakened by the shouts of his son, Rigoberto, warning him that some men had broken into the downstairs bedroom, he reacted defensively, thinking that it was the work of some of his enemies. When the men outside demanded that he surrender the house he responded by telling them he wanted to talk to the local authorities whom he knew personally since he did not believe the attacker's claims that they were Federal Judicial Police. When someone fired a shot he responded with his old shotgun that was no match for the weapons with which the Mexican agents were armed.

During the first moments of the gunfight a young Mexican agent, Juan Manuel Esquivel, was killed, the victim of misplaced rounds from a fellow agent's automatic weapon or a shotgun blast from Manuel Bravo; a question that will never be answered. This infuriated the federal officers as well as making it clear to Comandante Velasquez that he must do something to mask his hasty and mistaken actions. The house was breached and Manuel Bravo-Cervantes and his wife died in a hail of gunfire, Celia, the mother and grandmother, was shot in the back. Her son, Rigoberto, was killed downstairs, in his bed.

When the gunfire began a nearby neighbor hastened to inform a relative that someone was shooting at the Bravo house. The relative immediately called the home of one of Manuel Bravo's married sons in Zamora, Michoacan. The phone was answered by a daughter who passed the instrument to her father, Hugo Bravo-Segura. When Hugo heard that the family home was under siege he reacted immediately since, not only were his mother, father, brother and nephew at the house, so was his beloved son. Hugo called his brother, Manuel, who lived only a few blocks distant and told him to get his pistol for they must go to help their father. Manuel came to Hugo's house in the family station wagon and they made the trip to "El Mareño" in about thirty minutes only to be taken into custody by the Federal agents when they arrived. Then, beaten and tortured, they probably never knew the fate of their parents and brother before they met their own.

The wives of the two men were too worried about their own sons to be afraid of violating their husbands' orders to stay home. They got together in Zamora and went to the office of the Michoacan State Judicial Police to solicit their aid. Several police agents accompanied them to the farm where they were met by heavily armed Federal Judicial Police agents who disarmed the state agents and took the two women into custody. The women were placed in a small outbuilding at the farm, blindfolded, threatened, slapped around and questioned about their knowledge of the kidnapping of Enrique Camarena and Alfredo Zavala. They heard shouting and some gunfire and once thought they heard the voices of their husbands. Their ordeal ended the next day when they were released without explanation or apology and found their lives had been inexplicably and horribly altered forever.

Their sons were suffering from deep trauma requiring extensive psychiatric treatment just to remove the scenes from their minds; scenes they were unable to bring themselves to describe in detail. Their fathers were dead, their grandparents were dead, their uncle who they enjoyed so much, the uncle who had been injured when a horse kicked him in the head and the family did not have the money to have him treated properly, still it had not affected his mind, only made him kinder and more patient with them.

The wives of the two men were numb with shock, one of them said. "I don't know why, but they murdered that family."

The cover-up that began when the call for help was made had now cost lives. The count was six, the five members of the Bravo family and the MFJP agent.

Within an hour or two of the time the search team had stopped their activities in and around the Bravo ranch on March 5, a peasant, named Antonio Navarro-Rodriguez, stopped his bicycle on a small but well-traveled foot path some 800 yards from the farm. He dropped the bicycle on the bare ground, intending to cut some alfalfa on his father's small piece of nearby property, when he was stopped by a strong, unpleasant odor. He located the source of the smell, two large objects wrapped in plastic, and he observed the disfigured face of a human being through the wrappings. Unnerved, he hastened to tell the only person of governmental authority around, a rural constable in the nearby village of La Angostura.

Navarro and the constable returned to the scene, along with two of Navarro's friends, riding on the constable's tractor. The constable looked at the bodies and immediately departed to notify the authorities in Vista Hermosa. The mayor of Vista Hermosa, only too aware of the tragic events of the last few days, contacted the state and federal authorities, awaiting their arrival to accompany them to the site of the discovery.

They arrived to find the bodies had been uncovered by curious villagers, two male human cadavers in a state of decomposition, partially wrapped in large plastic sheets. The bodies were transported to Zamora, Michoacan, in the bed of a pickup truck where local pathologists performed the first of three autopsies on March 6. Comandante Armando Pavon was apparently informed of the discovery of the bodies early in the evening of March 5 and quickly traveled to Zamora without informing the DEA contingent. In fact, the U.S. authorities were not informed of the discoveries until after the next morning's news broadcasts, which somehow contained the information that the bodies had been identified as those of missing U.S. DEA agent Enrique Camarena and Mexican citizen Alfredo Zavala. Of course the bodies were in an advanced state of decomposition, bore no identification and the Mexican government had no dental records, no fingerprint charts nor any other information with which to make a positive identification.

My plans were immediately changed and I caught the first available flight to Guadalajara.

Edward Heath, Joe Gonzalez and Bobby Castillo had the unenviable task of accompanying representatives from the office of the Mexican Attorney General to the morgue in Zamora, Michoacan. One of the Mexican lawyers carried a Betamax video camera and recorded the bodies, the place where the bodies had been deposited, not interred, and the massacre site.

James Kuykendall

The cadavers had already been submitted to autopsies by the time the DEA agents arrived. The bodies were ultimately put through three autopsies. In several aspects, the three autopsies are different. The pathologists in Zamora were not under as much influence as their counterparts who later performed the autopsy in Guadalajara but they might not have been as well educated. The U.S. Navy pathologist who was sent later was not well versed in the kind of trauma to which the two men had been subjected and was tasked with examining a body that had already been subjected to two autopsies.

The Hospital Civil, where the autopsies were performed in Zamora, was as crude and primitive as the surrounding countryside but the doctors, according to their reports, attempted to perform their gruesome task with professionalism.

After the usual legal preamble common to Mexican criminal investigations, the official report of the incident makes reference to the fact that the two bodies were in white plastic bags and that both bodies had bindings on the arms and legs.

The description of the autopsy begins:
March 6, 1985 at 2:45 AM:

EXTERIOR EXAMINATION An individual of the masculine sex, about 45 to 50 years of age, 1.67 meters tall, ruddy complexion, skull of normal condition, lacking hair on the frontal part of the skull with light brown hair on the remainder. Wide forehead, small, straight nose, the iris of the eye a light brown color with only the left eye present. A large mouth, possibly with thin lips, a square jaw and a round face. Dressed in gray pants, a light brown shirt with black and red stars, a white "VIP" brand sweatshirt, white or cream underpants with two snaps in front, cotton undershirt with a "V" collar, "Fruit of the Loom" brand, size 42-44 large and light brown socks. Noting the absence of different teeth the following are mentioned; the third molar of the upper left jaw, and the last two molars of the lower right jaw. Lastly is found a filling of the first molar of the upper right jaw.

EXTERNAL LESIONS
>1. A deep hole can be felt on the left side of the forehead area of the skull.
>2. Multiple large bruises on the lower abdomen.
>3. The rectum bruised and dilated, caused by a cylindrical object.

UPON OPENING THE BODY CAVITIES

The cranium:
>The brain in a state of decomposition, the left temple fragmented as well as the base of the skull.

The neck:
>Shape and size normal, trachea and bronchial tubes bruised and discolored.

The thorax:
>The lungs reduced in size and shape, the heart normal in size and shape.

The abdomen:
>The liver, pancreas, spleen, kidneys, reduced in size and pale in color, the stomach and bladder empty.

CONCLUSIONS
>The cause of death of this unidentified male, approximately 45 to 50 years of age, was asphyxiation by suffocation.
>And in relation to the second unidentified body:

EXTERNAL EXAMINATION
>The body of a male individual, approximately 30 to 35 years of age, 1.75 meters tall, eyes colored dark brown, with a dark colored beard about 3 millimeters long, dressed in white under-shorts with long legs and with no visible mark, with the feet bound with curtain cord and blindfolded with adhesive tape which also covers the mouth.

EXTERNAL LESIONS
>1. A deep hole can be felt through the front wall of the skull.

2. There is an oval shaped cut, 6 centimeters by 6 centimeters, through the skin, muscles and tissue * * *********
3. There is an oval shaped cut, 4 centimeters by 7 centimeters, in the rear of the third distal of the right forearm, through the skin, muscles and skin tissue.
4. There is an area of ecchymosis and dilation of the rectum, caused by a cylindrical instrument.
UPON OPENING THE BODY CAVITIES;

IN THE SKULL   Upon separating the skin, and removing the skullcap, we find the brain and cerebellum in a state of liquefaction, gray in color and with the base and cranial cavity fractured.
THE THROAT   Shape and size normal,
THE CHEST   There appears fractures of the fifth, sixth and seventh ribs on the left side, the lungs are diminished in size and volume, the heart is normal in size and volume.
THE ABDOMEN The liver, spleen, pancreas and kidneys are of diminished size and volume, the stomach filled with a yellow, semiliquid substance, the bladder empty.
CONCLUSIONS;

The cause of death of this male individual of approximately 30 to 35 years of age, was death by asphyxiation, and he has been dead about 20 to 25 days, taking into consideration the influences of the area where he was buried.

The pathologists in Zamora said the injury to the forearm was produced by a bullet, they did not mention the hole in the top of the skull.

The MFJP ordered that the bodies be transferred to Guadalajara and the three DEA agents returned via the Mexican government helicopter. Heath was totally shaken and, for once, angry with the Mexican officials. We were all angry that day.

The DEA requested assistance from the FBI and agents experienced in the collection of forensic evidence were dispatched. The bodies were placed in the morgue in Guadalajara, just as primitive but larger than the facility in Zamora. The staff was overburdened at the time, as there were many victims of a bus accident, all requiring a legal autopsy.

Another problem surfaced. Even though the MFJP had taken over the investigation there was, in fact, no Mexican federal law against the kidnapping or murder of a foreign diplomat or official. The crime would have to be prosecuted under Jalisco state law, by the Jalisco state attorney general's office.

Someone in the DEA office, probably one of the indispensable secretaries, recalled that Kiki had visited a local dentist several times. The dentist was located and Alan Bachelier picked him up. The dentist took his records with him to the Hospital Cruz Verde, but the MFJP denied entry to the DEA agents, admitting only the dentist. The dentist entered the morgue about 10:15 PM on March 7. He later said that although he had identified the body of Enrique Camarena within fifteen minutes, he was not allowed to leave until 1:00 AM.

The second autopsy took place that same day at the morgue in Guadalajara, the pathologists obviously more educated, and perhaps more experienced. Their findings were somewhat different.

Drs. Tomas Alejandro Herrera-Perez and Luis Salgado-Salinas examined the body of an unidentified male, about 55 years of age, with abundant dry and semidry mud over the surface, signs on both wrists that indicated the subject had been bound, (but not the ankles), multiple bruises to the abdomen, the skull fractured by blows and the thyroid cartilage in the throat fractured. No mention is made of any anal violation. (The bindings on the bodies had been removed in Zamora.)

The two doctors concluded that the cause of death were the multiple blows to the head and body or asphyxiation due to the fracture of the thyroid cartilage.

Their examination of the body of an unidentified male about forty years of age found evidence that the wrists and ankles had been bound, that the broken ribs and damage to the right wrist were postmortem and that there was a hole in the left front part of the skull which was beveled both on the entry and exit sides. Again there is no mention of any anal violation. They do mention a light beard and mustache.

They concluded that death was caused by the trauma to the skull or asphyxiation, or both.

In the same report but as a separate operation, the two doctors conducted an identification examination on the two cadavers.

Utilizing removable denture plates provided by the family of Alfredo Zavala-Avelar, they positively matched the plates to the body. They also were advised that Captain Zavala had an operation as a young man, resulting from a severe injury suffered twelve years earlier in a practice parachute jump, which was required in his profession. The doctors found the surgical scar. They concluded, with certainty of 100 percent, that the, up until then, unidentified individual, was Alfredo Zavala-Avelar.

Then, using the dental charts provided by a dental surgeon, Dr. Luis Rodolfo Gallo-Ortega, they positively identified, 100 percent, the body of the, up until then, unidentified male, approximately 40 years of age, as that of Dr. Gallo's patient, Enrique S. Camarena.

When the FBI forensic experts arrived, DEA agent Shaggy Wallace transported them to the morgue. The Mexican officers would not allow them to enter and examine the bodies. At one point the agents were told that the forensic team should put its equipment back into Agent Wallace's car since as they would not be allowed to make their examination. The word was relayed to the consulate and Heath placed a hurried call to Mexico City, talking to someone in the Directorate of the MFJP who assured him that the

U.S. agents could enter the morgue. But again the guards refused to allow the FBI agents to enter. Heath himself rushed to the morgue and bullied past the guards to confront various Mexican officials and medical technicians, finally securing entry for the experts from Washington. The official making the decisions to limit access was one Eduardo Alfonso Figueroa, a lawyer from the Federal Public Ministry (the equivalent of the U.S. Attorney), who made himself scarce after Heath's call to Mexico City had apparently stirred things up.

It was a scene from a bad dream with bodies from the bus wreck lying on every table. The old building was much in need of repair with bare light bulbs hanging down to illuminate the interior. But the two FBI experts went immediately to work, examining the remains of the fallen DEA agent, removing every minute particle of matter foreign to the body, always under the watchful, and suspicious, eyes of the Mexicans. The agents also brought with them a fingerprint chart with the prints of Enrique Camarena, taken when he had hired on as a DEA agent in Calexico, ironically, he had been fingerprinted by agent Harvey Varenhorst, who had transferred out of Guadalajara in 1984. Positive and legal identification was made.

When they tried to perform the same exercises on the body of Captain Zavala they were stopped. Zavala was not a United States citizen, they were told, and, therefore, they had no authority to touch the body. They acquiesced, but at every opportunity, when no one was too interested, they did as much as they could, removing dirt particles and carpet fibers from the cadaver.

Even as they were finishing their unenviable tasks, another U.S. technician was arriving in Guadalajara. DEA had obtained the services of a pathologist from the United States. Navy doctor Jerry Spencer performed the third autopsy on the body of Enrique Camarena and, perhaps because of Heath's complaints, he was allowed to examine the body of Alfredo Zavala-

Avelar. Spencer's conclusions were substantially the same as those of the doctors in the two previous autopsies.

The hole in Kiki's skull, which, according to the pathologists, was not caused by a bullet, was the probable cause of death, but there had been much trauma, many broken bones, both pre-and postmortem. The condition of the body, especially after three autopsies, prevented more accurate analysis. Dr. Spencer also examined the body of Alfredo Zavala and concluded that, in his opinion, there was no evidence that either of the two men had been buried alive.

Prior to his work, Dr. Spencer had not been informed of the findings of the other pathologists, so he was surprised to hear that the two men had been bound, hand and foot. He said that he had seen no evidence of that. He also said that he did not see anything to suggest that they had been violated.

Although the partially decomposed condition of the bodies had diluted the features of the faces, the men could be recognized, although with some difficulty. His wife readily identified Captain Zavala's clothing as clothes she had personally cared for. The other body was clad only in underwear but Kiki had used jockey type underwear of an unusual style, and that was the type found on the body.

While Kiki's features were those of a man in repose, the face of Alfredo Zavala was contorted, as if in terror, and his hands were separated in front of his body, in a position of defense, as if trying to ward off something threatening. The bindings on his wrists were loose, broken as if by superhuman effort.

Almost thirty days had passed since the probable date the two men were murdered. No one really had a plausible explanation for the condition of the bodies. Someone's theory was that the ground was cool, the weather moist. Someone else said the weather was dry, and that was the reason. But the fact remains that the bodies were not as decomposed as they should have been after that much time, buried in an unmarked grave. There was a rumor that the bodies had been exhumed earlier, to be offered to the authorities in exchange for the reward of $50,000.00 DEA was offering for information on the disappearance of the agent. But negotiations had broken off, without explanation. There were several facilities in Guadalajara that had refrigeration units large enough to hold the bodies and the manager of one of those facilities was murdered a few days after the bodies were discovered. No connection was ever made.

    Mika Camarena had left Guadalajara some days earlier, to be with her three sons in San Diego, waiting word, and hoping. It had been hard for her to leave, but her boys needed her. Now there was nothing left to do but send Kiki home.

Chapter 7
DRAGNET

The giant aircraft had arrived just before dawn so that it was sitting on the concrete apron as the sun rose. The U.S. flag painted on the fuselage was out of place there, foreign, but comforting to some of the people arriving. The wide, heavy wings drooped low and provided shade for the people as they gathered for the brief ceremony. The air force crew, dressed in their flight suits, went about their tasks of readying the airplane for the flight, as if oblivious to the drama. A few of us would make the trip to San Diego and Calexico for the ceremonies and funeral, those remaining had another job to do.

Capi's funeral would be held in Guadalajara, the Consul General and the DEA contingent would represent the U.S. government there. The Ambassador and his wife, the U.S. pathologist and three of Kiki's co-workers, as well as the DEA agent-in-charge from Mexico City, were to be on the airplane to the United States. Kiki's body, placed in an imposing metal casket, was transported from the morgue in an old Cadillac hearse escorted by the Federal Highway police, blocking traffic, the fifteen miles to the airport. At the airport the Mexican Federal Judicial Police were conspicuously absent, and there was no one of importance representing the Mexican government.

Kiki's grandmother and an aunt were welcomed among the group, which would accompany the body on its final journey to Mika and home. The tiny old lady was a perfect picture of the other Mexico, the impoverished, abused masses.

Along the chain-link fence bordering the airport apron, were several hundred Mexicans. Some were employees of the consulate who had not been allowed to join the official group and others were simply curious onlookers. But there were dozens who were friends of Kiki, who had come to pay their last respects. U.S. Ambassador John Gavin said a few words, a priest offered a prayer, everyone took a deep breath to sustain themselves and the brief ceremony was held.

Six of the agents carried Kiki's flag-draped coffin from the hearse to the belly of the plane, their eyes streaming tears. There was no fanfare, no drumbeat, just six men, six DEA agents, on foreign soil, carrying the body of their fallen comrade. In the strained silence their shoes scraped loudly on the tarmac, one softly calling cadence and commands. The criteria for being a pallbearer? Those who had a blazer or sports jacket. No one had come to Guadalajara with a suit packed in his luggage. It was hard to believe we had tried so hard and failed.

While we were standing under the wing waiting to board, the word came that a young woman, a teenager actually, named Sara Cosio-Martinez had been kidnapped. The family automobile had been forced off the street, the rear window smashed with the butt of an AK-47. Sarah's mother was slapped around for resisting, then Sarah was spirited away by a group of unknown, armed, men. But the family was sure it had been the work of Rafael Caro-Quintero. The trafficker was infatuated with the girl and had spirited her away once before, in December of the previous year, prompting a countrywide manhunt by the federal authorities, in no small part because Sara Cosio's uncle was the national President of the PRI, Mexico's ruling political party.

Even as the U.S. Air Force crew pushed the C-130 at half the speed of sound toward the international airport in San Diego, the Mexican government was moving to quiet the storm. Unbeknownst to anyone in the U.S. government, the legendary MFJP Comandante, Florentino Ventura, had arrived in Guadalajara with orders to make arrests and stop the bashing

Mexico was receiving in the foreign press. DEA had repeatedly asked that Ventura be assigned to the investigation but had been refused.

Kiki's body was taken to a forensic facility in San Diego and x-rayed, but no other procedure was performed, because of the condition of the corpse.

The body was cremated, as per the wishes of Mika Camarena.

The ceremony at the Catholic Church in the quiet village of Calexico, California brought thousands of people to silently pay their respects and share the grief of the family. There were federal law enforcement representatives from all across the United States, and from every state and local police organization for hundreds of miles, including Mexicali, Baja California. DEA headquarters was strongly represented, the contingent headed by its new manager designee, Jack Lawn. Administrator "Bud" Mullins did not attend, having retired from federal service when Kiki's body was found.

In the overflow outside the church, listening to the services over loud speakers installed especially for the occasion, were the father of "Luis Valiente", a friend of ours who was shot in Guadalajara on September 29, 1984 by one of "Don Neto's" henchman, and "Miguel Sanchez", who helped find the Marijuana plantations in San Luis Potosi in September of 1982. Stalwart and brave men, they couldn't keep from crying as they tried to convey to me their feelings for Kiki Camarena. In those days just being there was dangerous for them.

The first anyone knew about Florentino Ventura's activities came from an official news release by the Mexican government. Twenty-four men, all but one current and former members of the Jalisco State Judicial Police, had been picked up and were interrogated, confessing to complicity in the crime and to narcotics trafficking activities. One of the arrested men, Comandante Gabriel Gonzales-Gonzalez, had died while in custody. The government said he had died of a heart attack. His widow said he had been tortured to death.

¿O Plata O Plomo?

The surviving arrestees were in Mexico City. MFJP Comandante Armando Pavon had been placed under house arrest and was also in Mexico City. The investigation had effectively been moved to Mexico City so the foreign press followed the investigation. Things quieted down in Guadalajara, the Mex-Feds had their orders; do not move without authority from Mexico City.

The director of the MFJP, Manuel Ibarra-Herrera had not yet been replaced but it appeared eminent. Ventura was reporting directly to the A.G's office, an obvious affront to Ibarra, who had replaced Ventura with Miguel Aldana-Ibarra, his first cousin, when Manual Ibarra assumed the position of Director of the MFJP in 1983. DEA's allegation that Manuel Ibarra had been responsible for allowing Juan Mata-Ballesteros to escape in Mexico City hadn't helped him. The government needed to quell the outcry.

The Mexico City television stations had almost around the clock coverage now, reporting on the arrests. Two comandantes of the Jalisco State Police had been arrested, Gabriel Gonzales and Benjamin Locheo. Twenty-one others, including some ex-members of the force, and Adan Camberos, the son of "La Comanche" were also in custody.

As soon as the legal seventy-two hour period passed, during which the government could hold suspects incommunicado, they were paraded before the television cameras and, to a man, they repudiated their statements, saying they had been tortured to secure the confessions. They all showed signs of the brutal Mexican treatment, which accompanied the traditional interrogations. Each had deep marks across the bridge of his nose where adhesive tape had been wound to blindfold them. Some had severe bruises and still others displayed red marks around their wrists from handcuffs and ropes used to bind them.

In Guadalajara we had watched, and listened, as the suspects retracted, one after another, their confessions. But we didn't really know to what they had confessed. It would be some time before the written declarations would be available for us to read. Some of us walked to a small sidewalk café on Avenida Chapultepec named "Los Rusos." The weather was beautiful and we were discussing the latest developments in Mexico City when the funeral procession carrying the body of state police comandante Gabriel Gonzalez-Gonzalez passed slowly in front of the café, just one block from where the tragedy had begun, at the U.S. Consulate. But the shadow of the cover-up had already started spreading. The count was now seven, the Bravo family, the MFJP agent at the Bravo ranch, and Gabriel Gonzalez.

Ford Motor Company manufactures automobiles in Mexico. Perhaps because of an agreement they have with Mexico, they didn't market their cars within the country with the same model names they used in the United States. Consequently the top of the line model, in 1984 and 1985, the Mercury Gran Marquis, was sold in Mexico as the Ford Gran Marquis. It was absolutely the most expensive and luxurious automobile you could legally own in Mexico at the time. Unless you were especially influential, it was the most ostentatious car anyone could drive. The traffickers had practically cornered the market on the Gran Marquis.

DEA Agent Alan Bachelier picked up information on March 25 concerning a black Gran Marquis that was alleged to have been used in the kidnapping of Kiki. The source of the information said that the vehicle was the property of Cesar Fonseca, a cousin of Ernesto "Don Neto" Fonseca. The source stated that Cesar Fonseca, assisted by his half brother, Tomas Fonseca, "El Tomasin", had hidden the vehicle in a partially constructed cinder-block house just outside the periferico; near an area know as "El Coli." The automobile had allegedly been hidden for about a month.

The DEA had an aircraft in Guadalajara at the time, a residual from the period in which so much equipment had been dispatched to help in the search. We commandeered it, no problem really, since the pilot was anxious to do something other than check the oil on the expensive craft, and overflew the area to look for the house.

¿O Plata O Plomo?

It wasn't hard to find. You could see the car from the air. I radioed to the ground units to tell the MFJP Comandante, Silvio Brusolo, that we were going to raid the house and invite him to join us. When they told him, he replied that he would have to call Mexico City for permission. The agents told him where to find us when he got his permission. Brusolo grabbed his AK-47 and hurried after the DEA agents, he could tell they were serious.

No one impeded our entry into the house; the car had been driven into what would have been the living room of the small two-bedroom concrete block dwelling. If ever competed, it would have measured no more than eight hundred square feet. Concrete blocks had been stacked up to hide the vehicle from curious passers-by but children in the sparsely settled neighborhood had removed some of them and the automobile was clearly visible. It was a black Ford Gran Marquis with Durango license plates, number FXX-879. The agents, now assisted by the Mex-Feds, found that the partially completed structure belonged to the father of Cesar Fonseca's common-in-law wife. This fellow quickly volunteered the information that Cesar Fonseca had hidden the vehicle about twenty-two days before.

A tow truck was summoned and the vehicle removed to the yard behind the MFJP office where the doors and trunk were taped shut. The DEA agents initialed the tape in order to preserve the chain of custody.

Since we were in the area, I wanted to investigate another of the properties owned by the traffickers, specifically Ernesto Fonseca. When we were returning from our over-flights of the state of Zacatecas in 1984, made to confirm information about marijuana cultivation, flying over the western portion of Guadalajara in our approach to the airport, I asked Capitan Zavala, who was piloting the small rented airplane, to circle a truck yard, which we suspected was utilized by "Don Neto" to store trailers used to haul marijuana to the border. Several trucks and trailers were parked behind the twelve-foot high walls of the compound and we saw a large house in the rear center section of the yard. I took several photos. The house sits inside and to the rear of the large, walled lot of about three acres in size.

Convincing Brusolo to join me in inspecting the house wasn't difficult. He could see it was going to be done whether he went along or not. He wasn't about to let a U.S. agent do that. Apparently the lessons learned at the Mareño ranch had impressed him as only he and Comandante Alberto Arteaga accompanied me through the twelve-foot gate. Running from trailer to trailer for cover, we approached the house and entered through the back door. There was only one man in the house, a caretaker, who pleaded ignorance of the identity of the owner.

Brusolo summoned his agents and they began to search the house, without positive results. Someone commented that the house was constructed strangely, it was built on a mound of dirt and had a tall concrete base, and perhaps it had a basement. A search for the door was initiated and, in a closet, beneath a linoleum covering, they found it. It didn't appear to have been opened in years. The basement was over twelve feet in height, with a concrete floor and walls. A metal staircase led down to a metal catwalk that traversed the room about six feet above the floor. The room was exactly the size of the house above. There were lights hanging from the ceiling and, at the throw of a switch, they illuminated the basement. The room was empty and dry. A close examination revealed marijuana seeds in the corners of the room, but the seeds appeared to be very old.

Infamous in the annals of the drug traffic in Mexico is the homosexual Cuban, Alberto Sicilio-Falcon. Sicilio-Falcon had built a house in Guadalajara with a large basement where he stored guns and marijuana; a high wall surrounded the property. After Florentino Ventura arrested him, the house passed into the hands of Ernesto Fonseca. The address of the house was Number 8, Periferico.

The address of the house we raided that day was Number 8, Periferico.

¿O Plata O Plomo?

FBI agents were dispatched to Guadalajara and meticulously lifted fingerprints from every conceivable surface on the automobile, then conducted a minute search of the interior, under the hood and inside the trunk. They removed the carpet from the trunk and vacuumed the floorboards.

This automobile closely matched the description of the Gran Marquis seen by the veterinarian south of the city on February 7. Further, it had been hidden by a trafficker, the half brother of Ernesto Fonseca, "Don Neto," so chances were very good it had been used in the kidnapping of either Kiki or Capitan Zavala.

Since the veterinarian had seen the car prior to Capi's kidnapping it was more likely that it had been used to transport Kiki. Cesar Fonseca, who was nicknamed "El Cheshire", possessed some kind of police credential and, although related to Ernesto Fonseca, was reputed to be one of Miguel Felix's henchmen.

A bill of sale in the glove compartment indicated the vehicle had been sold by Country Motores (Country Ford) on the 11th day of October of 1983 to Salvador Cortez-Barajas at an address of Federacion 326 in Guadalajara.

During March, messages were received from the DEA office in San Jose, Costa Rica, telling of a group of very wealthy, and mysterious, Mexicans who had purchased some expensive, secluded houses near San Jose. The DEA office in San Jose was not sure they were connected with the kidnapping but they were monitoring their activities closely. Apparently these Mexicans had access to several aircraft to ferry them back and forth to Mexico.

DEA in San Diego, California, advised that an informant had received information indicating that Rafael Caro might be in Costa Rica.

The Mexican government placed telephone taps on the Cosio family, trying to locate Rafael Caro-Quintero should the family receive word from, or about, Sara.

James Kuykendall

    The two efforts paid off, the Mexican government reported that Sara had called her mother from Costa Rica as she was lonely and missed her family. Sara was, after all, only seventeen years old, in spite of her mature, Veronica Lake hairstyle, and voluptuous figure.

    Combining the Mexican government's information together with what the DEA office in Costa Rica had gathered, it was evident that the suspicious mansions were, in fact, the hiding place of the missing Sinaloa trafficker.

    On April 4 at 6 AM, the Costa Rican authorities moved in, arresting Rafael Caro-Quintero, Sara Cosio-Martinez and four others. Reportedly one of the bodyguards fired a shot but no one was injured. The Costa Rican swat team did put a lump on the head of a rent-a-cop outside the house.

    The other four people in the house were Rafael's bodyguards, cooks and general flunkies. They were identified at the time as Miguel Angel Luna-Vega, Jose Albino Bazan-Padilla, Jose Luis Beltran-Alvarez and Juan Francisco Hernandez-Ochoa.

    Rafael Caro and Sara Cosio were surprised in bed together, the brave trafficker cooperating with the officers but telling them they were mistaken, that he was not Rafael Caro. He produced documents to show that his name was Marco Antonio Rios-Valenzuela.

    Sara contradicted him and part of the search was over.

    The Mexican government immediately began to pressure the government of Costa Rica to hand the trafficker over to them so they could prosecute him for kidnapping. The DEA wanted him in the United States but, incredibly, there were no charges against him. One of the major drug traffickers in the world and there had never been charges filed against him in the United States, highlighting yet another mistaken policy of the United States government.

    Inside DEA, written status reports had to be maintained and upgraded periodically on fugitives and indicted persons outside the reach of

U.S. authorities. The policy had been to not seek indictments unless the arrest of a trafficker was imminent.

Sometimes traffickers have bad luck. While the governments were attempting to resolve the problem of venue, the house, or houses actually, owned by the trafficker were searched and otherwise processed by the Costa Rican police; a surprise visitor arrived to see his old friend, Rafael Caro-Quintero.

Jose Leonardo Contreras-Subias, a really dangerous trafficker from Sonora and Sinaloa pulled up in a car and knocked on the door. Two people were with him, two more Mexicans. Juan Carlos Campero-Villanueva and his wife, Violeta Estrada, said they had been flown in from Guadalajara for the express purpose of providing company for Sara since she was homesick for her friends and someone her own age. The habits and vices of the low-class traffickers had begun to grate on her, in spite of the lavish gifts Rafael Caro had given her, expensive clothes, jewels, even a red convertible, a rarity in Costa Rica. Like Rafael Caro's business manager, Jorge Leon-Keschner, Juan Carlos Campero and Violeta Estrada were employees of Country Ford, the auto agency in Guadalajara. They were promptly arrested and included in the group.

Leonardo Contreras-Subias was a tall, ugly man with a grotesquely crooked nose and he was wanted in Mexico for the murder of an MFJP officer in Tijuana. The circumstances surrounding the murder were cloudy, but it was related to the seizure of 16 tons of marijuana in a warehouse in Tijuana. Contreras-Subias had allegedly put two men, MFJP agents, in the trunk of a car and set it afire. One of them died. Contreras-Subias said that he had just arrived in Costa Rica from Venezuela, where he owned a ranch. Of course he professed his innocence of any crime except, perhaps, ill-timed visits to old friends.

A subsequent investigation would determine that Subias-Contreras, and the young couple from Country Ford had actually been on the private

James Kuykendall

airplane with Rafael Caro and Sara Cosio when the trafficker fled Mexico in early February. One of Caro-Quintero's many henchmen had contracted a Costa Rican smuggler named Werner Lotz to pilot his aircraft to Mexico and transport the group to Costa Rica.

While the law was being researched to find a way to prosecute Rafael Caro in the United States for the murder of the DEA agent on foreign soil, the Mexican government convinced the Costa Rican government to turn "Rafa" over to them. Ventura and his group of officers flew to Costa Rica in two jet aircraft to bring the suspects back. Hardly pausing to turn off the engines on the airplanes, the return trip was made in record time.

The jets' arrival in Mexico on April 5 received as much fanfare as that expected for a rock idol or movie star, in spite of the Mexican government's control of the press. The media had managed to whet the Mexican public's appetite. Cars and vans from every television station in the city, and the foreign media, met Ventura's group. The television cameras followed the automobiles as they sped though the crowded downtown streets toward the offices of the MFJP.

The young woman, the niece of the head of PRI, was released to the custody of her parents, who made statements that they bore no ill will against the trafficker who had kidnapped her.

Ventura invited DEA to participate in the interrogations of the traffickers the next day.

A telephone call from the embassy in Mexico City summoned me to attend the interrogations, and a quick flight on Aeromexico brought me to the harrowing taxi ride to the U.S. embassy.

Three DEA agents made the trip from the embassy to the MFJP offices, Edward Heath, Bobby Castillo and I. We were escorted inside and security was tight. There were members of the foreign media milling around outside on the sidewalks and many onlookers. The prisoners were nowhere in evidence.

¿O Plata O Plomo?

Inside Comandante Ventura's office there was confusion, telephones ringing, aides running in and out, and the comandante looking tired but neat, fresh from a bath and perhaps a small nap. For no apparent reason, Ventura began to give orders furiously, to have cars brought around to the rear of the offices, not offering any explanation to the U.S. agents. Then, just as mysteriously, we were ushered into waiting vehicles, and a van pulled up to receive the prisoners from somewhere in the bowels of the building. The caravan then screamed out of the compound, with armed men guiding us out into the city streets where we raced to a remote part of the sprawling city. All the while Ventura was talking to the other vehicles on the car radio.

The ride ended at a metal gate, jerked wide open by other armed men who were obviously awaiting our arrival. The three vehicles entered the enclosure and the gate was closed, shutting us off from the outside, and the press. The place was not unknown to me, it was Ventura's private shooting range, with facilities to cook and drink while engaging in target practice, and I had even participated once myself. There was also a small glassed-in area with tables and a bar.

We got out of the automobiles and the MFJP officers helped the blindfolded and handcuffed prisoners out of the van and into the building. Each man was carefully guided down the concrete walk and up the stairs to a waiting chair. The officers milled around for a while and a typewriter was set up in order to record what was gleaned from the interrogations.

Ventura began to tell us what he had learned from the prisoners. However, it did not appear that he was in any hurry to begin the interrogations, which was why we were there. In response to my questions, wanting answers to the riddles we had left behind in Guadalajara, he became agitated and stated that my theory didn't correspond to what he had discovered in his investigation. Ventura then ordered everyone back into the vehicles and we returned to the MFJP offices downtown. Heath and Ventura had a private conversation and the interrogations were set for later in the day.

At 7:00 PM Comandante Florentino Ventura sat down beside a desk where a young man was already seated at a manual typewriter. He had an aide bring a chair and place it in front of the desk and three chairs were placed behind this chair. These chairs were for the use of the DEA observers. Ventura then indicated that he was ready to begin and the first man was brought in.

Blindfolded and handcuffed, he identified himself as Rodolfo Lepes-Montes, 33 years old, from Pijuamo, Jalisco. He stated that his profession was that of a truck driver and that he owned his own truck. Lepes-Montes said he had come to Costa Rica to deliver checks to Jose Albino Bazan-Padilla, another of those arrested. The money was to pay off a drug deal. The checks, totaling $195,000, had been sent by one of Rafael Caro's associates in California, a man named Jesus Diaz De Leon aka "El Cachas". "El Cachas" allegedly lived in Montebello, California and had a business importing Mexican products to sell in the United States. "Cachas" was rich and owned at least ten trucks and trailers. Lepes-Montes was staying at "Cachas" apartment at the Condominios Villa Gerritos in Mazatlan when he was called by "Cachas" and told to go the house of Jose Albino Bazan-Padilla and pick up three checks for $50,000 each from Bazan's father and take them to Albino Bazan in San Jose, Costa Rica. He was to fly via LACSA airlines flight #645 on April 3 and meet Albino at the airport in San Jose. Upon his arrival in San Jose, he turned over the three checks and $45,000 in cash to Albino Bazan. The checks were from the Comermex Bank in Culiacan, drawn against an account in the Ervine Bank in Miami, Florida. Bazan gave Lepe $2,000 and a return ticket in the name of Juan Francisco Hernandez-Ochoa, a name used by Lepe-Montes as he had purchased a false passport under that name about two years earlier. Lepe-Montes accompanied Bazan-Padilla and a local Costa Rican girl to the mansion where Rafael Caro and the others were enjoying their daily routine of whiskey and loafing. They drove out in a Mercedes Benz automobile with Bazan behind the wheel.

Rodolfo Lepes-Montes said he knew nothing about the kidnapping or murder of Enrique Camarena and Alfredo Zavala. He added that his current address was Rinconada Girasol #3679 in Guadalajara. The address was significant, it was located a bare two blocks from the former residence of DEA agent Roger Knapp and a telephone registered at that address had surfaced in the investigation in the United States into the trafficking activities of Jesus Padilla and Emilio Quintero-Payan. The telephone bill at the house averaged $2,000 a month, mostly calls to San Antonio, Texas and San Diego, California. Lepe-Montes said he had been at several parties with the Caro-Quintero group in Guadalajara and had met many important people in the traffic at those parties. Those he mentioned were Jose and Emilio Quintero, Rafael's three brothers, Jorge, Miguel and Mario, and a man named Arturo Alatorre. Lepe-Montes remembered "Cachas" telephone in California, 213-722-9944.

What with the many breaks called by Ventura to answer the telephone and give instructions to his officers, the second interview didn't commence until 11:00 PM.

Younger than the other man and slighter in build, Jose Albino Bazan-Padillo said he was from Comadero Cosala, Chihuahua but lived in Culiacan where he worked in an ice factory owned by his father. When he had visited a brother, Miguel Angel, in Los Angeles, California, some two years earlier, he was introduced to a man named Jesus Diaz De Leon, who used the nickname of "Cachas" and was a big marijuana trafficker in the L.A. area.

"Cachas" had connected Jose Bazan with Rafael Caro-Quintero. Apparently impressed with Jose Bazan, the traffickers had trusted him enough to allow him to handle their money. According to Jose Bazan, he had purchased the homes in Costa Rica for Rafael Caro-Quintero. He said he had paid about $850,000 for the Villa California, $250,000 for another house near

Isksu and $500,000 for a third near Coronado. Jose Bazan said he had two brothers who had served time in prison on charges of trafficking in drugs but he became belligerent and uncooperative when asked about his involvement in the kidnapping of the DEA agent. Comandante Ventura dismissed him and left to talk on the telephone, not returning until about 2 AM.

The next man the Mex-Feds led in to be interviewed was not the one we expected. Tall for a Mexican, about 6 feet 1 inch, with an athletic build, his highlighted hair disheveled, and still blindfolded, Rafael Caro-Quintero was placed in the chair in front of the desk and immediately began to profess his innocence of any crime, interrupting Ventura, who was trying to ask questions about his background.

Ventura told him to answer his questions as they were asked and the interview began. It was not an interrogation; Ventura never raised his voice, never disputed him, never accused him of anything and treated him with undue respect. Rafael Caro said that he was born in La Noria, Sinaloa and was 29 years old. He said he had a first grade education and was employed as a cattle rancher, living at Paseo Virreyes #818 in Guadalajara. He gave his telephone number in Guadalajara as 15-86-87. He said that he left La Noria when he was 18 years old to live in Culiacan and work as a truck driver. After a year or so, in 1976, he had started to plant marijuana in small plots around Culiacan like everyone did. In 1981 he began to expand and in 1982 he planted in Sonora, near Caborca and La Cienega. He was producing 5 to 6 tons annually and selling to two men from the United States, Jaime Mendez and a man named Enrique, whose last name he couldn't remember. He started working with Ernesto Fonseca and Juan Esparragoza and, beginning in 1984, he planted in Chihuahua.

He stated that his two U.S. buyers, Jaime and Enrique, died in a plane crash in the mountains of Chihuahua in 1984, and he knew nothing more about them. In 1982 he had met with the MFJP Comandante in Sonora, Moises Calvo, and arranged for protection for his fields, paying Comandante

¿O Plata O Plomo?

Calvo 5 million pesos each month to stay away from his plantings. The payments were delivered to Moises Calvo's home.

The marijuana plantations in Chihuahua were the biggest he had planted. He said that he had as many as 37,000 people working for him for 10 days at a daily salary of 2,500 pesos. He planted from June to October to harvest from September to December but he stated he had never personally visited the plantations in Chihuahua. His younger brother, Jorge Luis, made the arrangements for protection in Chihuahua with the military and with the MFJP Comandante, Alberto Arteaga. Rafael said they paid 6 million pesos monthly for each of 3 ranches where the marijuana was planted. Ten million pesos were sent each month from the Multibanco Comermex at Plaza del Sol in Guadalajara to Comandante Arteaga in Chihuahua.

Rafael Caro-Quintero said that he had estimated his profit in 1984 from the plantations in Chihuahua alone would have been 100 million dollars!

This interview was being conducted on a very polite level by the same man who was earlier ordering the prisoners about with abrupt authority. Ventura allowed one of his clerks to remove Rafael Caro's blindfold and the trafficker turned around to face the U.S. agents seated behind him, grinning insolently.

Either Ventura had lost control of the situation or had never been in control. This man was menacing, not so much in his physical stature as in the fact that he could so manipulate people with his wealth. It was obvious that the famous and fearsome Comandante Florentino Ventura had been compromised.

The three U.S. agents got up and walked out, with Ventura following. He was visibly upset with us. Edward Heath was so angry he couldn't express himself but did manage to say, in Spanish. "This is bullshit! I'm going to call the attorney general." Ventura watched us walk out of the MFJP offices.

James Kuykendall

At 4 00 PM I talked to Edward Heath. He said he was going to the Mexican Attorney General's office to try to straighten things out. I didn't hear from him again.

At 5 PM a reporter from NBC called me to ask what Heath was doing at the MFJP offices. Not knowing, I hurried over and asked for Heath, receiving the reply that he was somewhere inside. Eventually he came out and told me the Attorney General had assigned Sergio Saavedra to conduct the interrogations and they were so engaged. He also advised me to wait outside and he returned to the interrogation room that was somewhere below the main floor of the building.

Waiting wasn't easy, I convinced the guard to escort me to the place where the interrogations were taking place. Heath and Saavedra were surprised to see me. There were four other men in the room. One, an older gentleman I recognized as one of the "doctors" the MFJP always had around, to swear the prisoners had not been mistreated before they were turned over to the prosecutors, was seated off to one side and not actively participating in the events. Another man, wearing a shirt and underwear, blindfolded and handcuffed, was sitting on the floor against the back wall of the dungeon-like room. I recognized him as Rafael Caro-Quintero. There were two other men, MFJP agents, standing around awaiting instructions from Saavedra. Heath indicated that I could sit and watch but was not to ask questions, as my voice would be readily identified. On the floor in the middle of the room was a large reel-to-reel tape recorder, plugged into a wall socket by a long extension cord.

Twice in my life I personally saw the Mexicans subject a man to the infamous "calentada" meaning "heating up". The word has lost its true definition through the centuries but not its meaning. When the Spanish conquistadores wanted Moctezuma's gold, they burned his feet over an open fire to loosen his tongue. The modern Mexican law enforcement officers applied the same term to the administration of fiery mineral water into the nostrils of their victims. Holding the man's mouth closed and spurting the liquid into his nostrils, or saturating a cloth held over his nose, death came by drowning or heart attack, if the torture was too prolonged.

Sergio Saavedra, the government lawyer, motioned to the two MFJP agents to do something to the prisoner. These two burly guys took Rafael Caro to a place in the middle of the floor and laid him on his back. One of them then straddled him and held his hands, still cuffed in front of him, against his chest. The other man knelt at his head and pulled his chin up, closing his mouth and covering it with his hand. He then shook a bottle of mineral water for a few seconds and appeared to spurt the liquid into the nose of the terrified man. The man on the floor reacted violently, struggling against the restraint. This went on until the bottle was apparently empty. The floor around the prisoner was wet with the contents of the bottle. Rafael Caro slowly rose from the floor, with a little assistance from one of the MFJP agents, and was guided over to a chair where his pants were draped over the back. He pulled his pants on and, again with some help, sat down in the chair. Saavedra began his interrogation or, I assume, resumed his interrogation.

I had no material with which to take notes, Heath did not take notes, and we did not receive a copy of the tape. Rafael Caro-Quintero admitted that he was a narcotics trafficker on a large scale and he admitted paying millions in bribes to the Mexican military, several MFJP Comandantes and to the zone coordinators of the DFS. He repeatedly denied any involvement with the kidnapping or murder of DEA agent Enrique Camarena. He was not asked about Alfredo Zavala. Saavedra exhibited his respect for the man's power by repeatedly asking him to swear that he would not seek revenge against those who were interrogating him under orders of the government. The questioning went on for about an hour before Caro-Quintero was led out of the room and replaced by another man.

Leonardo Contreras-Subias was seated at the chair previously occupied by Rafael Caro and Saavedra began to question him. He also admitted to being a narcotics trafficker and said that he had killed two Mexican Federal Judicial Police agents in Tijuana. He defended his actions by saying the two men had been sent to kill him by the MFJP group supervisor in Tijuana, a man named Irachi, because of confusion over a bribe. Contreras-Subias said he killed the men in self-defense and tried to burn the bodies to hide the crime. He stated that he was not in Mexico when the kidnappings took place in Guadalajara, having fled to a ranch he owned in Venezuela, bought with drug money. He claimed to know nothing about Rafael Caro's involvement in the kidnappings.

In 1987, while helping the Texas Department of Public Safety narcotics division on a cocaine investigation, I received information that one of the suspects in the case, a Colombian citizen, was hiding in a motel in Nuevo Laredo, Mexico until the heat was off over the cocaine seizure. I obtained the assistance of the Mexican Federal Judicial Police and, along with other U.S. officers, accompanied the MFJP to the motel where they gained entrance to the room of the suspect and detained him. The suspect produced documents indicating he was a Mexican citizen and began to tell conflicting stories to the Mexican officers. One of the DPS officers had seen the man on the U.S. side of the river earlier that day; a charge he denied. The MFJP Comandante sent one of his men out of the room for some "water."

The suspect was in his mid-thirties, six feet tall, 210 pounds, and in pretty good shape, a little older and a little stouter perhaps, than Rafael Caro had been in 1985. The motel room was small and cramped with nine of us in there including the trafficker. His hands were tied behind his back and one of the MFJP agents, with a practiced move, wrapped a sheet around the suspect's legs and wound it tight before straddling him. On each side another man grabbed the Colombian's arms and shoulders and held him tight against the bed. A fourth man sat almost on the man's head and held it tight while yet a fifth grasped his lower jaw and mouth and began shaking the bottle of mineral water vigorously. At the first squirt of the mineral water into his nostrils, the man almost heaved all five of his tormentors off the bed. They fought and constrained him and the administration of the water continued, with the comandante leaning down close to ask questions of the prisoner. "Where is the money you were going to pay for the cocaine? Where are your friends?" The MFJP agents took off their own belts to almost throw them off the bed in violent reaction to the water torture. The man administering the water placed a wash cloth over the man's face and saturated it with mineral water and the man gurgled and screamed as well as he could, fighting frantically to escape the abuse.

DPS Lieutenant Kenneth Maxwell and I stood and watched in horror the most brutal thing either of us had ever seen. There was no question of stopping it. This was Mexico, this was the Mexican way and the Colombian had placed himself in this predicament by acquiring the false Mexican identification. Max didn't realize at the time that I was beginning to question that last time I had witnessed the Mexican water torture and the other man's reaction to it.

The trafficker confessed, to everything, to anything, to stop the mistreatment.

The search for men likely involved in the kidnapping was not confined to Rafael Caro-Quintero. It was unclear in 1985, as it is today, just who was the principle force behind the decision. One man? A group of men? But there were major suspects, many of them, and one was Rafael Ernesto Fonseca-Carrillo.

Lawlessness reigned in western Mexico that year, and not just the variety doled out by drug traffickers. The beach resorts were suffering from unusually high rates of crime. Armed thugs were hi-jacking tour buses and stealing from tourists in broad daylight and the incident of rape of foreign tourists had grown to alarming proportions. In Puerto Vallarta, Jalisco's internationally known resort town, U.S. and Canadian women were being assaulted almost daily. The tourist trade was starting to suffer.

James Kuykendall

Easter is a busy holiday in the resort towns. The northern tourists flock in, eager for the sunshine. The Jalisco state government wanted to protect the industry so they sent reinforcements to the authorities in the area. From Guadalajara, members of the Jalisco state police anti-riot team traveled to Puerto Vallarta to assist in protecting the tourists, and the industry. The man in charge of this unit in 1985 was an army colonel attached to the state government, Pablo Aleman-Diaz.

A group of armed traffickers and DFS agents had moved into a large house in Puerto Vallarta, obviously hiding out. Some of the group just couldn't stay at home, it was too confining and they needed to have some fun, so they took off and hit as many clubs and bars as they could, drinking and snorting coke along the way. In the late hours of the day trouble started, a fight with someone as belligerent as they, and the police arrived but the men didn't want to be arrested. They had things to hide, so they fired a few shots at the officers and raced back to the house where they had been staying. The cops followed them and called for backup. The police reinforcements in town for the holidays arrived quickly, surrounding the rambling mansion with its high walls. The local police said they knew the place since it was used as a sort of safe house by the DFS and it was owned by the chief of police of a local village.

A brief standoff took place but the attacking force outnumbered those inside and the gates were breached. Inside the police found 24 men, many of them carrying police credentials themselves.

Three of the men were agents of the Direcíon Federal de Seguridad, (the DFS). Jose Salazar-Ortegon, aka "El Paton" was a comandante with DFS. He had worked with "La Comanche" as a manager in one of her nightclubs and married one of her daughters, he was also one of Ernesto Fonseca's most trusted bodyguards. Eliseo Soto-Martinez and Rafael Ruiz Velasco-Trigueros were DFS agents. (Velasco-Trigueros was assigned to the Guadalajara airport) and at least six of the men were agents, or ex-agents of the Jalisco state police. One of the men inside the house was none other than Ernesto Fonseca-Carrillo, aka "Don Neto."

There was a virtual arsenal in the house as well, including rifle grenades, remote control explosive devices and many automatic weapons.

Among the arrestees were Fonseca's brother-in-law, Jose Guadalupe Valencia, who fell with the old trafficker in Cuenca, Ecuador in 1973, and Fonseca's driver, horse holder and constant companion, Samuel Ramirez-Razo. The remainder of the band was just your usual collection of murderers, rapists, thieves and narcotics traffickers.

Since the military was represented among the authorities making the arrests, the detainees were quickly taken into their custody, transported to Guadalajara, and flown to Mexico City the next day, April 8, 1985.

No one from Guadalajara was invited to witness the interrogations of these prisoners and DEA in Mexico City was only present when it was convenient to the Mexicans. Most of the information leaked to the press concerning the confessions was uncorroborated. Allegedly Fonseca confessed, and "Sammy" as well. But Fonseca said that it was Rafael Caro's idea to kidnap the DEA agent and he became angry when he learned of it and fought with Rafael, telling him it had been stupid to kidnap a U.S. agent, Fonseca said he had not been present when the DEA agent was killed and knew nothing about the details. In short, Fonseca accused Rafael of being the guilty party.

"Sammy" reportedly supported "Don Neto's" story, saying they had gone to Rafael Caro's house where they found the kidnapped agent bound and blindfolded. Fonseca became angry and slapped Rafael Caro before they left the house. But "Sammy" allegedly confessed to being one of the four men actually dispatched to kidnap Enrique Camarena, returning to Rafael Caro's house with the agent. He stated, however, that he had nothing to do with his murder. But, "Sammy's" confession contradicted the confessions of the Jalisco state police officers and those of Rafael Caro's henchmen. The other men arrested with Fonseca either weren't interrogated about their part in the murder or their confessions weren't considered important enough to be released to the press. They were just charged with narcotics trafficking and firearms violations.

The DEA agents in Medellin, Colombia, were working on locating Juan Mata-Ballesteros, Miguel Felix's cocaine supplier. Mata's wife was a member of a major cocaine trafficking family in Colombia. The traffickers often married within the trade. Colombia seemed to be a good place to hide, after his government-assisted getaway in Mexico City.

In early March of 1985, Mata's wife arrived in Bogota from Spain and was met at the airport by several influential men who helped usher her through Immigration and Customs checks without being inconvenienced. Nancy Marlene Vasquez was escorted through the checks by the former head of Colombia's DAS, the Directorate of Security, a well-known dope lawyer and a criminal court judge. Surveillance was initiated and lost, but her presence helped convince DEA that he was somewhere in Colombia.

Their perseverance paid off and Mata-Ballesteros was located in Cartagena, Colombia, in April. Mata's children arrived in Cartagena on board his two private aircraft. Surveillance was initiated but failed to result in the location of Juan Mata. The Colombian police and DEA continued their investigation and surveillance on several apartments and residences in Cartagena until they saw what looked like a narcotics transaction in the works. A coordinated raid with the Colombian national police on April 30 resulted in his capture. As the raiding party entered the luxury residence, two men ran out the back, one escaped and the second failed in his attempt to jump the second of two walls behind the house. Juan Mata had a Venezuelan passport in his name, several thousand dollars in U.S. and Colombian currency and a Smith and Wesson semi-automatic pistol. He said he had nothing to do with the murder of agent Camarena and that he was obviously not a violent man or he would have used the gun they found on him. He later said that Miguel Felix had not been involved in the murder either and that Rafael Caro-Quintero had killed the DEA agent because he had been responsible for the seizure of several large shipments of narcotics belonging to Caro.

Mata also congratulated the DEA agents, telling them his capture was something no one else had been able to do for twenty years.

Mata was held, pretty much incommunicado, while an argument raged between two factions within DEA. One calling for the return of Mata to Mexico to stand trial for his implication in the kidnapping of Kiki whereas the other wanted him in the states where there was a warrant for his arrest since he had escaped from prison in the United States while serving time on a rather insignificant immigration charge.

The Colombian government was then willing to give him to whoever wanted him. The DEA Agent-in-Charge in Mexico City headed the group pushing to have Mata flown to Mexico, with substantial support from his friends in DEA headquarters. For eight hours the offer stood, until two lawyers walked in with a writ demanding their client's release. The Colombian government withdrew its offer because of fear of bad publicity resulting from not following the extradition laws to the letter. The opportunity had passed. The next step was to file formal extradition papers, which both the United States and Mexico did. While this legal proceeding was mired down in the courts and foreign ministries, Mata bribed his way out of prison and escaped in March of 1986, reportedly paying one million dollars to the prison officials who aided him.

Colombian authorities found documents in the residence in Cartagena, which indicated that Mata owned 17 ranches with approximately 2,000 employees and 13,757 head of cattle. The land alone was valued at more than 65 million dollars. But Mata and his wife also owned several construction companies and apartment buildings.

He surfaced in his native country of Honduras and paid off everyone in sight, first having an old murder charge disposed of, which was what had prevented him from returning to Honduras earlier. A court of appeals irrevocably acquitted him of any implication in the murder of a businessman and his wife in 1978. Mata professed his intention of living forever in his native country and dedicating himself to his three principal pursuits, livestock, tobacco farming and humanitarian projects.

Juan Ramon Mata-Ballesteros kept to himself but must have felt he had made the right payoffs because he eventually ventured outside the compound where his house was located, to jog in the mornings. Pressure was exerted by Washington, the Honduran military wanted guns and equipment. One morning Mata was jumped outside the compound by Honduran military police and flown to the Dominican Republic where he was delivered to U.S. marshals for the last leg of the journey, to answer charges in the United States.

In the riots that followed in Honduras, protesting the illegal extradition, at least nine people died violently. Add those to the dead in Mexico and the toll rises to 16 people dead from violence related to the kidnapping and murder of the DEA agent.

Clutching an apple in his handcuffed palms, Juan Mata, still dressed in his jogging clothes, faced the television camera as he walked off the airplane in John Kennedy Airport in New York City. Looking dazed, the brave doper was next to tears as he told reporters, "me sequestraron" (they kidnapped me).

Juan Mata was lodged in the maximum-security penitentiary in Marion, Indiana, awaiting trial on the conspiracy to murder and related drug trafficking charges, which had finally been filed against him.

CHAPTER 8
#881 LOPE DE VEGA

The existence of the interrogation tapes came to light after the arrests and interrogations of the evil, old trafficker, Ernesto Fonseca, and twenty-four others, in Puerto Vallarta on April 7. But something else came out of those arrests before the tapes surfaced. Comandante Florentino Ventura's brutal interrogations of the Jalisco state police officers did not reveal the place where Kiki Camarena had been taken after his abduction, although one of the state officers had allegedly confessed to being involved in the actual kidnapping and others confessed they had been at the house, or farm, (there were different descriptions of the place in the alleged confessions) where he was taken. All the arrested state officers were lifelong natives of the city of Guadalajara but somehow they could not provide an address. And they were in custody for a month before Fonseca and his henchmen were found at the resort city.

Rafael Caro's arrest in Costa Rica also preceded Fonseca's but the interrogations of Caro and his men had not provided an address either, in spite of the rough treatment that Caro and his followers allegedly received. This seems even more illogical when the house would be represented to be a purchase made by Rafael Caro.

On the day following Fonseca's arrest, DEA was told that the Mexican government now had the address of the house where Enrique Camarena was taken following his abduction, which one of the men arrested with Fonseca had allegedly provided.

DEA in Washington, D.C. again contacted the FBI for assistance and a team was assembled to fly in and process the site. However, the Mexicans did not give us the address until two more days had passed. The forensic investigators from the FBI were already en route from Washington when the address was passed to the Guadalajara DEA office by the DEA office at the Embassy.

On April 12 at about 4:00 PM, DEA agent Ralph Arroyo stopped at the office of the MFJP. He surprised everyone by entering Comandante Brusolo's office unannounced. He interrupted Brusolo's conversation with two women, two rather officious looking young women, who were closely guarding some plastic bags they were carrying. The comandante said they were forensic specialists from Mexico City and they had been at the house where agent Camarena had been taken after he was abducted. He added that the two "chemists" had arrived the previous evening and had spent the morning at the house. In agent Arroyo's presence the two women asked Comandante Brusolo for tickets, or the money to purchase tickets, for their return to Mexico City.

Brusolo asked the two "technicians" to remain and talk with the soon to arrive FBI forensic team and, at this time, introduced Arroyo as a DEA agent. The two women made it plain they did not want to talk with Arroyo and stated they were under orders to return immediately to Mexico City. They hurriedly left Brusolo's office without the money for the tickets. Arroyo said the plastic bags appeared to contain cloth material as well as papers and cord.

With the FBI forensic team due to arrive that day, the 12th of April was tense for us all, waiting anxiously for the call from Mexico City to provide the address. The call came at 3:30 PM and several of us drove over to the house. We had never been there before but it was only one block off a street we traveled daily. When we arrived the NBC television crew was already across the street with their camera resting on its tripod and aimed at the front of the house. The Mex-Feds had leaked the address to them but would not allow them to enter the grounds.

The address? 881 Lope de Vega.

James Kuykendall

A corner lot, the side street is named Sol, the house has entrances on both streets, a traditional driveway and garage on Lope de Vega and a large metal gate for automobiles on Sol. The grounds occupy about half the block and are surrounded by an eight-foot wall, not unusual in Guadalajara. The house has two stories; it is shaped in something of an "L," with a small swimming pool or pond inside the "L." There is a covered area on the opposite side of the pool and in the very rear of the grounds, which abut the street parallel to Lope de Vega; there is a tennis court. A small one-room structure with a bath, perhaps servant quarters, sits between the main house and the metal gate along the Sol Street wall. The house itself had three bedrooms upstairs and one on the main floor. A formal living and dining room, a large kitchen and maid's quarters complete the building. At the time the furniture looked new. It was what would be called "ranch" or "western" in the U.S. The kitchen was large but a terrible mess, with dirty dishes stacked everywhere. There were carpets on the downstairs bedroom floors and one upstairs room was locked.

Comandante Brusolo was not at the house but arrived within a few minutes. Several other MFJP agents were there. They were not exactly awaiting our arrival but neither were they surprised to see us. We wandered around the house and grounds but did not touch anything. The grass had been mowed recently, the swimming pool was full of filthy water and just inside the metal gate off of Sol Street, under a carport, there was parked a beige four door Volkswagen Atlantic (the equivalent to the Volkswagen Dasher sold in the U.S.). The car had no license plates.

We sort of looked at the place with suspicion and, perhaps, even reverence, for all we knew the Mexicans might be telling the truth for once. This might be the place where our friend had died. The four man FBI forensic team arrived at the Guadalajara airport at 5:00 PM, accompanied by DEA agent Bill Coonce, recently named by headquarters to supervise the investigation into the kidnapping and murder of Kiki. The investigation had been officially named "Operation Leyenda!"

¿O Plata O Plomo?

At the time the investigation was still under the Cocaine Investigations Division of DEA, and DEA had fought to keep control of the investigation, the FBI wanting to assume the case since they were empowered to investigate assaults and violence against federal officers.

After leaving their bags and equipment at the DEA office, the visitors were taken to 881 Lope de Vega. The team introduced themselves to the Mex-Feds and got to work. It was late so the work stopped at dark and everyone made plans to begin early the next day. The FBI agents were meticulous in their search for whatever minuscule clue might have been left behind. They vacuumed the rugs, saving everything. They scraped paint from the walls, cut samples from the carpets, picked up every piece of paper and impressed the hell out of everyone by their thoroughness. The black fingerprint powder was present on every conceivable surface when they finished.

From late on the 12th and throughout the 13th they scoured the grounds and buildings. Looking inside a small storm drain near the tennis court, one of the FBI agents extracted a bent and doubled license plate. The Mex-Feds were dogging the FBI agents and one of them immediately called Comandante Brusolo over to look at the find. Brusolo demanded the plate and it was turned over.

Later a registration check found that the license plate belonged to the Volkswagen Atlantic, it was registered to Martin Sauceda-Lopez at Chimalpopoca #320 in Guadalajara. The automobile, a 1984 model, was bought for cash on 11/23/84 from Automotriz Vallarta. An investigation verified that the address, #320 Chimalpopoca, existed but the residents of 11 years had never heard of Martin Sauceda. Inside the trunk of the Volkswagen the FBI agents found two small pieces of paper. Lodged within the folds of the truck liner, they were almost overlooked. One was a receipt from a man's clothing store, "Constantino's S.A.", for the alteration of two suits. The customer's name was Amado Beltran and the receipt was dated 2/2/85. The other was a receipt from a grocery store, "Gigante" at the Plaza del Sol shopping mall, dated 2/6/85 for a total of 3289 pesos, the items purchased were not listed.

Again, the FBI agents meticulously vacuumed the automobile and dusted it everywhere for fingerprints. To date only the fingerprints of Jose Luis Beltran-Alvarez, arrested in Costa Rica with Rafael Caro-Quintero, have been matched with palm and fingerprints found on the outside of the Volkswagen. The car had few kilometers on the odometer and was in almost new condition.

The forensic experts, back in Washington, D.C. would eventually determine that carpet fibers from the house were of the same type as those found on the cadaver of Alfredo Zavala and that human hairs vacuumed from the small building behind the main house were almost certainly those of Enrique Camarena. At least the odds were calculated at one in 5000 that the hairs matched those of Kiki. Additionally, hairs found in the Volkswagen had the same characteristics.

Another find at the house situated at 881 Lope de Vega was a thin, clear plastic bag of the type that clothes are placed in at a dry-cleaning establishment. The FBI agent brushed the bag aside as insignificant the first time he searched one of the closets. When he made his last and final search of the house he found that the bag had been moved from the closet shelf to the floor, probably by another agent. This time he placed the cleaner's bag in his collection of items to be carried to Washington for further processing. This bag would have great significance later. A pillowcase found in one of the bedrooms would be found to match the sheet that had allegedly been found on DEA agent Camarena's body. Rope, window sash cord actually, identical to that which the Mexicans said had been used to bind the two men, was also found in the house.

MFJP Comandante Silvio Brusolo told DEA agent Arroyo that the house had once belonged to a man named Guadalupe Zuno, an ex-governor of the state of Jalisco and the father-in-law of an ex-president of Mexico, Luis

Echeverria. Guadalupe Zuno had been dead for several years, according to Brusolo, and the house was left to the Zuno family, specifically Alvarado Zuno-Arce. About four months prior, Brusolo said, the house had been sold to Ruben Sanchez-Barba, the owner of a real estate company, Casabella Constructadora, located on Avenida Vallarta.

Comandante Brusolo said that he had located Ruben Sanchez-Barba and sent him to Mexico City to be interviewed. Sanchez-Barba's story was that during the first week of February several armed men had thrown out all of his workmen and moved in, which he could not prevent.

Allegedly the house was being maintained at the time by a poor family who had moved in three days prior to the arrival of the MFJP. Agent Arroyo interviewed the caretaker, Jose Martinez-Hernandez. He said he had been hired by a contractor named Ramon Cepeda-Arrellano and was to be paid 10,000 pesos to care for the house.

An inspection of the swimming pool was put off due to its filthy condition. When the team broke for a late lunch on the 14th the Mex-Feds were told that the pool would be searched later. Upon returning to the house the team was shocked to see the pool empty and clean. The MFJP insisted they had found nothing of significance.

Next to the pool was a covered area, a sort of patio. On a small table there was a telephone, a multi-line type of instrument, which was not functioning at the time. Through its own sources, the Guadalajara DEA office learned that the telephone number was 22-98-90. However, the number was registered to the house using the address on Sol Street, 2492 El Sol, in the name of Ramiro Nuñez-Rodriguez.

Long distance telephone tolls for the period from November of 1984 through the time of the search were obtained. The tolls showed 25 calls in November and December to numbers in Mexico City and Mascota, Jalisco. Mascota is a small town two or three hours from Guadalajara. No calls had been made from the telephone in January 1985. On two days in February, the 6th and 7th, 44 long distance calls were made. There were no tolls either before or after those dates in February and no further service to the telephone after that date. The numbers called on those dates were not called in November and December nor were the numbers noted in November and December of 1984 among those called on February 6th and 7th of 1985.

Inquiries through friends revealed that the house actually belonged to, or had belonged to, Jose Ruben Zuno-Arce, commonly known as Ruben Zuno. The Zuno family was prominent, not only in Guadalajara, but throughout Mexico. Ruben Zuno's father had once been the Governor of Jalisco and a former Mexican president, Luis Echeverria, was married to Ruben Zuno's sister. Ruben Zuno-Arce's eldest brother was closely acquainted with Fidel Castro, the Cuban dictator, and his youngest sister had founded a learning institute with leftist persuasions on the Pacific coast a few miles north of Puerto Vallarta.

But Jose Ruben Zuno-Arce was known to the Guadalajara DEA office for another reason. In February of 1982, just a few days after my arrival in Guadalajara as the agent in charge, Kiki Camarena placed a "lookout" with U.S. Customs advising that the owner and pilot of a small airplane, Jose Ruben Zuno-Arce, was suspected of utilizing the airplane to smuggle drugs to the United States.

Zuno-Arce was allegedly living in San Antonio, Texas but making frequent trips to the town of Mascota, Jalisco where he maintained a residence.

On March 25th of that same year, Kiki reported to me that Jose Ruben Zuno-Arce had made threats against the source of the information, accusing him of working for DEA and even naming Kiki as the DEA agent who had placed the lookout, causing Zuno's airplane to be searched upon his arrival in Del Rio, Texas, from Mexico, en route to San Antonio.

Concerned because the "lookout" had obviously been compromised, we sent a message to DEA headquarters asking that the incident be investigated. Our thought was that the U.S. Customs inspector conducting the search had indiscreetly revealed the source of the "lookout". A surprise telephone call from San Antonio, Texas, just a few days later, offered another explanation. A DEA agent who had somehow befriended Jose Ruben Zuno-Arce called Kiki inquiring into the particulars of the information about Zuno-Arce. He was a little too insistent. Kiki was edgy about that afterward but we could not prove anything and, as so frequently happened, no one investigated the incident in the U.S.

When I made out my list of suspects for the combined MFJP/DEA search team that first week in February 1985, I included Ruben Zuno-Arce's name, recalling the 1982 incident.

Aside from the original information alleging that Ruben Zuno was involved in the drug traffic, the only other thing we knew about him was that he had killed two Mexican Federal Judicial Police agents under suspicious circumstances.

Guadalajara's drug magnates had so much money they had to look for ways to spend it and there was always someone willing to help. Real estate was a favorite. Since most of them had come from very humble beginnings, they wanted the biggest, the loudest, the brightest and the most expensive. Miguel Felix owned at least one real estate company himself and utilized others.

A family, named Sanchez-Barba, had a real estate company named Terra-Nova, which provided service to Ernesto Fonseca and Rafael Caro, among others. The Sanchez-Barba family was related to the student activist turned dope dealer, Javier Barba-Hernandez.

After several million dollars were seized in California as illegal drug proceeds, several members of the Sanchez-Barba family sought out the DEA and offered their information and services in exchange for the return of the money.

James Kuykendall

One of the family members, Ricardo Sanchez, even agreed to testify for the U.S. government in any judicial proceedings.

During several lengthy interview sessions they identified luxury home after luxury home they had acquired for Rafael Caro-Quintero, Ernesto Fonseca-Carillo and their associates. One of these houses was located at 881 Lope de Vega (or 2492 El Sol).

Their story was that they were constantly looking for houses for Rafael Caro as he was having trouble with his wife and he did not like to stay in one house too long. He also liked big houses with swimming pools and large yards, usually half a city block, or more, as he liked to host loud parties with a lot of people. Allegedly, Ruben Sanchez-Barba, one of the brothers who owned Terra Nova, approached Jose Ruben Zuno-Arce and asked if he would like to sell his house. The witness claimed that Zuno was not told who the buyer would be. When Zuno agreed, a price was negotiated and the house was turned over in January of 1985. Rafael Caro was not happy with the house and made Sanchez-Barba paint the interior of most of the rooms and put in new furniture.

Guillermo Sanchez, "Willie," another of the cooperating witnesses, offered another interesting story concerning the house on Lope de Vega. After Rafael Caro-Quintero occupied the house, on February 6, he found the telephone did not work and called Willie to complain and demand it be fixed. Willie went to the house late on the 7th, accompanied by two men, a friend named Jorge Gomez-Espana, and a Guadalajara doctor named Humberto Alvarez-Machain. They met with Rafael Caro-Quintero and listened to his complaints. While they were there they saw a large number of Rafael Caro's bodyguards, as usual, armed to the teeth. Willie, afterward, sent a man to repair the telephone, which still gave trouble and required yet another trip by the repairman to mend it.

The Sanchez brothers gave the interviewing agents the addresses of many houses they had purchased for the traffickers, which added to DEA's growing database of information about the Guadalajara drug cartel.

Another of the houses they had bought for Rafael Caro-Quintero was a large two story home on Naciones Unidas, where Rafael Caro's brother-in-law, Jose Ramon Elenes-Payan, lived with his family.

DEA went to work and found Jorge Gomez-Espana, then quizzed him to see what he recalled about the visits to the house at Lope de Vega. His recollections were pretty much the same but he added something. When he and Willie left the house, on one of the trips, they gave a ride to two men wanting a lift to the Hyatt hotel. One of the men was named Rene Verdugo, Willie apparently knew him, and the other was simply addressed as "comandante."

The Hyatt Regency hotels are a U.S. company, even though Mexican law requires that controlling interests in Mexico be in the hands of Mexican citizens. It was easier to deal with a U.S. company. The hotel records confirmed Jorge Gomez's recollections, Rene Verdugo, from Mexicali, had been at the hotel, along with another man, last name Nieblas, on February 8 and 9, 1985. A subsequent investigation revealed that "Nieblas" was chief of police Arnulfo Nieblas of San Luis Rio Colorado, Sonora.

The interrogation tape labeled "copia 2" is very weak, or faint, and much care must be taken when listening.

Kiki responded to a question, but the question itself is unintelligible. "I do not know him but in Mexicali they say there is a person who helps to cross marijuana, let me try to remember."

"Yes, remember, I'll give you time." Was the interrogator's response.

Kiki said, faintly, very faintly. "Rene Verdugo."

With few notable exceptions, the 44 calls made from the house on Lope de Vega during those two February days were made to known drug traffickers or their associates, many of the numbers already of record with DEA at the time the calls were made.

On February 7th two calls were made to telephone no. 65053 in Mexicali, Baja California. The number was listed to Inmobiliaria Puerto San

James Kuykendall

Felipe, a real estate agency. Traffickers like to have real estate agencies for fronts; this one was a front for a well-known local trafficker named Rene Martin Verdugo-Urquidez.

Whether or not the house was the actual site of the interrogation is still open to argument but the calls made on those two days in February were to known traffickers or numbers likely used by known traffickers. It is pure speculation whether the traffickers were being called to elicit questions to be used by the interrogators, or to summon them to Guadalajara for a meeting. On February 6th, Kiki was not in their hands and there were no calls made from the house after February 7th.

Many of the telephone numbers were of record with DEA from prior investigations, in Mexico and the U.S. Only eleven calls were made on the 6th, the remainder on the 7th. The telephone records were not detailed enough to tell us the time of day the calls were made. In other words, which calls were made after 2:00 PM on the day Kiki was abducted.

On the 6th and 7th calls were placed to telephone numbers registered to Francisco Tejeda-Jaramillo, one number in Durango, the other in Tijuana. Francisco Tejeda was a narcotic trafficker/DFS agent associated principally with Miguel Felix and he had been mentioned by the informant from San Diego who passed along the information that a group of men from Tijuana were in Guadalajara looking for "la leyenda".

A call on the 7th went to the Rancho Camino Real in Nautla, Veracruz that was owned by Arturo Izquierdo-Hebrand, an old-time trafficker and the brother-in-law of the ex-chief of police of Mexico City, Arturo Durazo. The Rancho Camino Real had figured prominently in the investigation into the activities of Miguel Felix and Juan Mata since it was the site of one of the airfields used as a stopover to transport cocaine from South America to the United States.

Other calls went to known traffickers as well as telephone numbers not previously encountered by DEA. One call on the 7th was made to a telephone number in Los Angeles, California, subscribed to by one Jesus

Camberos. By the time the number was investigated, Camberos no longer lived at the address and he was never identified. Toll records from the house in Los Angeles indicated that the occupants had made 338 toll calls to 89 different telephone numbers between January 19 and February 14, 1985. Many of these numbers were associated with the narcotics traffic.
Telephone tolls for the months of January and February, 1985 were obtained for virtually all the numbers called from Lope de Vega 881 and all showed the same pattern. Many calls were placed to telephone numbers associated with DEA narcotics investigations and many to the numbers called from Lope de Vega. However, the telephone number at Lope de Vega did not appear on any of those tolls.

James Kuykendall

Camelot restaurant bar parking lot

Sign at corner of Lope de Vega and Sol streets

CHAPTER 9
THE CIA TRANSCRIPT AND JUAN ANTONIO BRITO

The tape that didn't surface? Or the tape that never was? When Jack Lawn asked the Mexican Attorney General about the interrogation tape that had reportedly been seized from Ernesto Fonseca at the time of his arrest, he inquired about a tape, but didn't emphasize it. The CIA had received information about "a" tape. When Lawn, Ed Heath and Stephen Trott listened to a tape that same afternoon they had no reason to suspect there were others.

A few days later the Mexicans allowed Ed Heath to listen to that tape and several other tapes but they didn't turn over copies.

A month or so later the CIA obtained a copy of a transcript, in Spanish, of a recorded interrogation of Enrique Camarena. The transcript is in question and answer form, covers 43 pages and states that it covers side "a" and "b" and ends rather abruptly. I have read it many, many times and have no doubt it is a legitimate transcript of an interrogation of DEA agent Enrique Camarena.

The Mexican government did not turn that tape over to DEA.

The fifth tape given to DEA, the unintelligible one, is a copy of "copia 4" and is so faint as to be almost inaudible.

So why did the Mexican government turn over two copies of the same tape? And they weren't the original tapes either; they copied them before sharing them.

The interrogation on the transcript was the most damaging, politically, to Mexico. The Mexican Minister of Defense at the time, General

¿O Plata O Plomo?

Juan Arevalo de Gardoqui, is expressly named in the interrogation as being responsible for the protection of the traffickers in the state of Zacatecas but Kiki, in his statements, clearly said that the information came from an informant. The Mexican government must have felt something was damaging enough, or embarrassing enough, not to release the tape.

The transcript contains other information not found on the two tapes that were delivered into the hands of DEA. Most notable is that concerning the skinny dope king, Miguel Angel Felix-Gallardo. The other two tapes contain little mention of him but Kiki is interrogated at length about the activities of Felix-Gallardo and, obviously, our knowledge of those activities. At two of the trials in Los Angeles the interrogation tapes of Kiki were offered into evidence but the transcript was ruled inadmissible because its source could not be substantiated. The information in the transcript seems to place it before either of the two tapes in order and the language used by the interrogator is cruder, crueler than that found on the tapes. Perhaps it was a different interrogator but without a voice, there is no way to know.

"I'm going to have to tie him to keep him upright." A statement from one of the interrogators.

"Whitey, tie him tight, so he can't even talk." From another.

"With a Tehuacan he'll let it all out." From yet another interrogator, referring to the Tehuacan brand name of mineral water.

And so the transcript begins.

The interrogator asks. "What training did they give you?"

Kiki answers. "A three month school, they teach you some American law, firearms and personal defense."

"Do you want to die?"

"No, I have children!"

The questions, laced with expletives, continue. The interrogators query him about the automobiles in the office, the cars assigned to the DEA agents, and even his personal car. They have information about a wiretap operation we worked, or tried to work, with the MFJP, in 1984. They knew the automobiles we had at that time. But even the transcript appears to lack continuity. The interrogation must have continued for hours, days!

The interrogators persisted in their guise, obviously transparent to Kiki by then, that they were police.

The interrogator said. "If we can find the person who gave you the telephone number he can lead us to Miguel's house."

The interrogator asked. "Look, one of them we can find, give me your informants, what are you waiting for? Don't you want to go? You are going to tell me tomorrow or the next day, why not now and you can go sooner?"

Questions and statements made by the interrogators indicate that they had been watching, or trying to watch, Kiki for at least three days.

Question: "And a Dart, model K, that you were in yesterday, or the day before?"

Kiki denies knowledge of the car.

Question: "A Dart K, or a Le Baron, you were in it yesterday or the day before?"

Again Kiki tells them he doesn't know the car.

Question: "Yesterday, or the day before, you were in it, look, we have a lot of time in this investigation, you're just playing dumb or you don't want to cooperate?"

Kiki tells the interrogators repeatedly that our efforts in Mexico are sincerely hampered by our lack of authority and our inability to legally carry weapons. His answer also seems to indicate that the interrogation began soon after he was picked up.

"No, look, sir, you have to understand, we, as you saw just now when you detained me, I am not armed and I am not looking for anyone, I know they have protection."

Other statements made by the interrogators offer some information about their identity, their origin and the date of the interrogation.

¿O Plata O Plomo?

Question: "Look, dummy, spit out the addresses, there is no problem, it's understandable, you're worried about your safety, you're worried about yourself, in another hour we are going to bring a doctor, you continue cooperating and there is no problem."

Question: "Look, remember, these things are going to be checked out, you aren't going to be here just one day, it could be three or four days."

Question: "You bastard, we are not from here, how are we going to know the streets, don't' be kidding us."

The transcript ends with more questions about an informant we called Juan Garcia, who had lived for a time in Zacatecas, then it ends abruptly. There were five cassette tapes in the package I delivered to Washington, rather cheap cassettes actually, and obviously not the originals, but copies. The cassettes were labeled,"Copia 1", "Copia 2", "Copia 3", "Copia 4" and "Copia 5."

"Copia 2 and copia 4" were the two tapes which contained the interrogations of "Kiki" Camarena.

"Copia 2" preceded "Copia 4" in content and it was also somewhat less intelligible. And the actual recording on the tape was shorter, maybe half as long.

The very first voice was that of a man, in Spanish, asking. "Let's see, where is the house?"

Then Kiki's reply, very weakly. "I think it's on Topacio".

The questions and answers are obviously the continuation of an ongoing interrogation, not anywhere near the beginning. The tapes and the bodies, almost the only clues. Edward Heath said he had listened to five tapes, or tried to; one was completely unintelligible. One was the tape he had listened to in the presence of DEA Administrator Lawn, the interrogation of DEA agent Enrique Camarena, "copia 2". And there was the second cassette recording of the interrogation of Kiki, "copia 4". "Copia 1" contained radio conversations from the DEA office in Guadalajara, overheard and recorded on March 5 and 8 of 1985. The voices of several of the DEA personnel are clearly heard on the tape, including my own.

"Copia 3" was a real puzzle for a while. The Mexicans had told Heath that it was the interrogation of an FBI informant and his wife. There was some speculation that it was a man we had heard of briefly during the days before the bodies were found, an FBI informant who had provided some information about large-scale marijuana trafficking in Mexico and had professed to know Rafael Caro-Quintero. The FBI confirmed that their informant had failed to contact them after their last meeting.

On the tape the interrogators asked the man's name.

He answered. "Antonio, Juan Antonio."

The FBI said that was a name used by their informant.

Antonio Brito asked to be in the middle of this band of thieves and he was well aware of their methods, but he probably never thought he would become a victim of those same methods.

I didn't hear the tape of Antonio Brito's interrogation until August of 1985 but by then I was sure of his identity. Listening to the tape confirmed it, and helped corroborate much of what we had learned about the large-scale marijuana traffic.

Brito surfaced about Feb. 20, 1985. At least he surfaced to those whom he had talked to before, the U.S. Border Patrol.

DEA had only heard of him in passing, as a possible Cuban refugee working for the DFS around Piedras Negras, Coahuila. It was also reported that he was a fugitive from the state of Texas, using an alias of Antonio Vasquez. He had also been identified to us as a DFS agent working around Zacatecas and providing protection for the traffickers cultivating marijuana in that area. But that was in mid-1984.

In fact, his true surname was not even Brito but he had been born in Cuba and had lived for a while in the United States.

He must have felt some heat or he wouldn't have sought out his old contacts; things had been going well for him.

¿O Plata O Plomo?

He made contact through a U.S. Border Patrol agent he knew and after several telephone calls offering to exchange interesting information for some unspecified consideration, he agreed to meet with U.S. Agents concerning what he knew about the drug traffic in northern Mexico. The Border Patrol notified the FBI. While we were busy in Guadalajara in February, the DEA office in Mexico City was contacted by another agency offering some information that might be of some help. The Federal Bureau of Investigation said they had an informant who was allegedly very well informed about all the large-scale marijuana trafficking in Mexico and who might have some knowledge of the kidnapping. The FBI was planning to meet with their informant for a series of debriefings.

The information was timely to the search for Enrique Camarena and DEA was invited to send a representative to the meetings. But the personnel in Guadalajara were working night and day and there was no one to spare. Consequently, the DEA representative who went knew little about the investigation in Guadalajara or about the major traffickers centered in Guadalajara. When he arrived for the meeting the DEA agent was not provided with the man's identity nor was he told that the man had been working with the DFS. Even with the life of an agent at stake, the infamous interagency rivalries would not be put aside.

The meetings took place in a hotel in El Paso, Texas, on February 26, 27 and 28. The DEA representative was only allowed to participate during one day of the interviews.

Juan Antonio Brito had his new and very young wife with him at the hotel but she was not present at the debriefings. In three days of interviews he had much to tell. Those present didn't understand most of it, which was unfortunate, as it might have helped clear things up more quickly. By zealously guarding their source of information the FBI did not have access to the knowledge that the Guadalajara DEA office had spent years accumulating.

James Kuykendall

When the results of the interview were relayed to Guadalajara there was nothing of apparent interest to the investigation at hand, that of finding a missing agent and informant. Several notorious traffickers were identified, along with some ranches and houses and a motive was suggested, that the traffickers might be angry about the seizure of the large marijuana processing area of Bufalo, Chihuahua in November of 1984. But the informant had stated, at least according to the message, that he had never heard the traffickers mention retaliating against DEA.

Brito told the U.S. interviewers that he had been working as a DFS agent for several years and, since 1983 was under the command of Rafael Aguilar-Guajardo, the DFS co-coordinator for northeastern Mexico. He was stationed at Piedras Negras, Mexico under a comandante called "Champion" until February of 1984 when he was told to go to Guadalajara and work under the DFS Comandante there. In truth, Brito could not have been a legitimate agent, since he was not a Mexican citizen, but the people handing out DFS credentials over-looked things like citizenship if the applicant had some skill that they could put to good use Because the DFS Comandante in Guadalajara, Federico Castel del Oro, had recently been shot several times by one of his own men, ironically with the surname of Camarena, over a difference of opinion about how to divide some bribe money, the Sub-director of the DFS in Mexico City, Alberto Estrella, had come to Guadalajara to temporarily manage the office, if that den of thieves could be called an office.

Brito probably liked the assignment. He had a wife there, the DFS secretary, whom he had met and married during a previous tour at the city when he had worked under Comandante Rogelio Munoz. He also had a child, a son, with that woman.

Shortly after arriving in Guadalajara he was sent to Zacatecas to work for a murderous DFS Comandante named Miguel Angel "El Negro" Vielma, guarding marijuana plantations, which belonged to "the family" and their associates. Vielma had previously been a Federal Judicial Police agent and during an assignment in Hermosillo, had killed his partner in a gunfight over money. He had spent some time in prison over the incident.

Brito spoke perfect English and found favor with the traffickers and the DFS bosses because of that ability. Brito hung around Fresnillo and Zacatecas. In Zacatecas he worked for Vielma and DFS Comandante "Ñoño" Nuncio but Nuncio was killed when he piled up a motorcycle on the highway. The motorcycle was mourned as much as Nuncio among the local sporting crowd, as it had been the winner in a hotly contested, and waged upon, match race staged by the traffickers between Fresnillo and Zacatecas. The federal highway patrol had blocked the highway and provided security for the race.

Until the raids by the Mexican Federal Judicial Police in that area in May of '84, Juan Antonio Brito lived at the Motel "El Bosque" in Fresnillo along with several other DFS agents, protecting the traffickers and their crops. He regularly hung out at a safe house in Zacatecas that a big dope trafficker named Ramiro Mireles-Felix had provided to the DFS.

After the raids and arrests in Zacatecas in the spring of 1984, the authorities felt it was inappropriate to allow massive marijuana cultivation until the publicity died down so Brito went to live in Torreon, Coahuila and guard the fields in Coahuila, Durango and Chihuahua. While living at a motel in Torreon with other DFS agents, he met a young woman from the border town of Reynosa and she moved in with him. By this time he had ascended in importance and was in charge of some of the family's operations in the north.

Rafael Aguilar-Guajardo and the Caro-Quintero organization had fields of marijuana planted near Morelos, Coahuila and Bufalo, Chihuahua, along with many other locations he couldn't recall exactly.

In the late summer of 1984 the Mexican army discovered some fields near San Fernando, Chihuahua, which belonged to the organization but the seizure was never reported. During Brito's three days of interviews in El Paso he told the agents that MFJP Comandante Miguel Aldana and his men had stolen some of the marijuana in Bufalo before it was burned and Rafael Caro-Quintero was outraged and had threatened to kill Aldana's family.

Right after the raids in Zacatecas were made in May of 1984, Rafael Caro-Quintero appointed his brother-in-law, Jose Ramon Elenes, as his man in charge of the fields in northern Mexico, replacing "El Negro" Vielma. Guadalajara DEA's notice to the GOM in May of 1984 that the DFS Comandante, "El Negro" Vielma, was in cahoots with the traffickers rendered him useless to the traffickers since the government was trying to distance itself from that operation.

As was the practice, the man on the scene, being the general manager of the operation, was called "El General" by his subordinates. Brito was apparently well liked by Jose Ramon and visited him often at his home on Naciones Unidas street in Guadalajara.

Brito said that in September of 1984 he visited the fields near Bufalo, Chihuahua with Rafael Aguilar and another DFS agent named Jorge Salazar.

In addition to his brother-in-law, Ramon Elenes, Rafael Caro had another man known as "the doctor" who was in charge of his operations in another part of Mexico but the doctor had been killed in Guadalajara. Brito was actually referring to Juan Antonio Fonseca-Solares alias "el doc".

Juan Fonseca died on November 20, 1984 during a bloody encounter with the local police. He and his companions had visited a Chinese restaurant and, upon leaving, got into a fight with the security guard, who called the police. The police arrived a little late but put out the description of the cream-colored Gran Marquis on the radio. Other police units found the vehicle and began a lengthy pursuit when the driver failed to pull over. As a result of the high speed chase, the Gran Marquis hit a concrete median less than a block from the Jalisco governor's mansion and lost a wheel, rendering it inoperable. At that point the gunfight began in earnest. The Gran Marquis was fully armored and the occupants had automatic weapons, while the police officers had only handguns. But the windows on the Gran Marquis did not open so the people inside had to open the doors to return fire, which finally enabled the police to get the upper hand. "El doc" was killed, along with his wife, Doris Elenes de Fonseca, who was the sister of Rafael Caro's wife. Another male occupant in the Gran Marquis died and "el doc's" brother and sister were wounded. One city patrolman lost his life as well. The bodies of the traffickers were taken to the morgue to await an investigation. The following day, Sergio Espino-Verdin, the Guadalajara head of the Federal Political Investigations used his authority and that of a local doctor, Humberto Alvarez-Machain, to transfer the bodies from the morgue to a funeral home.

On January 23, 1985 Brito reportedly met with Rafael Caro-Quintero and DFS Comandante Tomas Morlett-Borguez at the La Longosta restaurant in Guadalajara. No one discussed kidnapping or killing anyone but Rafael Caro was angry over the losses in Chihuahua. Brito claimed that Morlett was in Guadalajara with a large group of men, on an assignment for the traffickers. Brito gave the interviewers in El Paso the addresses of two safe houses that DFS and the traffickers used in Torreon along with the corresponding telephone numbers. He also provided several names of local officials involved in providing protection for the traffickers in the area. They were the comandante of the DFS, the director of the state judicial police and the comandante of the MFJP.

Antonio Brito also told the interviewing U.S. agents that one of the traffickers was a Durango state police officer that lived in the safe houses and worked with the traffickers in Torreon. This man drove a black Ford Gran Marquis and was named Cesar. Brito's interviewers weren't at all knowledgeable about the drug traffic in Mexico but perhaps it was bureaucratic competition that prevented them from being completely open with the DEA at the time of the interview.

The interviews were terminated on a high note of expectancy. Brito was to telephone the FBI agents the following week after he had learned the locations of several large marijuana plantations, which was what the agents were interested in since they planned to travel to Mexico and locate the fields.

Brito didn't make the phone calls, and calls to his motel in Torreon were answered with the news that he had moved and left no word on how to find him.

According to all the information available, the five cassette tapes relative to the disappearance of Kiki Camarena on February 7 in Guadalajara, had been discovered in the house in Puerto Vallarta where Ernesto Fonseca had been arrested on April 11. One of the tapes was the interrogation of a man who had disappeared sometime after February 28 in a distant part of Mexico. The questions left no doubt about that.

One tape, two interrogations! Brito's recorded on one side, Brito's wife, or mistress, recorded on the other.

Once again, I found myself listening to the words of a man talking under the obvious threat of, at least, great bodily harm. Brito had cause to know that their threats were serious.

The voice of the interrogator was soft, requesting information, not demanding it. The voice didn't seem to be the same as that of any of Kiki's interrogators.

"On the 26th and 27th, you were where?"
Brito answered. "In El Paso."

The interrogator asked him whom he had met with in El Paso and Brito provided the names. He was asked who he had "given up" (informed on) among the "federales".

Brito said. "The one that was the former comandante here."
The interrogator asked. "Juan Manuel?"
Brito said. "Yes."

(Note: Juan Manuel Castro-Prado had been the DFS comandante in Torreon, Coahuila, at the time Kiki was kidnapped. Juan Manuel Castro-Prado died mysteriously in the early nineties, his body dumped outside of

Torreon, without shoes. The state attorney general determined it was suicide!)

One of the interrogators, (there were at least three,) asked Brito to tell them what the men in El Paso had wanted. They asked if he had been questioned about Jorge Salazar (Note: Jorge Salazar, alias "El Paton" was a DFS comandante in Guadalajara and the right hand man of Ernesto Fonseca), about Morlett (Note: Tomas Morlett was the DFS Comandante in Oaxaca.) and about R-1, (Note: R-1 was the radio call sign used by Rafael Caro-Quintero. He even had a heavy gold bracelet with the legend inscribed in diamonds).

Interrogator #1 asked Brito. "And the darker one, with the dark glasses?"

Interrogator #2. "Short, with prescription glasses?"

Interrogator #1. "Who is he?"

Interrogator #2. "And a short fat one, that you introduced yourself with, as you arrived? Who are they?"

Brito answered. "That one, that one is. (And Brito provided the name of the American agent)."

The very people now conducting the interrogation had observed Brito's meetings with the FBI agents in El Paso, Texas! Neither Brito nor the U.S. agents had been aware of the surveillance.

Brito complained about the handcuffs being too tight and the interrogators told him that he would be in a better mood to talk when some of the pain had subsided. At one point he was admonished severely by one of the interrogators to talk, to "say the words", as if he might have nodded his head in response to a question and the interrogator wanted to make sure the answer was recorded. Often, during the interrogation, the sound of metal doors closing can be heard in the background, sounding like those you might find in a jail or prison.

Interrogator #2. "Does your wife, the one you just married, have knowledge about all this?"

Brito answered. "She knows that I went to talk to them."

The opposite side of the tape is a recording of the interrogation of a young woman, obviously Brito's young wife. She confirms the trip and the meetings in El Paso but said that she was not present during the meetings and knew nothing of what was discussed.

During her interrogation the woman professes that she does not know very much about her husband, only that he works for the Judicial Police and that his boss is "Kennor". (Note: "Kennor" was a nickname, origin unknown, for Jose Ramon Elenes-Payan, Rafael Caro-Quintero's brother-in-law, who was in charge of the family's marijuana operations in northern Mexico in the latter part of 1984).

Her voice is pleasant, she sounds young and she was cooperative to her interrogators. She also vanished.

The existence of the tapes was not publicly disclosed, even the United States government kept the secret while it pushed to get copies. The great earthquake struck Mexico City on September 7, 1985, and afterward the Mexican government asked DEA for copies of the tapes, explaining that the originals had been lost in the earthquake.

Finally, in February of 1986, the Mexican Attorney General publicly admitted that tapes of the interrogation of Enrique Camarena existed.

The first tape is very short and consists of the recorded radio transmissions between DEA agents and the DEA office in Guadalajara. The radio traffic took place on two dates, the 5th and 8th of March. The recording of the radio traffic on the 5th was between agents at the Guadalajara airport and the DEA office in Guadalajara. The agents at the airport were waiting for Ed Heath, Joe Gonzalez and Bobby Castillo to return, by helicopter, from the morgue in Zamora. After they arrived at the airport, Heath reported in to the office over the radio.

¿O Plata O Plomo?

    The traffic on the 8th is again between agents at the airport and the office. This traffic concerns the arrival of the U.S. Air Force C-130 to take Kiki's body to the states.

    The recordings were taken from some kind of monitor, or a radio, left out, perhaps on a table, in front of the recorder. Sounds of birds, trucks, a television show, someone washing dishes, even a baby fussing, can be heard in the background. This tape, also, was found with the others.

    What is the significance of these two tapes being found together with the two tapes of Kiki's interrogation? Kiki was almost certainly subjected to the brutal interrogation within the first two days of his detention. Brito was interrogated after February 28 in a city almost five hundred miles away. The radio traffic was recorded in Guadalajara during the first week of March. Yet all these taped recordings were apparently found together in Puerto Vallarta in early April.

    The massive search for the kidnappers of the U.S. agent hadn't hampered the traffickers at all, or their DFS allies. Kiki had told the inquisitors of a man named Juan from Reynosa, who had been in Zacatecas and helped us with information about the traffickers. Did this information lead them to look inside their ranks for traitors? Did they eavesdrop on their own telephones in Torreon thereby catching Juan Brito reaching out for his old contacts? Like the other tapes, it ends abruptly.

    It is significant that the information given voluntarily by Brito to the US agents in El Paso and the information coerced from him by the interrogators is essentially the same.

Chapter 10
INNOCENTS ABROAD

In the weeks before DEA Special Agent Enrique Camarena was abducted the Guadalajara newspapers had run brief stories on the recent, unexplained disappearances of some other United States citizens, disappearances investigated by officers of the State Department from the consulate. Kiki was not the only American missing in Guadalajara but the DEA was not involved in those investigations.

December 2, 1984 was a bright; clear Sunday morning in Guadalajara, "just another day in paradise," as the expatriates were fond of saying. For four young people, two married couples, from the United States, it was a day to spread the word of the particular brand of Christianity they believed in, that preached by the Jehovah's Witnesses.

Dennis and Rose Carlson had arrived barely two days earlier, driving in from Redding, California. Ben and Paula Mascarena had been in Guadalajara for about two years, doing neighborhood calls, knocking on doors and passing out literature such as the church's "Watch Tower" magazine. Ben and Paula had invited the Carlsons down to stay with them.

There was a large group of Jehovah's Witnesses in the city passing the word in every neighborhood, and with some success. Many Mexicans were trying the new church and liked the open friendliness of the members and the demonstrative services. Most of the missionaries were from the United States but there were a number of Canadians as well, and, as none were endowed with great wealth, they sought shelter where they could. Many were camped in small RV's and tents south of the city on the highway to Manzanillo. The Mascarena couple had been staying in a small house belonging to a man named Gerenger, like themselves a native of Nevada. In fact, Ben Mascarena had worked for Gerenger at his casino and restaurant in Nevada. But, for some reason, they were uncomfortable with the owner and had commented to their friends that they wanted to leave the house, perhaps even to return to the United States.

They were not the only members of the Jehovah's Witness contingent who were thinking of leaving Guadalajara. Several of the missionaries had been harassed in the city and they felt they were under surveillance at the park where they were camping. In addition, some large, armed men had rather brusquely questioned their right to be promoting their faith in the area, and had advised them they were in violation of their immigration status in the country. They had backed up these words with some official looking credentials. The more knowledgeable among the missionaries said they thought the armed men were DFS agents.

The previous Sunday, November 25th, the Mascarena couple, along with several others of the group, had been engaging in a door-to-door campaign in the "Arcos Sur" neighborhood in the western section of Guadalajara. On this day, they were assigned to return to the same neighborhood and took their friends, the just-arrived Carlson couple, with them. They drove to the area in Dennis Carlson's car, a Dodge Omni, with California license numbers 765-YGL. It was, as previously mentioned, the 2nd day of December 1984.

A retired Mexican Army General lived in that neighborhood and he had vehemently protested the presence of the missionaries. He had shouted at several of them and threatened them with prison, or worse, if they didn't leave Guadalajara, and Mexico. He somehow linked their religion to anti-government activities and wanted them out.

The two couples had hardly begun their morning practice of knocking on doors, perhaps they had chatted with the occupants of three or four houses, when three cars arrived at the location, stopping with a screech of their tires and disgorging their occupants, several rough looking men, who quickly and quietly rounded up the four missionaries, herding them toward the waiting automobiles and pushing them inside, before departing rapidly.

The few witnesses on the street that morning said that the men spoke very little to the four missionaries, but firmly ushered them into the cars, the women in one, and the men in another. The three cars utilized by the abductors were described as small, perhaps one was a Volkswagen Caribe, yellow or beige in color. There were six men in the group of abductors, one witness said.

One of the women, possibly Rose Carlson, had shouted to an elderly lady nearby "Take their license numbers". But the old woman wasn't wearing her glasses and could not make out the numbers. The witnesses agreed, however, that there was no struggle between the four missionaries and the six men, almost as if the missionaries believed the men were some type of government official. The three cars sped away as quickly as they had arrived and the four people disappeared.

Left parked on the side of the street, the only physical evidence that the two couples had actually been there was the Carlson's vehicle. The dust raised by the rapid departure of the small cars settled on the hood. The Dodge Omni would wait forever.

Someone among the Jehovah's Witnesses stoked up the courage to report the matter to the police and, on Monday, the United States Consulate was informed. An officer from the consulate referred the matter to the Jalisco State Police, homicide division. The comandante in charge of the homicide division was Gabriel Gonzales-Gonzales, the man who died in March 1985 while being interrogated by Florentino Ventura!

The United States Department of State has no trained investigators among its ranks and, therefore, throughout the world, relies on the local police agencies to search for its missing citizens or to prosecute wrong doers for offenses committed against them.

The police made a half-hearted attempt to investigate the disappearance of the couples, but more effort was concentrated toward intimidating the remaining missionaries. This had the desired effect. The missionaries pulled out but many were harassed on the trip from Guadalajara to the U.S. border.

Mr. Norman Carlson, Dennis' father, traveled to Guadalajara to try and determine what had happened. The U.S. Consulate assigned their police liaison officer to accompany him on his visits to the authorities. The Jalisco State Police were polite but knew nothing. However, he had to visit another Mexican government agency to gain the release of his son's effects.

The Consulate officer took Mr. Carlson to Mexicaltzingo St. #2173, the office of the Direcíon Federal de Seguridad, the dreaded DFS. There, a stern faced and unsympathetic Mexican official received them. Ushered past heavily armed men and up a staircase faced by a two-story tapestry depicting a Bengal tiger, they entered the office of the comandante of the Guadalajara branch of Mexico's feared secret police.

Dressed in a business suit and with the air of an inquisitor, Luis Cruz-Mera, who said he was the man in charge, acknowledged Mr. Carlson's identity and the purpose of his visit to Guadalajara. After listening to the Consulate liaison officer interpret the father's concerns, Cruz-Mera suggested to Mr. Carlson that the four young people were hiding somewhere. Perhaps they had committed some crime in the United States? Maybe they were involved in the drug traffic? So many gringos are, you know! After this rude tongue lashing Cruz-Mera gave his permission and Mr. Carlson was accompanied by two burly DFS men to the apartment where his son and daughter-in-law had spent their last nights before vanishing. Afterwards, several of the missionaries told Mr. Carlson that these same two DFS agents had harassed them prior to the kidnappings.

The theory informally suggested by the Mexican government to explain the disappearance of the four missionaries has been that they knocked on the door of a house in the neighborhood owned by a major drug trafficker. The trafficker suspected the four people to be DEA agents and ordered them taken. However, such a house has never been identified and, formally, the Mexican government does not admit the abduction even took place. In spite of the witnesses, their position is; without bodies there is no crime.

One of the witnesses to the abduction was an elderly man. Extremely moved by what he saw, he was confined to his bed for a few days, in danger of a heart attack.

The neighborhood is quiet and modest, the people of a low income level, and few own automobiles.

On his feet again, the elderly gentleman was waiting to catch a bus when a car stopped in front of him at the bus stop. A man in the car, recognized by the old man as one of the participants in the kidnapping, threatened him with bodily harm or death if he didn't hold his tongue.

Certainly the traffickers owned many houses in Guadalajara but the ones actually occupied by the drug kingpins themselves were large and expensive. No such house exists anywhere near the corner where the kidnappings took place. It was a quiet Sunday morning. The missionaries had been at the location only a few minutes, maybe half an hour or so, and the houses they had visited that morning are easily identified. The kidnappers didn't spill out of the interior of some notorious hide out. They arrived in three automobiles, with their target well defined.

No trace of these four human beings has ever been found.

Carlos Solana-Macias, an official from the Mexican government, allegedly the tourist Department, visited Dennis Carlson's family in northern California, sympathetic about their loss while expressing alarm about the damage being done to the Mexican tourist industry by the adverse publicity from Guadalajara. But Solana-Macias really was seeking information, trying to determine what the family actually knew. Was there something potentially damaging to Mexico's image that had not been published?

Sometime during the initial stages of the search for Enrique Camarena an MFJP agent asked one of the DEA agents if Kiki was missing a toe on one foot. No explanation was given for the inquiry. The DEA agent sought the answer among Kiki's close friends. My response was no, there was no damage to either foot.

The DEA agents in Guadalajara were not privy to the details of the investigation into the disappearance of the four missionaries. The state department handled that and did not feel the need to consult with DEA.

Several years later I learned that Benjamin Mascarena had lost a toe on his left foot to frostbite. Now no one can remember who the agent was who raised the question.

Ten days prior to Kiki's disappearance two other United States citizens vanished without a trace in Guadalajara.

John Walker had been in the war in Southeast Asia. He was wounded in that war and received a pension because of the wound, which crippled but did not debilitate. He started a career as a newspaper journalist but wanted to write novels. Walker moved to Guadalajara because he could afford to live in the cheaper economy on his pension and began to research a proposed novel based on the drug traffic. He had rented an apartment in a private home and lived there with his wife and daughters until his wife, Eve, returned to Minnesota with the girls. John then spent more time enjoying the city than writing, but the novel wasn't forgotten.

Albert Radelat came to Guadalajara to visit his friend, John Walker, for a few days, moving into John's quarters and joining him in exploring the city's bars and restaurants. Albert had met John the previous year when he was checking out the privately owned Autonomous University of Guadalajara as a place to continue his dental education. The two got along well and enjoyed their time together. Albert was the son of a doctor who fled Castro's Cuba. Albert decided instead to return to the United States to resume his education.

On January 30, 1985, Albert Radelat telephoned his parents in Fort Worth, Texas, and said that he would be returning one day late, on the 31st instead of the 30th, as previously planned. But Albert wasn't on the plane the next day. One of their favorite places had been a small restaurant frequented by the American students at the university. The owner of Uncle Sam's Bar and Grill looked for his friends at John's apartment. When the landlady told him they hadn't returned to the apartment since the evening of the 30th he became concerned and informed the police.

Albert's parents also called Guadalajara to check on their son. When the calls failed to produce results, Dr. Radelat went himself.

Dr. Felipe Radelat had qualities unlike many people. Just managing to escape arrest in Cuba, he left behind a successful practice and great personal wealth. He had started anew at the bottom in the federal public health system in the United States and became a medical director at a federal correctional institution. After retiring from a career in public medicine, he opened a private family practice and later joined a group, sponsored by Rotary International, which provided free medical aid to children in third world countries. Dr. Radelat had performed hundreds of surgical procedures to repair cleft palates of impoverished Mexican children.

In Guadalajara Dr. Radelat talked to the owner of the house where John Walker had rented a modest apartment. The landlady said she remembered that Albert had asked to use the telephone on the 30th, (John did not have a telephone in his apartment) to call his parents. After he made the call she had invited him to have lunch with her and her fiancée. During the meal Albert had commented that he intended to invite his friend, John, to eat a seafood dinner that night at a nice restaurant, as it was his last night in Guadalajara.

Dr. Radelat was shown the apartment rented by John Walker. It had not been disturbed, even by the police investigators, who had not shown much interest in the mysterious disappearance of the two men. Lying on one of the beds were his son's unused airline tickets for the flight home. The suitcases, packed for the trip, sat on the floor.

¿O Plata O Plomo?

Just as Norman Carlson had done two months before, Doctor Felipe Radelat talked to U.S. Consulate officials and to officials from the Jalisco state attorney general's office. At the consulate everyone was sympathetic but sympathy wasn't what he needed. They did help, eventually, to secure meetings with representatives from the state attorney general's office, but the only information anyone had was that John Walker's car, a green 1975 Ford Galaxie with Minnesota license plates, had allegedly been found on February 17, legally parked, near the Holiday Inn.

Dr. Radelat had an advantage over Mr. Carlson, he spoke fluent Spanish, and he also was not a member of a radical church, distasteful to the largely Catholic Mexican officials.

Eve Walker, John Walker's wife, had returned to Guadalajara and was working as hard as Dr. Radelat, trying to stir up sympathy for her plight, talking to the media and to the police, but having just as little success.

Daily blasts against Mexico by the U.S. newspapers and television newscasters were not helping the families of the two missing men in their quest. The intense, and at times frantic, search for Enrique Camarena and Alfredo Zavala had consumed the attention of the press and infuriated the Mexican government. As each day passed without news of the missing DEA agent, the foreign media attacked the government with more fervor, accusing it of corruption, apathy, collusion and whatever. This did not cause them to be benevolent toward the two desperate families.

In March, following the discovery of the bodies of Kiki and Captain Zavala, Dr. Radelat and his wife traveled to Mexico City where he had acquaintances, seeking help among the Rotarians and in the Cuban community. One of those acquaintances, like Dr. Radelat a refugee from Cuba, had an influential Mexican friend in the publishing world who arranged a meeting with a very powerful figure in Mexican politics. In his luxurious offices on Avenida Insurgentes, Miguel Angel Nazar-Haro welcomed Dr. Radelat and the publisher. Dr. Radelat understood that Miguel Nassar was some sort of private investigator. He was completely unaware of his background.

The former director of the Direccíon Federal de Seguridad listened attentively to Dr. Radelat's account of the disappearance of, and his frustrating search for, his son and John Walker. Afterward Nazar said that the case was too politically sensitive and he did not want to get involved. As the two men were leaving his offices Nazar called the publisher back and talked privately with him for a few minutes. The publisher later told the doctor that Miguel Nazar had said to tell the doctor not to be too optimistic about finding his son alive.

A father searching for his son is a determined man, and a man with the character of Dr. Radelat is fearless in his search. His persistence earned him an interview with another imposing Mexican personality.

MFJP Comandante Florentino Ventura was once again in the news. Already famous for his highly publicized daylight gun battles against international drug traffickers in the seventies, Ventura had a fearsome reputation and had gained the respect of many U.S. law enforcement officials. Assigned to take over the troublesome investigation in Guadalajara, he had arrested twenty-five men and obtained confessions linking some of them to the kidnapping and murder of Kiki Camarena. Dr. Radelat sought an interview with Ventura, hoping to convince him to include the disappearance of Alberto and John in his investigations. He was advised to go to the office of the attorney general where he would be received by Ventura. He did as instructed, taking his wife with him, in the hope that Ventura might already have some information, gleaned from the men arrested in the roundup in Guadalajara. Upon their arrival, however, Mrs. Radelat was excluded from the interview with the explanation that the meeting was for Dr. Radelat alone. Two MFJP agents took Dr. Radelat to Ventura's offices, several blocks away, while Mrs. Radelat had to wait at the AG's offices.

Night had fallen and it was easily 9:00 PM by the time the three men arrived at Ventura's offices. But this is not unusual in Mexico City where people regularly take three-hour breaks at midday and work late. Florentino Ventura introduced himself to Dr. Radelat and then had him sit and wait while Ventura made several telephone calls in his presence. It was at least 2:00 AM when Ventura himself, accompanied by four of his men, armed with machine guns, escorted Dr. Radelat back to the attorney general's office where Mrs. Radelat was waiting.

While at Ventura's office, Dr. Radelat had told Ventura about his investigation into the disappearance of his son. Ventura had Dr. Radelat dictate his story to a secretary. He then told Dr. Radelat he had no business conducting investigations in Mexico and that the police would take care of everything.

Returning to Guadalajara and carrying photos of both men, (he had obtained a photo of John Walker from John's wife) Dr. Radelat started looking for anyone who might have seen his son or John that last night. He went to the large intersection near the Holiday Inn, located on Avenida Lopez Mateos and Mariano Otero, to question hotel clerks, night watchmen and taxi drivers. A cab driver at the taxi stand adjacent to the Holiday Inn said that he remembered the two men. About three weeks previous, in the early evening, they had started to park their car in a space reserved for the taxis. He had advised then of their error and directed them to a place across the street near a lumber company. One man, the shorter of the two, was driving and moved the car while the other man, who the taxi driver said resembled the photo of Albert which Dr. Radelat had displayed to him, exited the car and waited near the taxi stand. The two men then entered a cafe called "Caramba". The taxi driver said that the driver of the vehicle looked like the photo of John Walker. He added that both men were wearing jeans and the shorter man was wearing a black jacket. Later that evening he saw them leave the restaurant and walk up the street in a northerly direction. He did not see them again. The following day Dr. Radelat returned to the offices of the Jalisco state attorney general and spoke with the state attorney general himself, Jaime Ramirez-Gil. He informed him of his conversation with the taxi driver and of his son's plans to eat at a seafood restaurant and suggested that the police inquire at restaurants and discothèques around the area of the Holiday Inn. Ramirez-Gil told Dr. Radelat to talk with the comandante of the homicide division of the Jalisco state judicial police, Gabriel Gonzalez-Gonzalez, and give any information, which Dr. Radelat had developed. Ramirez-Gil also advised him to return to the United States and to stop playing detective. Dr. Radelat replied that he was only looking for his son and he was not going to leave. If he were deported he would return illegally, "just like the wetbacks that enter the United States" and continue to look for his son.

    He talked to Comandante Gonzalez-Gonzalez on the same day and passed along the information he had gathered. The very next day, the Guadalajara newspapers carried the story that the state judicial police had located employees of "La Longosta" restaurant who had given accounts of the torture and murder of two men who the police believed were the two missing Americans, John Walker and Albert Radelat.

    According to the witnesses, the two men had entered the restaurant late one evening where a private party was in progress. The restaurant had closed to the public at 7:00 PM. Realizing their mistake, the two men tried to leave but were detained by some of the men at the party and taken into the kitchen where they were tortured and murdered. Their bodies were then placed into the trunk of a car and driven away.

    Dr. Radelat had the opportunity to read the statements of two men identified as waiters at La Langosta restaurant. One of the men, who said he was an eyewitness to the torture and murder of the two young Americans, was identified by name and address. Dr. and Mrs. Radelat went to the La Langosta restaurant and asked for the waiter but they were told he no longer worked there. The good doctor drove to the address listed in the statement but could find no one there who had ever heard of the man.

¿O Plata O Plomo?

The La Langosta restaurant, located on Mariano Otero, just off of Lopez Mateos, was owned by the traffickers from Sinaloa. By some reports the infamous "Cochiloco" himself was the proprietor. It was basically a seafood restaurant, which specialized in serving food prepared "Sinaloa style."

Three statements were allegedly taken by the Mexican government, from two waiters and a night watchman. The statements bear the date of March 29 and 30, 1985. The watchman stated only that he had arrived at the restaurant about 7:30 PM, found many vehicles parked in front and several armed men outside, and decided to go next door and visit another watchman. During the evening he heard music and the sounds of partying from the restaurant but nothing more. About midnight he returned to the restaurant and entered where he was told by one of the waiters to clean up some blood on the floor of the storeroom. He stated there was a lot of fresh blood on the floor, but he knew nothing of the circumstances that led to it. The other statements were from the two waiters,

One said that he had been requested to work late for a private party and asked another employee to stay and help. Around 6:00 PM Rafael Caro-Quintero arrived with about 30 armed men. The group ate and drank heavily and was still so engaged at about 10:30 PM when two young men, apparently Americans, entered through the restaurant's unlocked swinging doors. When told the restaurant was closed they left but were brought back inside by some of the armed men stationed outside. They were then taken into a storeroom at the rear of the restaurant with Rafael Caro following. Caro returned after about five minutes to resume drinking. The waiter said that some of Caro's men told him the two intruders were tortured with ice picks. This went on for about an hour with Caro paying occasional short visits to the storeroom. Caro then left, accompanied by his men. The two Americans were pulled out of the storeroom with their feet dragging and their faces covered by rags. They were not moving. Caro's men took them from the restaurant and told the two waiters to clean up the blood in the storeroom and say nothing to anyone about what had happened.

When the waiter was shown photos of active and former members of the state judicial police he was unable to identify any of the photos as having been among Caro's men. He did identify Caro-Quintero and he identified photos of John Walker and Albert Radelat as being the two men who were tortured.

The second waiter said, in his statement, that a man he knew as Rafael Quintero had arrived at the restaurant at about 6:00 PM, along with 15 to 20 men, including a "norteño" band. The group remained after the restaurant's closing time of 7:00 PM. About 10:30 PM two men appeared at the door of the restaurant but withdrew. They were immediately forced back in by some of the men outside and questioned. Their identification was seized from them and they were beaten and stabbed in their legs. The two men fell to the floor and they were kicked brutally. Caro's men then pulled them to their feet, covered their heads and forced them to walk out of the restaurant. The waiter heard one of the men say, in English, "I can't see."

This man was unable to identify any of the men with Caro-Quintero from photos he was shown of active and former members of the Jalisco state judicial police. He did identify the photos of John Walker and Albert Radelat as those of the two men who were beaten and tortured that night. If the owner of the restaurant was ever identified or questioned that was not revealed. If the investigators ever looked for the musicians allegedly there that night it was not made known. The obvious discrepancies in the statements of the witnesses remain unexplained. The U.S. state department was never given access to the alleged witnesses, even after repeated requests for interviews.

Travel agents in the United States had ceased their touting Mexico as the place to visit and many tourists had opted to fly to Hawaii or the Caribbean after all the adverse publicity from Guadalajara. The Mexican government tried to repair the damage and they were aided to some extent by the U.S. government.

A resolution passed by the U.S. House of Representatives warned U.S. tourists that it was potentially dangerous to travel in the state of Jalisco because of the presence of narcotics traffickers. The governor of Jalisco, Enrique Alvarez del Castillo, cried foul. Although he had refused even to answer the U.S. Consul General's telephone call he now said there was a "defamation campaign' being waged against Jalisco state's tourist industry, a multi-million dollar business.

U.S. Senator Lloyd Bentsen and even Ambassador Gavin issued statements containing forgiveness. The situation, they opined, had improved and U.S. travelers could once again feel safe on Mexican highways. "More than four million Americans visit Mexico each year and relatively few of them encounter problems." Gavin said. Senator Bentsen stated. "The state department told me they're getting better cooperation out of the Mexican government."

During the three days that Rafael Caro-Quintero occupied the residence at 881 Lope de Vega, 44 telephone calls were made from the house. Almost without exception those calls were made to known drug traffickers. One of those traffickers, who received the most calls, was a man named Francisco Javier Tejeda-Jaramillo aka "Paco."

"Paco" Tejeda-Jaramillo was generally regarded as a member of Miguel Felix-Gallardo's organization. He lived in Tijuana, carried the credentials of a DFS agent and was a major figure in the drug traffic in that area. Three numbers called from 881 Lope de Vega were associated with "Paco" Tejeda. The fact that the numbers were in Tijuana had a lot to do with Tejeda's downfall. The DEA office in San Diego, California, has the responsibility of trying to ride herd on the activities of narcotics traffickers in that region of Mexico, an impossible task but one that has never been shrugged off. The traffickers love Tijuana because of its proximity to southern California, a major market for drugs and a playground for men with money. DEA agents just naturally love the challenge. San Diego always had more than its fair share of aggressive and resourceful agents. When some of these agents learned that a possible suspect in the kidnapping of Kiki was living in their area they began to plot his demise. Tips to the Mex-Feds were not followed up and it appeared that Tejeda had been told that DEA had acquired a more than usual interest in his whereabouts. The agents, however, persisted and, once again, from the capitol city came the troubleshooter.

Using information supplied by DEA in San Diego, Ventura and his men located "Paco" Tejeda and returned him to Mexico City for interrogation. Edward Heath and Bobby Castillo from the DEA were allowed to sit in on some of the interviews. In a written statement, turned over to Heath on June 11, Tejeda-Jaramillo confessed that he had been at the house on Lope de Vega when Samuel Ramirez and Ernesto Fonseca arrived at approximately 3:00 PM on February 7th with another man, identified to him as Enrique Camarena. Camarena's head was covered with a jacket or coat. The three arrived in a beige Volkswagen Atlantic. Jaramillo implicated Rafael Caro-Quintero, Miguel Angel Felix-Gallardo, Ernesto Fonseca-Carillo and Javier Barba-Hernandez in the beating of Enrique Camarena and in the decision to have both Camarena and Zavala "eliminated." Tejeda did not confess to any active personal involvement in the interrogations or murders of the two men. He stated that Enrique Camarena, unconscious from his beating, was carried out of the house on February 8th, sometime after 5:30 PM, and placed in the trunk of a blue 1975 Dodge Volare. Another man, identified as "el chango" Alvarez took an "I" shaped tire iron and struck Camarena in the head. Alfredo Zavala was then placed in the truck along with agent Camarena. Three men, identified as "el chango" Alvarez, Jose Refugio Alvarez, and Carlos Martinez drove off in the Dodge Volare to dispose of the bodies. The car was said to be the property of Jose Refugio Alvarez.

¿O Plata O Plomo?

According to Tejeda-Jaramillo the men were buried in Primavera Park, but he did not know where.

During the next five days, Tejeda-Jaramillo allegedly confessed to some participation in yet two different murders. DEA knew nothing about this interrogation or the confession. Nor did anyone else until Comandante Ventura arrived in Guadalajara on June 17th along with an enormous contingent, which included "Paco" Tejeda-Jaramillo. Acting in an extremely uncustomary fashion, Ventura requested assistance from the emergency medical people in Guadalajara, the "Cruz Roja" and the fire department. Or, perhaps, he just needed someone to dig.

Night had already fallen when the caravan of "Federales" and their helpers arrived at a remote area of the primitive park named "La Primavera". The property had been given to the state of Jalisco many years before by the Zuno family, prominent both in state and national politics. Much would be made of the coincidental, or maybe not so coincidental, fact that the house at 881 Lope de Vega had once belonged to one of the members of that family, Jose Ruben Zuno-Arce.

The searchers began to search, digging here and there, but not without direction, at least according to some of the diggers from the fire department. They were directed to several sites by "Paco" Tejeda and they were searching for the bodies of two Americans who were killed and buried there by the drug traffickers. Rain began to fall and everyone was drenched to the bone. "Paco" recalled something about the site, it was near a small arroyo. They found a familiar looking spot and began to dig. One of the excavators struck a boot buried in the mud. They began to dig more carefully and unearthed the two cadavers, or what remained of them, mostly just bones, but still in their clothing and wrapped in a rotten carpet and three tablecloths.

James Kuykendall

The remains were removed to the morgue in Guadalajara and the Mexican government made the announcement that the bodies of the two men had been located.

Dr. Radelat received a call from Comandante Ventura advising him of the discovery and he flew immediately, along with his wife, to Guadalajara. At the morgue he was asked to identify his son's remains. Albert had suffered a fractured jaw in his youth and Dr. Radelat found evidence of the fracture and subsequent repair. He found no evidence of foul play but the condition of the remains really made it difficult to determine that. John Walker's wife, Eve, identified her husband's remains from the leg injury he had suffered while soldiering in Vietnam. He had been seriously injured by an exploding land mine. Walker's skull had a large hole in the upper rear portion that appeared to have been caused by a blow administered by a blunt instrument.

The family asked the representative from the U.S. consulate if the FBI would send forensic technicians to examine the remains, the bindings, shrouds and clothing. The request was made on Friday, the 20th. The FBI answered yes, but that the agents wouldn't be available until Monday. When the Mexican government was informed of the families' desires, they responded by giving the families an ultimatum. There would be no such examination and if the families wanted to return the bodies to the United States they must do so immediately or they would be buried in Mexico.

The remains of the two unfortunate men were flown to the United States that day but their clothing remained in Mexico. The Mexican government gave the money and jewelry found in the grave to the men's survivors. According to the Mexican government there had been electrical wire found with the bodies that had apparently been used to bind their hands and feet. Later the same government said three tablecloths found shrouding the bodies were from the La Langosta restaurant and that the red carpet in which the bodies were wrapped came from the trunk of a Ford

¿O Plata O Plomo?

Gran Marquis automobile used to transport the bodies to the Primavera park.

Discrepancies? In abundance, and still unexplained! Once again there is the question of why the mind loosening interrogations of almost a hundred men had not disclosed this crime.

Once again DEA headquarters requested the expertise of the FBI. The agents traveled to Guadalajara to look at the site where the bodies of John Walker and Albert Radelat had been found. Soil samples had previously been gathered at the "El Mareño" ranch and at several ranches and large properties owned by the major traffickers but no match had been found with the dirt and debris gleaned from the bodies of Kiki and Capi. It took most of the day but the site was located, by this time the shallow grave had partially filled in, due to heavy rains in the late summer. The FBI agents dug and scraped, filling their evidence bags with any sign of the remains of the two murdered young men. At the laboratory in Washington, DC, and after exhaustive study, they would offer their opinion that the bodies of Kiki and Capitan Zavala could have come out of the same hole, so alike were the soil samples.

Both buoyed and bothered by the discovery of the bodies in Primavera park, the relatives of the missing Jehovah Witness missionaries hired a private detective in the United States to help them find a way to search the park for their loved ones, on the premise that the traffickers had also kidnapped them, mistaking them for informants or agents. The investigator proposed to use some electronic instruments to search any likely areas in the park. Toward this end they asked the U.S. State Department for assistance. The state department responded to a query from a California congressman with glowing praise for the cooperation they were receiving from the Mexican government in "resolving this mystery."

Their praise was short lived as the Mexicans began to plead bureaucratic duplicity as the reason the equipment could not be given clearance. The attorney general said the equipment could come in if customs approved. Mexican Customs said the equipment would have to be described and catalogs sent to the government to determine if its importation was prohibited. The embassy sent a cable to Washington, "It appears that Mexican government officials are not as forthcoming and anxious to cooperate as they would have us believe. More weeks of passing the buck and indecision are likely. Any guidance the department can provide will be appreciated." There was no guidance.

The private investigator did not get the authorization to bring in the electronics for his proposed search.

If, indeed, the traffickers had abducted and murdered the four missionaries and the two friends out for a night on the town, they had killed ten people in their desperate quest for the leak in their organization, Kiki, Capitan Zavala, the four Jehovah's witnesses, John Walker and Albert Radelat, and Juan Brito and his wife. The Mexican government was only responsible for seven deaths; the Bravo family, the young agent killed at the Bravo farm and Comandante Gabriel Gonzalez. But this tragedy was far from over.

CHAPTER 11
TROUBLE IN THE NORTH

The questions on the tapes, those asked, or demanded, of Kiki, invariably returned to, or were centered on, the activities of Ernesto Fonseca-Carillo, Rafael Caro-Quintero, Juan Esparragosa-Moreno and others who we believed to have been principally involved in the cultivation of enormous plantations of marijuana and the transportation of hundreds of kilos of cocaine. Over and over the interrogators asked about these men and what Kiki knew about them their activities. And Kiki tried to satisfy their demands. He told them what we had done in the states of Zacatecas and San Luis Potosi.

In retrospect perhaps it wasn't so strange that almost everything we did seemed to be related to the "family". Of course, in the beginning we didn't realize how influential the "family" was.

In June of 1982 we were having a meeting in the office in Guadalajara. The attendees were the best informed at the time on the activities of the group of traffickers which everyone, even the traffickers themselves, called the "family" and which appeared to be controlled by a sinister and shadowy man named Miguel Angel Felix-Gallardo. The meeting was related to an intelligence probe called "Operation Broker", created to gather as much information as possible about Felix-Gallardo's organization.

Joan Bannister, an intelligence analyst in Mexico City at the time who was very well versed on the subject, and Tony Rizzivuto, an agent stationed in Los Angeles, also with much knowledge on the subject from a previous tour in Mexico, were discussing the case with Butch Sears, who was the case agent for the Guadalajara DEA office.

James Kuykendall

Since I was not much more than an interested observer, trying to learn from their experience, it was no loss to the meeting when I was summoned to a telephone call, which removed me from the discussions. A man, who identified himself as "Miguel Sanchez", was on the line and asked to meet with me. He stated that the agent-in-charge of DEA in Laredo had sent him.

Needing a respite from the strong differences in opinion surfacing in the meeting, I agreed to see him. He said that he was calling from a pay phone nearby so I left the building and then returned to the Consulate through the library door with "Mr. Sanchez" in tow. We talked for a few minutes to get acquainted and he advised me that the reason for his visit was to seek my help in obtaining a visa to enter the United States so he could journey to Detroit and try to get some information on a heroin trafficking organization. He told me that he lived in Zacatecas, which was a part of our area of responsibility, so I began to question him about current events in that area and what might be happening in the drug traffic there. It really hadn't occurred to me to do anything but help "Miguel" get his visa and be on his way back to the U.S. but as we talked I developed a strong liking for the man and a real interest in what he had to say. Even though he had only rumors of something big, it was obvious that he had the experience and intelligence to recognize the likelihood that the rumors were based on fact.

Normal practice in DEA was that the agent-in-charge not control informants so I went to Kiki's office and asked him to join me in talking to our visitor. When we returned to my office "Miguel" extracted some slips of paper from his pockets and displayed them to us. He then proceeded to remove his eyeglasses from a shirt pocket and put them on.

"Miguel's" appearance in those days, partially as a result of financial hard times, was slightly bizarre. He was wearing some well-worn blue denim pants, mustard yellow cowboy boots with the longest pointed toes I had ever seen and a faded checkered shirt with patches on both elbows. The hat he had removed upon entering the office had at least a five-inch brim and the eyeglasses he had just donned were missing the left lens. "Miguel" was of medium height and weight, about fifty-eight years old and well burned by the desert sun. He had an impish smile that wrinkled the corners of his eyes.

Kiki and I looked at each other with a grin and listened to his story. Just as I had, Kiki was getting interested. Our new friend told us of a man in Zacatecas who had confided that he was going to plant a big field of Marijuana of at least one hundred acres. Even though this was unheard of at that time he made it sound possible and really whetted our appetite for more information.

About that time it became obvious that "Miguel" was not going to return to work for the Laredo office, at least not for a while.

We asked "Miguel" to come back on Monday and gave him fifty dollars for bus fare and expenses, since he was flat broke. "Miguel" became a good friend of ours and was very close to Kiki. It hurt him deeply when Kiki was killed. "Miguel" was not a young man, even when we met him, and he had seen his share of the brutality that is an everyday part of the drug traffic in Mexico He had survived some tough personal hardships but Kiki's death truly affected him. He was probably the most sensible informant I ever met, he didn't show too much instant wealth, he invested a little of what he earned and he enjoyed helping us. His only problem was that he didn't really like associating with the traffickers and, as dangerous as that was, preferred being with us, so he came to visit often, always bringing with him the most incredible information about the progress of the plantation in Zacatecas. It was said to be at least one hundred acres, well-guarded, irrigated by wells and with weekly deliveries of fertilizer for the crop.

We were having a difficult time accepting this information because the state of Zacatecas is practically a desert and, at the time, one of the most economically depressed states in Mexico. A drive through the state of Zacatecas reveals mile after mile of cactus-studded, arid wasteland. The people still farmed with horse drawn plows and there was almost no electricity outside the larger cities. There were few paved roads, inadequate schooling, massive unemployment, and Zacatecas was one of the states from which so many illegal aliens came to the United States. In short, a financial basket case with little hope for the future. Outside of some worked-out silver mines, there were no natural resources.

That the desert can bloom had been proven in Israel, Arizona, California and so on, but only with the outlay of enormous amounts of money. There are no rivers or lakes in Zacatecas, no large corporations to develop subterranean water sources and nothing to attract investments. So where could this enormous farm of marijuana possibly be and where could they find enough water?

Our instructions to "Miguel" were to try to locate the field, or fields, and then back off and we would watch it grow.

"Miguel" eventually became friendly with the trafficker who was the apparent owner of this plantation of marijuana. He identified him to us as Antonio Perez-Parga, a rancher from the small village of San Blas in central Zacatecas. Perez-Parga had apparently been involved in cultivating marijuana for about two years, with assistance and financial backing from some Sinaloa traffickers. "Miguel" determined that the fields were located somewhere near the town of Vanegas in the state of San Luis Potosi, just outside the boundary of the state of Zacatecas. He also gave us the not too unexpected news that the state and local law enforcement officials had all been paid off not to interfere with the fields. "Miguel" said he had been present when the traffickers delivered some guns to the comandante of the Federal Judicial Police for the state of San Luis Potosi. "Miguel" was told by Antonio Perez that he had loaned this comandante a tractor from the fields so he could do some work on his pig farm near the city of San Luis Potosi. We were really perplexed as to how we would ever be able to destroy these fields with the Federal and State police providing protection. But I think that we still believed at that time that there was some un-compromised level of government.

¿O Plata O Plomo?

The Mexican Government would eventually view our informants as spies and publicly label them as traitors but the only information we ever received about Mexican officialdom concerned corruption as it was related to the drug traffic. We were strictly concerned with the drug traffic and so instructed the people who helped us, but if public officials involved themselves in the traffic or in providing protection to the traffickers, we often became informed.

The first hint of the involvement of the "family" came with the news from "Miguel" that Antonio Perez was being financed and supported by the notorious trafficker known as "El Azul", (the blue one). His real name was, of course, Juan Esparragosa-Moreno and he was bad news. According to "Miguel" there were many also lesser traffickers from Sinaloa in the towns of Fresnillo and Zacatecas. He said they were having lavish parties, inviting all the local politicians, and bringing "bandas" (percussion musical groups) from Culiacan to celebrate all the money they were going to make that year from the marijuana fields.

By this time "Miguel" was spending a lot of time with Antonio Perez and his number one helper, Rodolfo "El Feo" (the ugly one). "Miguel" brought a picture of Antonio Perez and Rodolfo "El Feo" which Kiki showed to the others of us in the office. (That fellow was definitely "feo".)

Antonio Perez was a farmer/rancher who lived in a dirt street village of mostly adobe huts in northern Zacatecas. He was the "cacique" (political chief) of the village known as Rancho San Blas.

The village wasn't much, being located in a dusty, remote area of the state, but it had been the home of his parents and now he and his brothers were the big dogs in town and lived in the best houses and drove the best cars.

Antonio passed a lot of his time spending money and enjoying life in Fresnillo and Zacatecas with occasional trips to Guadalajara, Nuevo Laredo and Piedras Negras to look for buyers for the marijuana he was producing.

James Kuykendall

"Miguel" still wasn't positive about it but it certainly appeared that this wasn't Antonio Perez-Parga's first year in the marijuana cultivation business. He was well connected with the people who had to give their blessings to the operation. He had seemingly endless amounts of expense money and plenty of expertise in pot farming.

As he confided more and more in "Miguel" he told him of the armed guards at the site, the radio communications, the more than two hundred field workers, the fertilizers and insecticides used to produce a better crop, the deep wells drilled to provide irrigation, the agronomist who paid regular visits to oversee the operation and always of the fact that the authorities were in his pocket.

We advised "Miguel" to keep inquiring where to find this mysterious but gigantic plantation of marijuana and we patiently went about the other business of the office, working on drug cases as they surfaced and on the volumes of intelligence being generated on the activities of Miguel Angel Felix-Gallardo, Ernesto Fonseca-Carillo, Juan Esparragoza-Moreno, Juan Jose and Emilio Quintero-Payan, "Cochiloco", and the other members of the "family".

During this time I personally made several trips through Zacatecas, occasionally meeting with "Miguel" at a safe location to talk about progress on the case. I could not get over being amazed by the traffickers having picked this place to grow marijuana, the only apparently suitable areas being those near the few centers of population. However, we were not concerned, as the information was that the crop was not yet ready to be harvested.

Kiki was picked to be the temporary agent in charge of the office in Mazatlan for a month. During this time he renewed an old acquaintance with the comandante of the Federal Judicial Police in Culiacan, Manuel Espindola, who seemed to be getting along well there in spite of it's being the center of drug related violence. Kiki and Manuel Espindola had met some years earlier when Espindola assumed his post as a comandante at Mexicali, Baja California. Kiki was a DEA agent across the border in Calexico and he said that they had worked reasonably well with Espindola who showed some self-restraint against getting rich overnight.

Pete Hernandez was the liaison with "Miguel" during Kiki's absence. A few meetings were held with "Miguel" during the next two months and he told us that things were progressing well. The fields were growing and in absolutely no danger of being bothered by the Mexican officials. He still had not determined the exact location of the plantation so our instructions to him were to keep looking and try to fuel the confidence of Antonio Perez.

During the month of August I was in Mexico City as the acting country attaché (DEA's chief representative) while the agents in Guadalajara, and all over the world for that matter, went about their business of trying to disrupt the lives of narcotics traffickers.

The Mexican peso continued its downward trend and on August 9 you could buy 77 pesos for a dollar.

While I was trying to deal with the State Department types in the Embassy, the boys at the DEA office in Guadalajara had the opportunity to see one of the members of the "family" up close.

Kiki had returned to Guadalajara from his temporary assignment in Mazatlan and characteristically got right down to work. A very reliable informant had furnished the address in Guadalajara of Emilio Quintero-Payan, a notorious drug trafficker who had been involved with just about every kind of drug.

Ironically Emilio's neighbor was Manuel Espindola, the comandante of the MFJP in Culiacan. He owned a luxurious house in Guadalajara where his wife and family lived while he headed the office in Sinaloa.

In October of 1978 Emilio Quintero was arrested in Nuevo Laredo, Mexico, in connection with the seizure of 33 and a half kilos of heroin, a good amount by anyone's standards.

The bust occurred as the result of an undercover investigation put together by DEA agents. But the cautious traffickers refused to cross the river to complete the transaction, thus necessitating the help of the Mexican Federal Judicial Police with all the risks inherent in asking for their assistance. Emilio was arrested, along with his teenage paramour, a spirited little thing named Irene Navidad, and a number of henchmen, among them a notorious trafficker from Jalisco known as "matacien" (the killer of a hundred people). The Mex-Feds extended the investigation to Monterrey and Saltillo and arrested several others.

The MFJP comandante in Monterrey was Manuel Espindola.

Apparently a large amount of money changed hands because everyone was released after a two-week stay in jail. The judge said there was not enough evidence to indicate these people were involved with the seized drugs. It's anyone guess what ultimately happened to the heroin.

Armed with the address, Kiki drove by Emilio's house in the exclusive Colinas de San Javier district and, on one occasion, spotted a yellow Chrysler Cordova parked in the drive. All cops walk around with dozens of license numbers in their heads. Kiki was no exception, he wrote the number down and remembered it well afterward.

Kiki arrived late at work one day and parked in the lot behind the consulate, stopping to banter with the parking lot attendant. He started threading his way through the seemingly endless line of people trying to obtain visas to travel to the United States. He stopped in his tracks, his mind racing back in time, and retraced his steps to the parking lot. Sure enough, there was Emilio's yellow Chrysler jammed into the crowded lot.

Checking his notes in the office he confirmed that the car was the same as that seen at Emilio Quintero's house. Since he felt it was worth the chance he asked the consular officer to let him know if he encountered anyone with the surname of Quintero asking for a visa that morning.

Pay dirt! At mid-morning he got the call that a woman, with the surname of Quintero, accompanied by her children, was asking for a visa to travel to San Diego, California. Emilio Quintero owned a home near San Diego under another name.

¿O Plata O Plomo?

Kiki rushed downstairs and looked at the passport of the visa applicant, Guadalupe Irene Navidad de Quintero. The paramour from the Nuevo Laredo heroin incident!

Ol' Emilio had done the right thing and married the girl! Irene wasn't traveling alone, however, she had a girlfriend, her neighbor, wanting a visa to accompany Mrs. Quintero to San Diego. This lady also had her children along. Kiki asked the vise-consul to have the two ladies return to the consulate with their respective husbands and their bank books, under the pretense that they should show financial responsibility, insuring they would not become wards of the United States taxpayers. Kiki advised the other agents in the office what he had done and they waited anxiously to see if it would work.

The two women complied and returned shortly with their husbands. The DEA agents were waiting, cameras in hand. Skinny Emilio and a fat companion entered the consulate, obviously irritated, but complying with the vice-consul's request, presenting their bank statements to show solvency. The vice-consul copied the documents and, afterward, gave copies to Kiki. The fat man had presented credentials identifying himself as agent number 1179 of the Direcíon Federal de Seguridad. His name was Humberto Alvarez-Machain and his credentials were signed by Miguel Angel Nazar-Haro. Mr. Alvarez-Machain said that he was the next-door neighbor of Mr. and Mrs. Quintero.

When Emilio Quintero-Payan strode into the United States Consulate in Guadalajara as if he owned it, he left four bodyguards waiting outside on the street, their eyes swinging back and forth like windshield wipers, looking for who knows what. The DEA agents managed to get some pretty good snapshots of the four men.

Irene de Quintero and Alvarez's wife were issued their visas and allowed to continue on their shopping trip to the states. The four desperados returned to whatever they were doing and the pictures and copies of the documents were placed in DEA's files.

Afterward some inquiries were made about the fat man, Humberto Alvarez-Machain. He turned out to be a local doctor, a gynecologist, who hung out with the traffickers and the DFS. It was said he liked the scotch, cocaine and women that were always around.

Although the jury in Los Angeles, California, did not see this file in 1992, the judge certainly did.

On the tape labeled "copia 4" the interrogator asked Kiki, harshly. "Emilio what?'

Kiki answered. "Quintero?"

And, again the interrogator asked. "Yes, do you have a photo of him?"

"No, the only photo we have is from "El Alarma" When he was arrested in 1979."

And, from the transcript obtained by the CIA, the tape the Mexican government didn't turn over.

The interrogator said to Kiki. "Look stupid, give up the addresses. There is no problem, it's understandable, you are begging for your safety, you are worried about yourself, in another hour we are going to bring a doctor, you keep co-operating and there is no problem."

Kiki traveled to Zacatecas on August 24 of '82 to meet with "Miguel Sanchez" and check on the progress of the fields. He returned the following day with the exhilarating news that he and "Miguel" had pinpointed the fields.

They had followed Highway 54 north out of Zacatecas and across the desert for about 125 miles, then turned to the east at a small settlement (actually no more than a restaurant and service station) called San Tiburcio. From San Tiburcio they traveled another twenty-five miles through a small mountain range to the intersection with the north-south railroad tracks of "Ferrocarilles Mexicanos" where they run between Monterrey and San Luis

¿O Plata O Plomo?

Potosi. Near the small town of Vanegas, in the state of San Luis Potosi, they turned onto a dirt road and wandered north, very carefully now, fully aware that the marijuana growers would not take kindly to their kind of curiosity.

After a few hours of bouncing around in the jeep amid the dust and intense desert heat they were more than slightly thirsty. They stopped a Corona beer truck delivering to the villages in the area. They bought a few beers to quench their thirst and, while drinking the warm beer beside the road, inquired of the driver if he knew who the owners were of a farm in the vicinity employing a lot of out of town workers. The driver pointed out a farm on the horizon and said, "I don't know what he's growing but whatever it is, it sure is green". He further explained that the overseers wouldn't allow him to get too close to the fields and that he delivered a lot of beer there every week.

Kiki and "Miguel" bought a few more beers and thanked the driver. They located the farm and approached close enough to determine that there was a lot of activity, quite unusual for such a remote place. They then hustled out of there and compared notes.

The place was about where Antonio Perez had indicated, there was definitely a large, well-financed, farming operation going on with a large number of people employed and there was too much security for a legitimate operation. They felt they had found the long sought for plantation.

What was needed now was aerial confirmation.

I did not then, nor do I now, feel that we were wrong in unilaterally searching for and confirming the existence of marijuana fields, heroin labs, cocaine stashes or clandestine pill manufacturers. By September of 1982, it was obvious that we had to minimize our trust in the Mexican authorities. We had a job to do and corruption was the biggest stumbling block to that job. Corruption simply cannot be rationalized, once it starts, it spreads and it becomes the status quo.

James Kuykendall

A private airplane was needed and a private airplane was located, with a little help from friends. The pilot flew Kiki over the area near Vanegas, San Luis Potosi. They found the fields he had seen from the ground. From the sky he could see more, there were several tractors, at least two water wells for irrigation, many, many field workers, several buildings and acres and acres and acres of tall lush plants. It just had to be marijuana.

On September 3, Kiki flew over the fields again.

After first briefing an openly skeptical Assistant Attorney General, Samuel Alba-Leyva, Kiki boarded a small Mexican government airplane along with a pilot and two trained observers, both men with several years in the Attorney General's drug eradication program, and pointed out the plantation to them. One of the observers, government attorney Mario Alberto Cueva-Cerpa, asked the other if he thought the fields were marijuana. The other man, whose years of experience included hundreds of hours looking for marijuana and opium poppy fields in the dangerous mountain canyons of the Sierra Madre, replied, "No son manzanas." ("They aren't apple trees").

Now convinced, the Mexican officials pushed their small plane through the clear, blue, high desert skies to the Zacatecas airport and Mario Cueva telephoned Asst. Atty. General Alba-Leyva with the confirmation. Alba-Leyva told Cueva-Cerpa to go to San Luis Potosi and wait for the helicopters to be sent in from Guadalajara and Uruapan, Michoacan.

Early Saturday morning I received a call from Kiki about the previous day's events. He said they were sending helicopters in to raid the fields. David Burnett, the agent in charge in Mexico City, also called and advised me to contact attorney Hernandez, the head of the Guadalajara eradication program, and hitch a ride with him to San Luis Potosi.

At daylight Sunday morning we were pounding across the high plains of Jalisco in a Bell 212 helicopter. The trip took about two hours. Kiki, Eradication Campaign coordinator Cueva-Cerpa and the MFJP from San Luis Potosi, including the comandante who had allegedly borrowed Antonio Perez-Parga's tractor, met us at the airport.

¿O Plata O Plomo?

There is a beautiful hotel in San Luis Potosi where Kiki and Mario Cueva-Cerpa had already checked in and reserved rooms for us. The pilots, observers and crewmembers of the eradication teams stayed at the cheap hotels in town or slept in the helicopters and fuel trucks at the airport.

Just after dawn we left in the helicopters to Matehuala, about one hour's flight north of San Luis Potosi, and met with the Mexican army unit that was going to accompany us on the raid. Assistant Attorney General Alba-Leyva was also there, having flown up from Mexico City in a Lear Jet just for the planning stage.

After much confusion and arguing, the big helicopters were loaded with soldiers and MFJP agents and lifted up into the still, cool mid-morning air. I was riding in the second machine next to Kiki and he was anxious for us all to see the fields. He and I both had cameras along, as did Mario Cueva-Cerpa. The flight took us through the mountains and along the railroad tracks.

From at least fifteen miles away, Kiki pointed ahead and shouted above the noise of the turbine engines. "Hay esta."(["There it is").

Like an emerald on a white satin sheet, the dark green fields could be seen against the dry desert floor. For miles around there was nothing but scrub brush, cactus and dry ravines, with the mountains in the distance. The plantation was laid out in an orderly fashion with land being prepared for additional planting adjacent to the existing green fields of marijuana. As we approached the size of the plantation became more apparent. Perhaps two hundred acres of wheat isn't anything to a Montana wheat farmer, but two hundred acres of mature marijuana in the middle of a high desert is an awesome sight.

The big helicopters circled, raising huge clouds of dust as they landed near the bunkhouses while the small helicopters provided vigilance overhead. The soldiers and Federal Judicial Police agents jumped out while the machines were still hovering and charged the buildings with their weapons ready.

They shouldn't have bothered.

There was nobody home, just marijuana everywhere, a pothead's paradise. But no people, everybody had split, taking their vehicles, their tractors and almost all their personal belongings. One inoperable Ford pickup truck was left behind. In the makeshift bunkhouses there were metal cots to accommodate several hundred people. In the two well-stocked mess halls we found twenty, fifty-kilo sacks of beans, at least twenty sacks of tortilla flour, kilos and kilos of sausage and bacon, cases of soft drinks and beer, and every kind of canned food imaginable. Near one combination bunkhouse/mess hall there were fifteen head of cattle corralled, a shed containing more than twenty tons of fertilizer and the two acre marijuana seed bed from which the fields had been transplanted.

Hundreds of plants had already been placed in plastic containers to be planted in the ground we had seen being prepared nearby.

The plants were the sinsemilla (seedless) variety, which contain heavy concentrations of resin; the resin in turn contains the chemical THC, which is what causes the high so cherished by pot users.

The plants averaged 5 feet in height, with some as high as 8 feet; each plant was shaped like a Christmas tree and at least six feet in circumference. This was the type of marijuana being smuggled into the United States and bringing one thousand dollars a pound in U.S. markets in those days. As heavy as each plant was, there was a king's ransom spread out before us. Some quick math and a simple formula gave us these figures.

ONE HECTARE=10,000 square meters.
One plant per square meter=10,000 plants per hectare
(Actually they were planted about 90 centimeters apart)
90 hectares x 10,000 plants= 900,000 plants

¿O Plata O Plomo?

(Each plant weighed about twenty pounds, but reducing for shrinkage and removal of the stalks might cut the weight by fifty percent,) so; 900,000 plants x 10 pounds= 9,000,000 (nine million pounds)
9,000,000 pounds divided by 2,000 (one ton)= 4,500 tons.

This was the highest quality in sinsemilla marijuana, shipped by wrapping each branch, or "cola", in plastic wrap and then loosely stacking the "colas" inside thick cardboard boxes of the type used to ship eggs. (Obviously people selling plastic wrap and egg boxes were also making their share of money from this enterprise). This grade of marijuana was selling for $1,000 (one thousand dollars) per pound in the United States in 1982. A little more math then!
2,000 pounds (one ton) x $1,000= $2,000,000 per ton.
4,500 tons x $2,000,000= $9,000,000,000 (nine billion dollars)

Of course that is the best U.S, price and does not take into account expenses, but?

Even if the Mexican financier sold the marijuana for only $250 (two hundred and fifty dollars) a pound he would have received a gross return of $2,500,000,000 (two billion five hundred million dollars) And even if my math is a little off, it was still a lot of money.

Not bad in a country where the government was hocking it's citizen's sweat for several generations into the future by borrowing billions from foreign banks.

Marijuana of this quality really was selling for $1,000 per pound in the United States in those days and that damn sure wasn't the only field of marijuana in Mexico either.

As I walked through the rows upon rows of giant marijuana plants, it was obvious that the Drug Enforcement Administration's intelligence system had failed. This was no experimental farm. These were professional, experienced farmers producing quality crops with modern methods and, just as importantly, operating with almost total impunity. How long had the traffickers been cultivating marijuana like this? How widespread was the practice?

Inside one of the bunkhouses and under a cot, I found a spiral Scribe notebook. The MFJP agents had quickly gone through the bunkhouses and removed anything of value and whatever personal effects had been left behind, including anything that might have led to the people behind the plantation, so this was the only remnant of the people who had been working in the fields and living in the bunkhouses.

The notebook, filled with sad, romantic poems to an unidentified female, had belonged to a man from Silao, Guanajuato, and he had noted his occupation as "motero" (marijuana grower). How had he come to be here in the middle of the desert? Where had he gone?

The smaller helicopters arrived at the fields, those equipped with spray booms to apply the herbicide to the plants, but they did not spray that day. As evening approached, the attorneys and their two U.S. observers flew back to San Luis Potosi to spend the night in our modern hotel rooms. The soldiers and Federal agents slept on the cots at the fields.

The next morning we arrived late at the fields, about an hour's flight from San Luis Potosi. The small tank trucks, loaded with fuel and herbicide for the helicopters, had made it to the site the night before and everyone was preparing the spray helicopters for their task. This involved mixing the dry herbicide with water obtained from one of the three deep wells that had been drilled to provide irrigation for the fields. As we enjoyed a meal of tortillas, meat and beans, cooked at the mess hall by several of the soldiers, the helicopters flew back and forth spraying the fields. The plantation was so large that two machines were actually in the air at the same time, without risk of collision. This spraying continued for two more days. In answer to my concerns about the effectiveness of the weed killer, Attorney Mario Cueva-Cerpa pointed out that the tops of the plants were beginning to turn brown and this indicated they were dying. I hope so, because Kiki and I returned to Guadalajara on Thursday evening in a government airplane. The soldiers

¿O Plata O Plomo?

were to remain behind to uproot and burn whatever plants were not killed by the herbicide.

Kiki and I took many photographs. He was obviously proud of his accomplishment since nothing like this had ever been done before. We left the film in San Luis Potosi, with the Mex-Feds, to have it developed. When we received the pictures, all the photos in which any of the MFJP officers had appeared were missing, as well as the negatives.

In 1983 President Reagan personally recognized the crew of a U.S. Coast Guard cutter for having seized over two hundred tons of Colombian marijuana during their operations throughout that year. I don't think anyone told him that they were planting gardens that size in Mexico.

On my next visit to San Luis Potosi I learned that the Mexican Government had not issued an arrest warrant for Antonio Perez-Parga, had not attempted to determine who owned the property nor had they inquired into the deep wells drilled at the farms. In Mexico it is illegal to drill a water-well without a permit from the Secretaria de Aguas y Recursos Hidraulicos (Secretariat of Water and Hydraulic Resources) and all drilling companies are closely regulated.

Soon after this I attended a training course in the United States and happened to stop by the Marijuana section in DEA headquarters. The agents there were all alarmed at the amount of marijuana being planted in the United States. They called it "domestic" marijuana. I couldn't get over the pictures they showed me of green houses and small plots hidden among the trees in the national forests. They felt the production was so big; they wouldn't even look at my pictures.

I took the pictures to a conference in San Antonio, Texas, on the drug traffic in Mexico, and taped them to the wall in the conference room. An FBI agent named Jack Lawn attended the meeting as a sort of quiet observer. It was the first time I had met him, he had just been confirmed as the Deputy Administrator of DEA.

James Kuykendall

Again no one seemed to express any interest in the fields but one of the attendees did ask me "what does that show, Jaime"? I replied "corruption".

I really believe that the fields were so big that they just couldn't comprehend what it meant. Hell, it was hard for me and I had been there.

I should have tried harder.

CHAPTER 12
ZACATECAS REVISITED

During mid-1983 DEA Agent "Butch" Sears began to receive information that there were large fields of marijuana that were ready for harvest, or that soon would be, between Fresnillo and Zacatecas and in the regions to the north toward Concepcion del Oro in the same state. He had an informant, heavens knows how he located him, whom he fondly called the "bone picker" because his means of livelihood was to gather dry bones in the desert and sell them. People made buttons, small statues and other things out of the bones. Needless to say, it was a meager living.

Well, whatever else "bone picking" accomplished, it gave him a perfect opportunity to observe the well-organized activities of the marijuana planters just slightly off the roads and highways of the state of Zacatecas.

An impoverished old man pushing a broken-down wheelbarrow, gathering dried bones, just didn't constitute a threat in the minds of the boisterous machinegun toting bandits from Sinaloa who were trying to relieve the boredom of being in Zacatecas by amusing themselves with the bare-footed peon girls who lived in the adobe villages on the desert floor.

This old man, who probably wasn't over fifty but looked seventy, wandered slowly but surely noting locations in his memory and passing the information on to Butch. For sure this wasn't too fast or sophisticated a method, but marijuana doesn't grow overnight anyway. Besides, we knew that our problem wasn't the speed with which we received the information but what the hell we were going to do with it once we had it.

There was absolutely no doubt the authorities knew it was there. Helicopters from the Jalisco eradication program and the Durango eradication program were both assigned to fly over the area looking for cultivations and the deep green fields of marijuana were impossible to overlook in that desolate land. The conclusion was that they didn't over-fly or, if they did, nothing was done.

The "bone picker" related information to us, confirmed by other sources, that marijuana production was alive and well in Zacatecas. The locations he pointed out were the same although he wasn't in a position to know the identities of the planters or financiers. He was, after all, only a scavenger who no one noticed.

What he told us was that there were numerous fields of marijuana planted north of Fresnillo, west of the highway that runs from Zacatecas to Concepcion del Oro. The fields were large, from twenty to fifty acres in size.

He said that the traffickers were everywhere, speeding up and down the dirt roads in new pickup trucks while waving automatic weapons at everyone.

The newspapers in Zacatecas reported numerous shooting incidents that year and even detailed a shootout with local police at the main police station in
Fresnillo.

An ex-Federal Judicial Police officer, at the time employed as a state Police comandante in an adjoining state, told us that Fresnillo was jokingly being called, "Colombia" because of the abundance of marijuana being grown. He said there were places where the fields could even be seen from the highways.

In September, Butch passed the word to the comandante of the Federal Judicial Police in Zacatecas that there was a lot of growing activity in his area. The comandante replied that he would request the helicopters to check out the reports and take the required action.

Butch scheduled a trip to coincide with the arrival of the helicopters from Durango and I stopped off in Zacatecas, at his suggestion, to watch the fireworks. Butch was at the Mex-Feds' office in Zacatecas talking to the

¿O Plata O Plomo?

comandante and the eradication zone coordinator from Durango when I arrived. Butch said they had to check out some reported fields west towards the mountains before they could act on his information and invited me to come along. I jumped at the chance to ride along on the raid and we drove to the airport, located halfway between Zacatecas and Fresnillo, where the helicopters were waiting.

The Bell 212 was not new but the motors turned over promptly and the pilot and his navigator were meticulous in their pre-flight routine.

In the back of the big whirly-bird, Butch and I rode with the youthful looking coordinator and eight Mex-Feds. The MFJP comandante from Zacatecas was riding as observer in a small Bell 206 helicopter, which was trailing the big one.

As usual the clear blue sky took our breath away and the smell of adventure made our hearts race. The helicopters beat the air toward the Sierra Madre to the west, flying much too low. If the engines quit the pilot couldn't have possibly landed safely. But you don't express your concerns in situations like that lest your manhood be questioned, besides, who knows what waits at the end of the ride.

At the end of this ride were the mountains, and we rose up, over, and into them. And down into the deep treacherous, canyons. And out of those canyons and into others, with the canyon walls just feet away from the tips of the rotors, the cactus and scrub brush waving in the blades wash.

Of course the little 206 was above us and informing the pilot of our ship by radio where to turn and which canyon to fly into while we looked for whatever we were seeking. Butch and I weren't really sure what the object of the search was.

Since it was dry up there and the canyons were narrow, any marijuana field in those canyons was going to be very small. But the flight continued, into ever narrower gorges.

James Kuykendall

    The pilot and his observer in the small helicopter guiding our way must have had some difficulty in picking out which canyon we should follow as we suddenly found ourselves facing a blank wall, a classic box canyon, with only one way out, the way we had entered. The walls were so close the helicopter couldn't turn around, being longer than it was wide.

    The young, rakish looking pilot and his navigator were talking between themselves, with an occasional conference with the coordinator, and gesturing at the irregular walls of the canyon, which looked to be just inches from the tips of the rotating blades. After a few words with the pilot of the smaller helicopter hovering upstairs, our pilot looked at the navigator, then the coordinator, nodded his head, smiled, and changed the pitch on the blades of his machine. Then he pointed the nose of the Bell 212 almost straight up while increasing the velocity of the rotors. Now the flying machine was literally hanging down from the blades, gravity pushing us back against the seats.

    The helicopters blades were frantically biting at the thin mountain air, although their loud thumping was nothing to the pounding of the hearts of the sweating occupants, as the pilot slowly spun the machine around on an imaginary axis, constantly looking to gauge the distance of the blades from the rocky walls. When he was satisfied he had come all the way around he decreased the speed of the rotors, changing the pitch again, and pushed the nose forward until we were looking back the way we had come. The small field of scraggly marijuana we were apparently seeking was soon located and, when the helicopter set down in the two-acre plot that now looked like a football field, everyone gladly hopped out to settle their nerves. The little helicopter also landed and the comandante told us that he had some great photos of the maneuvers of our pilot. We all assured him that it had been exciting. Butch said that he was going to stay with the Mex-Feds who were going to search a small house nearby and question the occupants. I boarded the helicopter to return to Zacatecas to find that we were almost out of fuel. It was really anticlimactic though to have nothing to worry about but running out of gas on the return trip.

Butch rode with them all that day and the next while they looked for small reported fields in the mountains. Once they chanced upon some opium poppies growing in a remote mountain valley and landed to check them out. When they took off from a relatively large and open area the pilot clipped a tree with the rotor blade. This was the same pilot who had so expertly driven us out of our canyon trap.

Butch's helicopter rides did not include any trips to the northern part of the state where his information indicated that the large, cultivated fields were located. The excuse was that the helicopters had to return to Durango but would be back the following week and Butch was welcome to come along.

When Butch returned the following week, he was greeted with the news that the Federales and the Army had conducted raids on large fields in the middle and northern sections of the state and destroyed more than two hundred acres of marijuana while arresting dozens of people. Unfortunately no one of any importance was among those arrested.

Maybe, but if that was true, it sure didn't convince anyone to stop growing marijuana in the desert. And it sure didn't make Butch Sears happy to lose out on laying claim to a big bust. Our area of responsibility was divided into sections and each agent tried to outdo the other in developing information and looking for fields or laboratories. Butch didn't have a beach or resort area in his section so he tried harder.

In the fall of 1983 the U.S. State Department accomplished a spectacular diplomatic coup when they somehow convinced the Mexican government to send over half of the Mexican eradication campaign helicopters to the tiny country of Belize in Central America to spray the hundred or so small plots of marijuana that had been located there. This was treated as a major breakthrough, one source country helping another source country to destroy its illicit crops of marijuana. The helicopters were in Belize almost 3 months.

The marijuana harvest in Mexico begins in earnest in September and continues through January. This was because of the growing season and because the crop is planted to ripen in time for the big U.S. holidays from Thanksgiving through New Year, when America's potheads like to toke up seriously. That year there were only half the helicopters to look for and destroy the weed. That year Rafael Caro-Quintero's fortune reached nine figures.

Not everyone was ignoring the problem, though.

Kiki Camarena took off on vacation for Thanksgiving in the United States. He traveled to Calexico and San Diego by the longest route possible, through Juarez, Chihuahua and El Paso, Texas. His reason for the side trip was to visit his compadre, Pete Hernandez, who had transferred out of Guadalajara in June of that year. Pete had suffered burnout from the frustration of dealing with the corrupt Mexican system. He was learning to enjoy arresting crooks and putting them in the slammer, even though the judges and lawyers would probably let them out later.

Pete and Kiki couldn't get away from the job, even for the few days they would be together. Pete asked if Kiki would like to talk to an informant of the El Paso office who was knowledgeable of the Zacatecas area. "Hell, yes," Kiki answered. So they got together with the informant, we called him Juan Garcia. Juan told them he knew a man in Fresnillo, Zacatecas, who sold heroin for major suppliers out of Culiacan. This man, Manuel Chavez, was also reportedly overseeing some of the extensive marijuana cultivation being done in the state.

The informant, Juan, fidgeted in his chair and spoke animatedly about the operations there. The heroin came from Sinaloa, he said, from the infamous trafficker, Filemon "Chombi" Medina. The agents had heard of him, many times. Kiki was interested, excited, and asked if the informant wanted to work for him in Guadalajara. The informant responded in the affirmative and the deal was set. He told Kiki that he was, himself, originally from Culiacan and knew many traffickers. He certainly looked the part, with a big mustache, wavy hair, western clothing, (complete with Iguana skin boots), slim athletic build and the light colored eyes so common to the region. Juan was in his late thirties at the time.

Providing him with the address of the consulate in Guadalajara and the DEA office phone numbers, Kiki told Juan to go to Guadalajara and wait for him. He then finished his vacation trip to California, impatient now to return to the hunt.

Juan Garcia showed up in Guadalajara the next week, a week too early. Kiki hadn't returned, so I gave him some money, which he quickly spent on Scotch and women, mostly in a disreputable bar named "El Cue", downtown near the historical plazas and churches. Juan would not be easy to handle. He quickly became restless and wanted to move into action. More money, then I sent him back to Juarez with the orders to return in ten days when Kiki would brief him on his mission. Juan boarded the bus for the eighteen-hour trip to the border.

Money isn't all that motivates people to work as informants, some people do it for excitement, and for others it's just a more leisurely occupation than manual labor. But no one sticks around unless they like the agent, or agents, they are working with, it's a dangerous way to make a living. Juan came back, and Kiki was waiting for him.

Crowded into the small cubicle, which served as Kiki's office, they formulated the plan, which they would follow during the next several months, if we could obtain funding from the DEA office in Mexico City. Juan was to go to Zacatecas, move into a hotel and cement his relationship with Manuel Chavez, and then try to interest him in a new client for large quantities of heroin. Kiki, in an undercover role, would be the client. Juan was to remain in touch through the telephone. To this end we would have a new line installed without reference to the consulate and special instructions given to everyone in the office regarding procedures to be used in answering the calls.

While we negotiated with Mexico City regarding the funding, Juan moved into the "El Bosque" hotel in Zacatecas and started hanging out with the traffickers and DFS agents, which you really couldn't tell apart. Manuel Chavez was receptive to his advances and everything was looking up. Mexico City increased our operating expenses and we tried not to think about the money we would eventually need to make a large undercover purchase of heroin.

The stuff was going for about $6,000.00 an ounce and if Kiki was going to represent himself as a major dealer, he couldn't settle for an ounce or two.

When he wasn't drinking or romancing, C.I. Juan was digging into the operations of the traffickers in the state of Zacatecas. We nicknamed him "C.I." Juan, short for "confidential informant" to differentiate from someone else named Juan who was known to the office. It looked as if they had taken over. They were well organized, had consolidated their operations and they had a fifty thousand dollar line of credit at Conasupo, the government owned supermarket, and were making the Zacatecas tractor and automobile dealers very happy. Literally every law enforcement agency and the local military brass were taking payoffs to leave them alone.

Our friend, Juan, liked to talk and he liked Kiki, so when he called to report on the activities of the traffickers Kiki recorded the conversations. Juan detailed the areas being cultivated by which trafficker, or which group of traffickers, usually members of "the family." Juan might have been embellishing things a bit, but not too much.

Several trips to Zacatecas were made by the agents in the office, snooping around to see if Juan might be misleading us. The hotels were full of well-armed, arrogant, young men, dressed in western boots and hats, who slept late and spent most of their time drinking and dancing in the three discotheques in Zacatecas, carousing in the low class cat houses, or driving around the desert in late model pickups and Gran Marquis. Most of them bragged to the local young women they were DFS agents, readily showing their credentials to back their claim.

Our original plan was being followed, in spite of the information being passed by Juan about the large-scale marijuana production. Kiki and agent Butch Sears traveled to Zacatecas to meet with Manuel Chavez and negotiate with him for a quantity of heroin. We had now decided that the delivery of the heroin should take place in the United States. Arresting Manuel Chavez in Mexico wouldn't accomplish anything, if indeed we were able to find anyone to arrest him. Once again the major obstacle to modern law enforcement was old-fashioned greed.

On December 9, 1983 Kiki was introduced to Manuel Chavez by C.I. Juan. Kiki represented himself as a trafficker with the name of Javier Quintero and stated that he was interested in buying large quantities of heroin. Chavez was interested and offered uncut heroin, delivered in Durango for $7,500.00 per ounce. Kiki replied that he was interested but he wanted delivery made in the U.S. Chavez said he would think about it but they should continue to talk and maybe they could reach a mutually acceptable arrangement.

Without a firm strategy to follow in the investigation, we argued with Mexico City about funding for our operation, mostly Juan's expenses, and pleaded with Washington for "buy" money to pursue the heroin case.

Some correct procedures were followed, however. In addition to C.I. Juan and the "bone picker", information was now coming in from "Miguel Sanchez", the source of information for the big marijuana bust in 1982, and a man who worked for the SARH (the Secretariat of Water and Hydraulic Resources) in Zacatecas. "Miguel Sanchez" told us of a large farm north of the city of Zacatecas, near a small village named "Villa de Cos", which had recently been purchased by a trafficker named Ramiro Mireles. Mireles was unusual in that he was from Zacatecas and Guadalajara, not Sinaloa, but he was doing quite well in the dope business in spite of his ancestry. "Miguel Sanchez" said he had heard that Mireles planned to plant large areas of the farm in marijuana and then store the weed in underground silos, both as protection against possible seizure and as a hedge against falling pot prices.

C.I. Juan had already furnished information to Kiki concerning Ramiro Mireles. Mireles owned a row of houses in Zacatecas where the DFS "agents" were living. Since C.I. Juan was with them almost daily he was able to furnish the names of several of these so-called federal agents. Juan Antonio Brito was one who seemed to have the confidence of Mireles, as well as a lawyer named Nicolas Briseño. Two other, younger men, named Mike Ramos and Daniel Lucero, were also close to Mireles and Manuel Chavez. According to what these two had told C.I. Juan, they had been working for the DFS coordinator in Juarez, Rafael Aguilar. Rafael Aguilar had sent them along to help out in Zacatecas, probably to protect his interests.

The SARH employee, who will forever remain anonymous, passed information to us through a third party. Mexican government workers are not encouraged to join in the fight against drugs since this runs counter to many of the top officials' retirement plans. Large areas of Zacatecas had been declared off limits to SARH inspectors, they were told that they were not to venture into those areas as the soil was not suitable for cultivation, in fact it might even be toxic. Fearing for their jobs, the inspectors didn't openly snicker at these obviously misleading orders. They were as aware as anyone else that their state had been sold out to the drug traffickers.

Every project, large or small, involving water in Mexico must be approved by the SARH. Wells aren't drilled, canals aren't dug, and ponds aren't made, without SARH approval and licensing. All water-drilling companies are regulated by the SARH. In Zacatecas the traffickers needed that water for their crops. Our man from SARH told us that numerous wells were being drilled out in the desert without official permits. It was his duty to seek out unsanctioned wells and force compliance or shut down the drilling operation. Since the area had been officially declared off limits, he was forbidden to visit these reported well sites under the threat of being fired.

Well, why didn't he go over the head of the local manager, call Mexico City? Out of the question, the orders had originally come from the capitol city!

From yet another source we received confirmation that the trafficker, Ramiro Mireles, had indeed purchased a farm near Villa de Cos, called "El Caminero". The previous owner had discovered a number of keys he had failed to relinquish to the buyer and sent his son to the farm to return them. When the son arrived at the main gate he encountered armed guards. He explained the purpose of his visit. The armed men told him the locks had all been changed and the keys were no longer needed. They then advised him to leave and not come back.

No matter that our information was coming from a number of different sources, in our minds irrefutable, we still felt the need to observe these fields ourselves. Because of an agreement with the Mexican government, DEA wouldn't allow unilateral aerial confirmation via DEA aircraft. Apparently we were going to follow the rules even if the Mexicans didn't! They also would not allow Roger Knapp, who had a private pilot's license, to fly a plane over the area.

Undaunted, we sought other means.

Captain Alfredo Zavala worked for us, part time. The other part of his time was spent as a pilot for the SARH, ferrying officials around the country and doing whatever else they asked of him, such as finding illegal well sites. He was a retired Mexican Army officer, hence the title "Capitan". Capi provided us information about the comings and goings of people at the Guadalajara airport. It was in vogue at the time for the traffickers to have airplanes. Some of the traffickers, such as Miguel Angel Felix-Gallardo, put them to extensive use. Others just used them to travel. Most of the airplanes available to the major traffickers were kept in two hangars adjacent to the hangar where the SARH airplane, flown by Capi, was kept.

Capi said yes, no problem, when asked if he could hire a plane and give us a ride over the state of Zacatecas.

So it was that Kiki and I met Capi at the airport one day in mid-March, 1984 for the flight to Zacatecas. We followed the mountains north then, using the highways for reference, found the fields we had heard of. Lots of fields, mostly north and northwest of the city of Zacatecas, but there were also fields east of the main highway and even to the south, not far from the airport. These were cultivated fields, ranging in size from 5 to maybe 50 acres, in remote or isolated areas. At that time of the year most of the fields did not appear to be planted but, in some cases, small plants, just emerging from the ground, were visible. Each field, or group of fields, was complemented by a water well, the pump housed in a small shed clearly visible from our lofty vantage point. Power to the pumps was usually provided by electricity from lines that snaked across the desert from the highways. More often than not, the power lines bypassed villages without electrical power to bring the energy to the wells. In the more remote areas of the desert, the water wells that fed the crops, or proposed crops, were powered by internal combustion engines, also protected from the elements in small, metal roofed, sheds.

About two hours of this aerial observation was all we could manage before we needed to refuel. On the way back to Guadalajara Capi set the airplane down on the small runway of the airport serving the city of Aguascalientes. While the attendant was fueling the plane we marveled at what we had seen and how it matched what we had been told.

From Aguascalientes it was a short trip back to Guadalajara. We made our approach to the airport on the west side of the city so we could photograph a large, walled-in yard belonging to Ernesto Fonseca. Allegedly, this place, located on the Periferico, was used to hide trailers, which were utilized in the transport of marijuana to the border. Capi circled the yard a

¿O Plata O Plomo?

couple of times and I shot three pictures of the compound of about three acres square, enclosed by a ten foot high cinder block wall with a large gate opening to the Periferico. Inside and to the rear of the yard was a large house sitting atop a raised mound. Four trailers were parked alongside the south wall.

C.I. Juan continued to provide information about the trafficker's activities in and around Zacatecas and Fresnillo. He said that he had observed the delivery of 80 tons of "Fertimex" fertilizer to Manuel Chavez, fertilizer destined to feed the pot farms. He said that Rafael Caro-Quintero visited Manuel Chavez at his house in Fresnillo. The young, flamboyant trafficker came in a luxury van, accompanied by fifteen automobiles and pickups filled with armed men. At Chavez's house, a large party ensued, attended by most of the law enforcement people in the area. Caro-Quintero dispensed money to the men as if he were awarding bonuses for selling more chickens than anyone else!

Our quest for "buy" money finally paid off! While DEA wouldn't quibble about spending buy money for dope in New York City, it was reluctant to part with it in any other geographical area. Not surprisingly, many of DEA's upper management were New Yorkers. Sometimes being around for so long has its rewards. The head of DEA's heroin investigations desk was then a New Yorker. He and I had been classmates in the Treasury Agents School in 1966. He felt inclined to overlook the obvious shortcomings in our investigation, our lack of jurisdiction in Mexico and the corruption that hampered our every move. He approved the initial buy, which is to say he gave us the money!

Well, it turned out that Manuel Chavez had previously been introduced to another DEA agent by C.I. Juan. Chavez and the agent, in an undercover role, had discussed a heroin transaction but, for one reason or another, the deal was never consummated. Kiki told Chavez that the other agent worked for him as a heroin buyer and that Chavez should travel to

McAllen, Texas, to make the delivery of the heroin. Chavez agreed to the arrangements, talked to the undercover DEA agent on the telephone and traveled to McAllen as requested. On April 18, 1984, Manuel Chavez exchanged 6 ounces of uncut Mexican heroin for $45,000.00 in U.S. currency. In conversations with the undercover agent (U/ C), Chavez revealed that he had access to 55 kilograms of heroin. He provided no other details but expressed a willingness to deliver heroin in multi-kilogram lots to the U/C in the United States. He stated that all the law enforcement authorities, including the judges, in the state of Zacatecas were being paid off. Chavez said that he could guarantee the U/C agent's safety in Zacatecas and could guarantee the safe pickup of large quantities of marijuana by aircraft in Zacatecas. He said that Mexican Federal police would be used to load the planes. The U/C agent did not pursue a specific date for the heroin delivery as the Guadalajara DEA office had some ambitious plans for dealing with Manuel Chavez and the traffickers in Zacatecas. The proper procedure in this type of operation was to record conversations such as these. That procedure was followed!

    On April 19 Kiki once again flew with Capitan Zavala over the fields in Zacatecas. They located the ranch called "El Caminero" which had been purchased by Ramiro Mireles. Kiki later wrote that he had seen a field of marijuana of about 40 acres in area on the ranch. He said the plants were 3 to 4 feet in height. In addition to El Caminero they flew over many other locations, observing fields of vegetation in various stages of development. He also spotted a seed bed about one acre in size, near some fields being prepared for planting. Capi then turned the airplane south and they came home.

    C.I. Juan was instructed to stay close to Manuel Chavez and to get in good with the new DFS comandante, a vicious dude named Miguel Angel Vielma-Heras. He had replaced Aparicio Nuñez aka "el Ñoño" both as the DFS comandante and as the majordomo for Rafael Caro's extensive marijuana plantations in Zacatecas. Vielma had his headquarters in offices provided by Ramiro Mireles.

In late April Manuel Chavez offered to sell 40 tons of marijuana to C.I. Juan, or actually to Juan's boss, Kiki. Chavez said the marijuana belonged to Ramiro Mireles and was stored somewhere near Fresnillo, Zacatecas. Kiki traveled to Laredo, Texas, to meet with C.I. Juan. While in Laredo on May 8 and 9, they had telephone conversations, which they recorded, with Manuel Chavez in Fresnillo. Chavez reiterated his offer to Kiki concerning the marijuana. He said that Kiki could send someone to Zacatecas to inspect the marijuana and the clandestine airstrip where the ton quantities of marijuana could be picked up. Chavez said the price for the marijuana was $400 U.S. per kilogram, which included refueling the aircraft, use of the airstrip and police protection. Kiki and Chavez agreed that a representative of Kiki would travel to Zacatecas at a later date and, along with C.I. Juan, would inspect the marijuana and airfield. Kiki returned to Guadalajara. On May 11, C.I. Juan called to say that Manuel Chavez had access to 98 tons of marijuana.

This information was dutifully passed along to the Special Agent in Charge in Mexico City. Mexico City had the purse strings and was trying to micromanage our operation. But if we wanted the funds to continue we had to play ball, like it or not!

Imagine our surprise when Walter White called in late May ordering us to culminate the investigation in Zacatecas. No amount of pleading could change his orders. He apologized, saying he was merely passing along commands from the SAIC. Threats didn't work either. He reminded me that the operation had been taken from us when the funding was transferred to Mexico City. The explanation for the hasty change in plans followed. According to what Walter had been told, the SAIC had run into the assistant attorney general in charge of the eradication campaign at the offices of the Director of the MFJP. This lawyer, Jesus Sam-Lopez, had allegedly told the SAIC he was leaving soon to Zacatecas to oversee the eradication program in that state. The SAIC was concerned that Sam-Lopez would find the fields and the Mex-Feds would get the credit for the seizures instead of DEA. This entire line of thought was totally naïve. The fields were perfectly safe from detection, hidden as they were under the watchful eyes of the military and DFS. Our investigation had been minutely documented since its inception the previous year and we would have had no problem reporting to DEA that any discovery and seizure just confirmed our information, after all, the only recognition that any DEA agent, or office for that matter, ever sought was from other DEA agents. The public didn't understand us, anyway. And, we had such little respect for the opinion of the Mexican authorities that we certainly didn't seek, or want, their admiration.

    Walter said it was futile to disagree with the SAIC about this. He wanted the operation terminated. Besides, he had left for the United States and Puerto Rico, accompanying the head of the MFJP on a U.S. sponsored trip to learn about drug enforcement techniques! My arguments rejected, I told Kiki what he had to do. He responded in anger that he had put a lot of effort into the operation and needed more time, maybe two to three months. The opportune time was in the fall, perhaps as early as September, but no earlier. His rationale was sound and based on first-hand experience. The big harvest season began in September to satisfy the U.S. pot market during the fall and winter holidays. The weed heads liked to celebrate, stoned! The over-flights had shown that most of the fields had not been planted, or were planted to ripen in the fall. Kiki was upset, to say the least. He didn't often lose his temper but he was turning red in the face and venting his anger on me. Kiki had forearms like Popeye and had once decked my predecessor in the lobby of the Holiday Inn. I didn't relish the idea of a knot on the side of my head so I took most of his verbal abuse. When he calmed down, we took stock of where we were and began trying to salvage what we could of our operation. What we came up with would require great coordination, a lot of luck and some help from our friends.

¿O Plata O Plomo?

While Kiki looked for C.I. Juan, who was not always easy to find, I answered a summons to Mexico City to a briefing for the Mexican Deputy Attorney General, to tell him what we knew. A bitter pill! He was especially interested in the information about the SARH having declared the target area off limits to its inspectors. The Mexican officials just couldn't believe that something like this could be happening on such a scale, especially in Zacatecas, where the governor was a good friend of President Miguel de la Madrid. They asked, I answered. The cat was out of the bag and I wasn't going to tell them about the undercover deals we had cooking. The SAIC was gone and we were going to handle this our way, our way usually worked. I informed them of the illicit activities of their comandante in Zacatecas and told them of the protection afforded by the DFS, in the person of "el Negro" Vielma. Once again they just couldn't believe this; that Mexican law enforcement personnel were involved with the traffickers. Against my advice and that of Walter White, they decided they would order the MFJP Comandante, Galo Martin, to Mexico City during the period of the raids so he couldn't interfere. They pledged to be discreet; it would be for some routine, mundane, reason they said. The meeting adjourned with June 6 set as the date for the raids.

Kiki had already set our wheels in motion. C.I. Juan had passed word to Manuel Chavez to await Kiki's representative in Zacatecas, someone was coming to inspect the marijuana. In addition he ordered a large quantity of heroin to be delivered to the undercover agent in McAllen, Texas. The delivery was arranged for the same date as the planned raids on the fields, so DEA could capture Manuel Chavez in the U.S.

Everything was going along smoothly, if that was possible, considering that the Mexican government knew we had been withholding information from them. Then another surprising thing happened! Marijuana was growing all over the place in the state of Zacatecas and no one had previously expressed any interest in it, except us, of course. Walter White called to tell us to move the date up since a Mexican army general had been injured in a plane crash in Zacatecas. The small plane he was riding in had crash-landed in a field of marijuana, not far from the airport, and the army was now manually destroying the crop. The Mexican attorney general's office was allegedly concerned that the army would find and destroy all the fields, thereby robbing them of the credit for the discovery and seizure of the marijuana.

Okay! Kiki drove to Monterrey, and then accompanied C.I. Juan to Laredo. Walter summoned me to Mexico City for more meetings while the three other agents in the Guadalajara office; Butch, Roger and Harvey, packed their clothes for the trip, planning to meet with the MFJP somewhere.

A pilot was needed for some undercover work. A gruff voiced Texas DEA agent, working in Laredo, had an informant who was a pilot, or vice versa. He was contacted and flew in with his airplane. He brought another CI/pilot with him. The two agreed to carry C.I. Juan to Zacatecas for the inspection trip. In the meantime, the undercover DEA agent in McAllen was having his own telephone conversations with Manuel Chavez, cutting C.I. Juan out of the middle of the heroin deal, the classic method to prevent compromising an informant.

In relating the circumstances now, it seems pretty simple, but it was a nail biter then, hoping we could successfully pull off all three deals at once.

C.I. Juan and the two CI/pilots flew into the Zacatecas airport where they were met by Ramiro Mireles himself. Mireles received them, ushered them through the small terminal and into a waiting, white, Ford Gran Marquis. A large marquee on the dashboard of the automobile bore the legend, Miguel Vielma, DFS Comandante. A convoy of automobiles accompanied the three men when they left the airport. One of the pilots became uncomfortable at the display of so many firearms by the receiving committee and opted to remain with the airplane. Among the convoy was at least one official automobile of the Federal Highway Police. Just at the outskirts of the city of Zacatecas, Mireles pulled into a service station where they were met by a man driving a Chevrolet pickup truck. This man, addressed by Mireles as "Licenciado" (lawyer), indicated to the CI/pilot and C.I. Juan that they should accompany him. They rode with him to a road that looped around the city. He stopped the truck near a large house and they exited. He then knocked on the door that was opened by a young girl, maybe ten years old, and a woman in her fifties. The woman allowed them entrance and they walked through the house to an open patio. On the opposite side of the patio the three men entered a room stacked to the ceiling with cardboard boxes. The CI/pilot pulled down several boxes and examined their contents. The boxes contained sinsemilla marijuana, "colas" wrapped in plastic and carefully placed in the boxes. This type of marijuana was referred to as "manicured", no stems, just the resin-laden tops. The CI/pilot marked several boxes, to insure that the boxes would be part of the proposed delivery. The men then returned, in the pickup, to the service station and were driven by Mireles back to the airport. At the airport Mireles introduced the two informants to his own pilot and directed them to a yellow, twin-engine aircraft parked on the apron. The CI/pilot climbed into the co-pilot's seat while Ramiro Mireles, C.I. Juan and Manuel Chavez rode in the passenger section. The pilot flew the airplane north some thirty minutes before landing on a dry lakebed. The men disembarked and the CI/pilot expressed his total satisfaction with the site as a landing area. Mireles stated that planes as large as a 747 could land there without a problem. The informants observed many tracks in the sand, which appeared to have been made by airplane tires.

The airplane returned to Zacatecas and the men parted company. C.I. Juan told Mireles that he or Kiki would be calling to confirm the date for the pickup, as he knew Kiki was interested in buying at least twenty tons of marijuana. The three informants then returned to Laredo in their own airplane.

James Kuykendall

Kiki had a day before the planned raids. Calls to Manuel Chavez's house were initially met with confusion and anxiety from the man in Fresnillo. The MFJP Comandante had been recalled to Mexico City as had most of the DFS agents. Chavez didn't know what to make of it. Long hours and many phone calls later, Chavez indicated that everything was okay and the deals would go through as planned.

While the informants were inspecting the marijuana, the MFJP was assembling the men for the raids and the attorney general's office was fueling the helicopters for the flights to the airport at Aguascalientes, which was to be the staging area for the aircraft since the helicopters could only fly about three hours before needing to be refueled. A DEA agent from the Mexico City office and I traveled in a Cessna Citation jet to Aguascalientes, along with two of the coordinators who were in charge of the eradication portion of the raids. At the hotel "Las Trojes" we met the DEA agents from Guadalajara and the helicopter pilots and navigators from the permanent campaign. The MFJP agents were to fly into the Zacatecas airport directly from Mexico City and meet with us there. While this was taking place, Manuel Chavez was traveling overland to Reynosa, the Mexican city directly across the Rio Grande River from McAllen, Texas, to meet with, and make the heroin delivery to, the DEA undercover agent. During the early morning hours of May 26, Manuel Chavez arrived at the hotel "La Conchita" in Reynosa and called the undercover agent's hotel room in McAllen advising the U/C he had arrived and requesting the presence of C.I. Juan to assist in crossing the heroin into the U.S., something immediately complied with.

Since the beginning of recorded history, no Mexican Immigration Officer has ever attempted to stop a Mexican from crossing into the United States, legally or otherwise. That day one did! With C.I. Juan driving, he and Manuel Chavez arrived at the International Bridge from Mexico into the United States. A Mexican immigration official asked the two men for their Mexican credentials. When Chavez couldn't produce his, he was ordered out of the vehicle. A hurried conversation took place between Chavez and the informant. C.I. Juan was to deliver the one and a half kilos of heroin to the undercover agent and then bring the money to Chavez at La Conchita hotel in Reynosa. C.I. Juan arrived at the hotel in McAllen and told the DEA agents what had transpired. Kiki called the MFJP office in Reynosa and, without disclosing the name of the hotel, told him there were several men in a hotel in Reynosa with a quantity of heroin. The agents believed Chavez had more heroin with him as he had told the undercover agent, in his earlier telephone calls, he was bringing 300 ounces, approximately 18 pounds, with him to Reynosa. The MFJP comandante in Reynosa was out of town and the group supervisor, Hugo Rivera, would not act without orders from Mexico City. Kiki called Walter White at the embassy and passed his problem. Walter called the acting director, Colonel Rocha, and asked for assistance.

Rocha must have acted. The group supervisor provided all the help Kiki and the DEA agents from McAllen wanted. They raided the hotel, arrested Manuel Chavez, Mike Ramos and Daniel Lucero. They also picked up the young whore who had accompanied Lucero on the trip. Ramos and Lucero were carrying credentials identifying them as DFS agents. Their pickup truck was seized but there was no more heroin. Chavez, under interrogation, stated that Joel Medina, from Culiacan, was in Fresnillo with the rest of the heroin.

At the same time that Kiki was urging the Federales to hit the hotel "La Conchita", we were making the hour and a half drive from the hotel in Aguascalientes to the Zacatecas airport to meet the MFJP agents arriving by fixed wing aircraft from Mexico City.

The task force departed Aguascalientes at first light, as the helicopter pilots had to wait until they could see, and arrived at its destination about an hour later. The MFJP agents had arrived 45 minutes earlier, commandeered two large buses to use as patrol cars since they had no ground vehicles and were busy loading agents into the buses.

James Kuykendall

While DEA agents Butch Sears, Roger Knapp, Harvey Varenhorst and Ernie Lowe remained at the airport to ride in the helicopters while they searched the desert for the marijuana plantations, Miguel Aldana-Ibarra, the MFJP Comandante in charge of the enforcement operation, took me in tow and we charged off in one of the buses to raid hotels and houses, the names and addresses of which I had provided the day before in Mexico City.

The way this worked, we would pull up in front of one the cheap hotels and Comandante Ibarra would jump out with several agents behind him and secure the hotel. He then jumped back into the bus and we proceeded on to the next hotel. When we reached the last hotel on his list, he then ordered the bus driver to turn around and we returned on the same route, picking up prisoners. For the most part our prisoners were peons from Sinaloa and Sonora brought in to work in the marijuana plantations. They didn't know anything or anybody, they said. But there were only a fraction of the number of peons staying in the hotels compared to the previous week. Most of the workers had been told to go home for a while until things cooled down. At the Hotel Fortuna in Fresnillo, the manager said his best customers had checked out two days earlier and they didn't say when they would be back. These men were always armed, even when they visited the swimming pool and had the air about them of being some sort of police officers. He had been reluctant to ask too many questions!

Late in the day Aldana and I returned to the airport to find that Roger, Butch, Harvey and Ernie had been left to cool their heels all day at the airport. They had been told there was no room for them in the helicopters. Each time the helicopters had returned to refuel they requested to be allowed to board but no one seemed to have the authority to let them ride. Mario Cueva-Cerpa, the representative from the A.G.'s office who was in charge of the helicopters, was conspicuously absent and no one could find him.

Since the DEA agents were pretty well disgusted by this time, we left the airport and drove to the MFJP office in Zacatecas. Sure enough, the MFJP

¿O Plata O Plomo?

Comandante, Galo Martin, had been recalled to Mexico City, the secretaries swore they didn't know why. MFJP agents were putting their prisoners in every conceivable corner of the small offices and it was very crowded. Comandante Aldana told one of his supervisors to pull the buses up in front of the offices and park them at the curb, then use them to house the arrested men, mostly peons from the states of Sinaloa, Sonora and Durango.

Aldana called the acting director of the MFJP in Mexico City, Col. Rocha, and I called the embassy. We both received essentially the same news about the heroin bust in Reynosa. Aldana was surprised to learn that Kiki was involved in the case, which was obviously linked to what we were doing in Zacatecas and he wasn't very successful at concealing his displeasure. When we explained how the detainees in Reynosa were connected to what we were supposed to be doing in Zacatecas (we still had not seized a pound of dope) Aldana decided to have the prisoners brought from Reynosa to Zacatecas. After getting approval for his plan, he dispatched the Twin Otter, with several MFJP agents for escort, to the border city to bring back the three men and one woman.

While on the telephone with Walter White in the embassy he had told me of the trip taken by the two informants just two days previous when they had seen the marijuana stash in a ranch near Zacatecas. Walter passed on the directions to the ranch as he had received them from Kiki and, in turn, I passed this information to Aldana.

Aldana used his authority to commandeer a helicopter and again insisted that I accompany him. We followed the instructions from Walter and looked for a road, or highway, that looped around Zacatecas toward Guadalajara to the south, but without luck.

The Mex-Feds raided several small ranches in this manner, swooping down out of the sky and scaring the poor people half to death when they jumped out of the still descending craft to charge their humble homes, machine guns at the ready.

James Kuykendall

Attempting to salvage something out of the trip, I directed Aldana to the ranch we had heard of, El Caminero, north of the city near the village of Villa de Coz. Aldana ordered the pilot to change course and we found the ranch without difficulty as I had seen it before in pictures Kiki took on his flight with Capitan Zavala. Again no luck as the Mex-Feds searched the place from top to bottom.

An old man working there made a casual remark to one of the agents that he knew of another ranch that belonged to the owner of El Caminero. The agent brought the old man, easily in his mid-seventies, to Aldana and he, in his abrupt manner, ordered most of the group back into the Bell 212 to look for this new ranch. The old man, our guide, was trembling with fear but he was more afraid of the MFJP than of his first journey off the ground. He looked wild-eyed around him as the whirly bird picked up and pushed back south again. His usual mode of transportation was aboard a tractor, at considerable less speed, and it took quite a while for him to find his bearings. When we found the place, looking like a rundown hacienda, it was also apparent that we had found the place described to Kiki by the informants. Just off of a little used bypass south of the city linking with the main highway to Guadalajara, a house, arranged in a square, with a central patio.

Again the MFJP agents went about their now familiar drill of leaping out of the helicopter before it had come to a full stop and charging the house. Only this time they had me with them!

The place looked deserted but the old man insisted this was the place; he had driven here on his tractor. Under some trees in front of the house was a late model Ford Bronco. A sticker on the windshield indicated that the driver of the Bronco had authority to enter the facilities of Randolph Air Force Base in San Antonio, Texas. A stolen vehicle for sure, the place looked promising.

One of the agents knocked on the door of the house while others ran around back or waited to the side of the door for it to be opened from within. An older woman, perhaps in her fifties, opened the door and the agent identified himself. Aldana joined the agent at the door and motioned for the rest of us to follow. With the woman leading the way we walked through the house and out into the central patio. In a room to the rear of the patio we found dozens of boxes of marijuana, stacked to the ceiling. In the patio, overgrown and littered with junk, were airplane parts. In the house, in a cheap suitcase, were utility bills for a house in Guadalajara, in the name of Ramiro Mireles-Felix along with some automobile registration papers for a car in the name of Libra do Perez with an address in Rio Grande City, Texas. This address was well known in DEA, as was the name. Perez was a major drug trafficker in south Texas.

The comandante used the radio in the helicopter to call for help and another flying machine came to the ranch with additional MFJP agents, accompanied by DEA Agent Butch Sears. Leading me around like I had a ring in my nose, Aldana said that he and I were returning to town. Butch stayed behind to continue the search of the ranch and its surroundings.

Back at the MFJP station, the processing of the prisoners continued, pulling them one by one out of the buses, taking their statements, and returning them to the bus. Under Napoleonic law, as it is practiced in Mexico, everyone involved in an investigation is obligated to make a statement. There is nothing of the "if you decide to make a statement" that is a part of the so-called Miranda warning of the United States. In Mexico you will make a statement. True or false, coerced or voluntary, like it or not, a statement is mandatory. In the best of times, it will be accepted as is, but often the Mex-Feds wanted a confession as well and not everyone was willing to make a confession.

With something positive to report I called Walter White again and filled him on the marijuana seizure. Walt told me that Kiki wanted to come down to Zacatecas and join in the fun so the airplane flying to Reynosa to pick up Manuel Chavez and the two DFS agents was going to stop in

James Kuykendall

Monterrey to pick up Kiki as he was driving there to drop off a car he had borrowed for the trip to the border.

Just at dark Kiki walked in, grinning from ear to ear. He had caught a ride from the airport with the MFJP bringing the three prisoners and the girl. He had ridden on the plane with Manuel Chavez but hadn't talked to him. We filled him in on what had, and hadn't, transpired in our part of the investigation and he told us about the problems in Reynosa. We all decided to look for Mario Cueva at the hotel later and demand that the DEA agents be allowed to ride in the helicopters looking for marijuana fields.

The Mex-Feds were using some larger offices to conduct their interrogations and they had taken over some government facility above the basement offices where the MFJP was housed. In addition to the two MFJP Comandantes, Aldana and Lorrabaquio, an attorney had been dispatched from Mexico City especially to handle the prosecutions for our case. Licenciado Garcia-Torres had arrived long before the marijuana seizure was made, driving his personal automobile from Mexico City. Each prisoner was interviewed briefly by one of these three men before being turned over to someone else for more extensive debriefing. In addition to the people arrested in the hotels and several men, including the old man who had been our guide, picked up at El Caminero, there were some rather respectable looking gentlemen who the Mex-Feds were charging with firearms violations. The explanation was that they were somehow connected with the traffickers.

Lorrabaquio was talking to Manuel Chavez so I joined in the interview, without invitation, and started asking questions. Chavez was eager to talk and save his skin. Lorrabaquio was not eager to listen. Chavez began to spout names of major traffickers who had been the chief financiers in the plantings. The most frequently mentioned names were Rafael Caro-Quintero, Juan Jose Esparragosa-Moreno (El Azul) and Ramiro Mireles-Felix. Lorrabaquio wasn't having any! I asked him why he wasn't writing down the man's statements and he just looked away. I stamped into the office where

¿O Plata O Plomo?

Aldana was barking out orders to his men and complained about Lorrabaquio's lack of action. Aldana told me to talk to Garcia-Torres. Although Garcia-Torres was even more evasive, he did tell me that it was more important to make a strong case against the people who were under arrest, that there were many people arrested and everyone felt they had done a good job. An hour of arguing did no good, the conspiracy ended there, not one major trafficker was linked to the case, even though the Mexican government had sent 170 men to participate in the action in Zacatecas along with 12 helicopters and several fixed wing aircraft, with all the support personnel. The fix was in, big time, orchestrated from the Federal District!

Feeling betrayed, I walked outside and found the DEA agents huddled, talking to Butch. He had arrived with several trucks bringing the seizure from the ranch to be guarded at a yard nearby. We walking over and looked at the haul. Two large trucks were filled to the tops of their stake beds with manicured marijuana in boxes and sacks. The marijuana was estimated to weigh nine tons. Along with the weed the trucks also contained three metric tons of marijuana seed. Lined up in a row, five-gallon jugs of hash oil were arranged against one wall in the yard, some 200 liters of hash oil in all. On several of the boxes of marijuana Butch had found the initials left by the CI/pilot.

We had no estimate of the amount of bulk marijuana necessary to squeeze out 200 liters of hash oil but it must have been substantial. Three metric tons of marijuana seed was something else though. At one kilo of seed per acre it was sufficient to plant three thousand acres. Marijuana was not broadcast planted. The agronomists employed by the major traffickers in Mexico in those days were using seedbeds and transplanting the seedlings about one meter apart. One kilo of seed per acre was more than enough.

In spite of the quantity of drugs seized, no one among the DEA contingent slept well that night. A well-planned, and executed, operation had ended in anything but success. This was not the way we did things. Just removing the dope does not affect the dope traffic. Traffickers have to be kept on the run, constantly, until they fall.

The next day we boarded the helicopters, at last, and headed out into the desert. A couple of fields of marijuana were located and one seedbed. Disappointing, but the agents were not driving the aircraft and had no control over where the search took place. We will never know what we missed.

Conferring among themselves first, the comandantes and lawyers asked if the heroin seized in Texas could be turned over to them so they could use it as evidence against Manuel Chavez. They had nothing to link him to the marijuana seized at the ranch. This was not without precedent so we moved the request upstairs. Mexico City DEA, then McAllen and then DEA headquarters concurred, so a sample of the drug was retained by the McAllen office and the remainder was delivered to Mexican government attorneys and DEA agent Harvey Varenhorst, who flew to Reynosa for that purpose. They returned to Zacatecas with the evidence they said they needed for their judicial proceedings.

Since we were out rousting traffickers, Kiki thought it might be interesting to visit our old friend Antonio Perez-Parga, the guy who had been in charge of planting, cultivating and harvesting the marijuana fields we had discovered near Vanegas, San Luis Potosi, in 1982. Characteristically, the Mexican authorities had never arrested anyone in connection with that seizure, even though we had provided names and even pictures of Perez-Parga and his main man, Rodolfo "El Feo". Aldana complied with our request and the helicopter pilot sought out Perez-Parga's village, far out in the desert.

Near a large and picturesque adobe church was an open area where the first machine set down, blowing dust in every direction. The village children ran around the area in a frenzy, something this exciting only happened about every thousand years or so. The two largest houses in town belonged to Antonio Perez and his brother. Aldana and his troops searched the houses and adjoining buildings but found no dope. One small barn belonging to the Perez family was locked so the Federales opened it with a very large key. They backed a truck through the door. Inside was a new Yamaha motorcycle, which they liberated, along with the truck. Two MFJP agents left in the truck, taking the motorcycle, which Aldana decided was probably stolen. We were unable to find Antonio Perez or any of his family and no one in town was willing to admit to being "El Feo". Everyone who was asked indicated someone else, but any man in that village would have qualified.

Aldana was enjoying himself, walking down the center of the dirt streets, with his hand poised over his holstered pistol, he later said he felt like he was in a western movie. He felt so good he let the helicopter pilots carry several of the village children in rides over the nearby brush flats. When we left, the whole village came out to the edge of town, enduring the dust, to noisily wave and cheer the departing raiders. Of course, they hadn't lost a motorcycle!

The DEA agents left that night, and the next morning, driving back to Guadalajara without fanfare. The Mexican officials who stayed behind held numerous photo sessions with the local press, proclaiming loudly of their successful mission and the terrible blow they had dealt the drug traffic. The marijuana was burned, in a public display, on a deserted farm just outside of town.

The end result was certainly not what we had envisioned when we began the investigation almost 6 months earlier.

In October 9, I received a call from the MFJP Comandante in Zacatecas, Galo Gutierrez-Martin, who had been allowed to return to his post after the marijuana seizures earlier that year. Galo Gutierrez told me he and his men had made a large marijuana seizure on the "El Caminero" ranch and asked if I would like to come and witness the destruction of the weed.

James Kuykendall

Butch Sears had transferred out of Guadalajara without a replacement forthcoming, so I drove to Zacatecas and checked into the hotel.

The next morning I was up early and headed to the MFJP office when I got a message at the hotel desk to call home. My wife answered my call and told me Roger Knapp's government automobile had been riddled by machine-gun fire in front of his house. Roger told me about the same thing when I called him, adding that his children were eating breakfast at the time of the shooting and would have walked outside to wait for the school bus in just a few more minutes. He also said there was no reason for me to return to Guadalajara right away as he felt the threat was over and there were Guadalajara police swarming around the neighborhood.

The Mex-Feds took me with them to "El Caminero" and showed me a large hole in the ground filled with marijuana, the silo we had heard about from "Miguel Sanchez." The hole had been lined with plastic, the marijuana placed inside and more plastic placed over it before being covered with soil. There were more than 20 tons of marijuana in the hole. Several army officers, a few lawyers, the mayor and almost the entire MFJP contingent were present. Large quantities of diesel fuel were poured onto the pot and it was set ablaze. The obligatory photos were taken of the officials and the brief ceremony was over.

¿O Plata O Plomo?

MFJP agents uncovering the Gran Marquiz

La Langosta restaurant and bar

Chapter 13
RAFAEL CARO AND THE RIO YAQUI

The name that had confirmed, for me, the validity of the information from the CIA concerning the existence of the interrogation tapes was "Jesus Ramirez". On both tapes, as well as in the transcript later obtained by the CIA, Kiki gave the name to his interrogators as an informant utilized by our office, principally providing information about Rafael Caro-Quintero.

I'm certain, having known him so well, that the torture to which Kiki was submitted must have been extreme or he would not have told his captors the identities of those who helped us. I believe he also must have suffered greatly when he learned how cruel the Mexican officers were. If Kiki had a fault it was that he trusted the Mex-Feds, in spite of what we knew about them. There is no doubt that the interrogators, at the very least, had past experience in Mexican law enforcement.

When I met the man that we would call "Jesus Ramirez" no one really knew much about the mysterious trafficker named Rafael Caro-Quintero. Some people even doubted that he existed and were convinced that another man, Rafael Caro-Lerma aka "El Charel" was the trafficker about whom the Guadalajara office was constantly reporting. There was certainly enough prior, concrete information to support their theory. "El Charel" had been a trafficker for many years and DEA's files contained many references to him. Also he was married to Ernesto Fonseca's sister, Adela, and they lived in Guadalajara.

"Jesus Ramirez" blew that theory.

Where did he get my name and telephone number? I never asked him. He had something I wanted, information about Rafael Caro, and I wasn't about to offend him with such an irrelevant question.

¿O Plata O Plomo?

It was late in September 1982 when Paulette passed a telephone call to me from an unidentified male. The caller said he had some information I would find interesting and suggested that we meet. I agreed and suggested lunch at the small upstairs restaurant on the corner one block from the consulate; he said he would recognize me when I entered.

"La Terraza" is just a nice, quiet and modest restaurant with decent food. It overlooks Avenida Chapultepec and through the large windows you can see the statues placed along the gardens in the middle of the street commemorating the young men who died defending Chapultepec Castle in Mexico City from the invading United States army in the mid 1800's.

He knew me when I walked in and stood to shake hands. We sat near the window and apparently he was satisfied that he could trust me because he began to talk. Young and handsome, with the light-colored skin and blue eyes that are so common to Sinaloans, he said he was from there and wanted to offer his services in the form of information about a drug trafficker named Rafael Caro Quintero. He further said that he knew him personally and was aware of some large fields of marijuana that Rafael Caro was financing in the northern state of Sonora.

Well, there he was. The first person we had met who knew first hand that elusive doper. Rafael Caro was real. Were the rumors correct, about his wealth, about his influence? The young man said that Rafael was powerful, perhaps not as much as Miguel Felix but he was growing stronger and becoming richer every day. Rafael was associated with Ernesto Fonseca and Juan Esparragoza in trafficking marijuana from Mexico to every U.S. border state. He was also doing business with his two maternal uncles, Juan Jose and Emilio Quintero-Payan. For one so young, he said Rafael Caro was 29 years old, this fellow was running in fast company. A more frightening array of partners could not be imagined.

James Kuykendall

We really hadn't expected to hear about another large plantation of marijuana so soon after the discovery of the fields near Vanegas, San Luis Potosi. My interest was piqued, however. After all that was our business.

My lunch partner trusted me enough to tell me his name and said that he needed to dig more to try to find the exact location of the fields in Sonora so I asked him to call me at the office but in the future to use the name of "Jesus Ramirez" when he called. He promised he would call but I anxiously held my breath for the next few days until his call came and I introduced him to Roger Knapp.

We met at the same place and Roger's quiet confidence assured "Jesus" he could believe in us. It was agreed that he would call Roger in the future, or ask for me if Roger was not available. At this meeting "Jesus" told us he thought the fields were near a large river in Sonora but he still did not know exactly where. He added that Rafael Caro's brothers were in San Diego packaging and selling the marijuana produced on Rafael's farms. The meeting ended with his promise that he would call again.

His digging paid off and in mid-October Roger Knapp caught a Mexicana airlines flight to Culiacan to meet with the MFJP and try to locate the fields that "Jesus" had reported. According to "Jesus" the fields were alongside the "Rio Yaqui", north of the lake formed by the Alvaro Obregon Dam. The "Yaqui" has its source near the border and winds its way across the Sonora desert to trickle into the Sea of Cortez near Ciudad Obregon.

His flight was preceded by another meeting between Country Attaché David Burnett, Assistant Attorney General Alba-Leyva and me, Alba-Leyva stated that he was not convinced that these fields we were reporting existed and he was visibly upset at our sleuthing around Mexico looking for marijuana plantations. He did, however, agree to provide the DEA with an aircraft and pilot to look for the fields along the Rio Yaqui north of Ciudad Obregon, Sonora. But the message was clear. The Guadalajara DEA office was unfairly criticizing the Mexican Government's much heralded eradication campaign by suggesting that large fields of marijuana were growing throughout Mexico while the Government of Mexico (GOM) was reporting the success of their campaign.

The comandantes usually cooperated only because they were told to so do by their superiors in Mexico City, which turned out to be the case here. On the date of his arrival Roger went to the offices of the MFJP in Culiacan but the comandante told him to come back the next day since an airplane was not available to make the over flights necessary to look for the fields.

When Roger returned to the MFJP office the following day he met another official from the United States. Cesar Bernal, of the U.S. State Department's Bureau on International Narcotics Matters who was also visiting the Mexican narcotics officers in Culiacan. He was accompanying two Colombian officials on a U.S. sponsored tour of the Mexican eradication effort. Roger explained to Cesar what he was doing in Culiacan and Bernal asked him, in front of the MFJP Comandante, if we (DEA) had found the fields by over-flights.

This was a sensitive question since DEA was prohibited from operating its aircraft in Mexico without GOM approval. Roger replied that an informant had provided the information, but the looks from everyone present clearly showed they didn't believe him. Cesar Bernal and the two Colombian officers boarded some, U.S. purchased and donated, eradication campaign helicopters and were whisked away to look for small hidden fields in the rugged mountains of the Sierra Madre. This was the standard horse and pony show for visitors being shown an overview of the much touted, State Department sponsored, campaign.

DEA agent Roger Knapp and the MFJP Comandante climbed into a single engine airplane for the flight over the Rio Yaqui in southern Sonora. North of the city of Ciudad Obregon is the large lake formed by a man made damn across the Rio Yaqui. This is scrub brush country but like any other part of the great western deserts if you add water you can grow anything. Above the lake the river flows year around and that's where Roger confirmed his information.

The little Cessna aircraft followed the river for miles and the fields kept appearing, sometimes on the east bank, sometimes on the west bank, sometimes both. Since there was no airstrip in the area the airplane returned to Culiacan and Roger returned to his hotel room to await the next move by the Mex-Feds. The comandante said that he had to call Mexico City for instructions and Roger should call back the next day.

Back in Guadalajara "Jesus Ramirez" called the office and passed the information to me, to give to Roger, that the traffickers were feverishly harvesting as much marijuana as they could before the Mex-Feds were forced to go in and destroy the fields. The raid had already been compromised.

Roger Knapp returned to Guadalajara with the news that he had not been allowed to accompany the Mex-Feds to destroy the fields. He had estimated there were 165 acres of mature marijuana plants in the fields he saw.

Through an independent, and highly confidential, source of information we confirmed what "Jesus Ramirez" had said. Much of the marijuana had been moved out while the MFJP stalled Roger in Culiacan. How much? We'll never know.

"Jesus Ramirez" kept telling us about the wild, young multi-millionaire named Rafael Caro-Quintero.

Rafael Caro-Quintero was a true product of the Sinaloa drug traffic and the personification of the Sinaloa drug trafficker.

He was married to the daughter of a powerful trafficking family. His own father was killed in a drug dispute and his brothers and sisters were a part of his organization, all with the blessings of his widowed mother. When we first heard of him, his mother and sisters were living in a large but not eloquent house on a street named Plan de San Luis in Guadalajara, just inside the periferico. He then was using the name of Pedro Santos Coy and was a rising star in the Mexican underworld.

His two maternal uncles, Juan Jose and Emilio Quintero-Payan, were impressed with his fierceness and had given him invaluable assistance in the trade. His paternal uncle, Rafael Caro-Lerma, also helped him greatly as well as another family member by marriage, the drug-lord Ernesto Fonseca-Carillo.

Rafael Caro-Quintero's fortunes were greatly enhanced in January of 1983 when Ernesto Fonseca's favorite son, Gilberto Fonseca-Caro, was killed in Tijuana in an altercation outside a stadium where he had just attended a boxing match. Gilberto Fonseca was accompanied by a bodyguard who was also a DFS agent. After exiting the sports arena where the boxing match had been held, Fonseca's group encountered an unknown individual urinating on his parked vehicle. A fight ensued, which Gilberto was apparently losing, so the bodyguard fired two rounds to even things out but his aim was bad, or good, depending on your point of view. His first shot grazed the urinator and the second struck Fonseca in the upper arm, passing through his torso and killing him instantly. Outraged over the death of his son, Ernesto Fonseca ordered the bodyguard killed.

The younger Fonseca had been married to Sylvia Fernandez, the daughter of
Mexico's most notorious heroin chemist, Eduardo "Lalo" Fernandez, alias "El Professor". The beautiful young widow did not have long to grieve, however, as Rafael Caro began to court her in earnest, taking her on trips around Mexico to visit his enterprises, impressing her with rides in his Lear jet, purchased in the United States and registered to a well-known Mexican business man. The jet would eventually be seized in Brownsville, Texas, and pressed into service as transport for the attorney general of the United States, Ed Meese.

James Kuykendall

Rafael Caro just naturally fell heir to Ernesto Fonseca's favors. Ernesto could see that he was a man after his own heart. Rafael was a devoted womanizer who loved to punish his enemies. He also loved money and had a nose for cocaine. And he had a knack for making his followers like him.

Business administrators for honest businesses weren't easy to find in Guadalajara in those days. The best were leaving their more legitimate jobs to work for unheard of wages in the employ of the traffickers. A fringe benefit was that you could steal all you wanted, as long as you didn't get caught. The traffickers had so much money they couldn't possibly keep up with it and didn't really want to, but they reacted violently when they stumbled upon a follower who hadn't been loyal to them. "Country Ford" was the newest and biggest Ford dealership in Guadalajara, a real showpiece. The owner, at least the visible owner, was a young businessman who allowed his manager, Jorge Leon-Keschner, to work for Rafael Caro.

The interrogator asked. "And that administrator that you talked about? Do you know where he is?"

And Kiki answered. "Him, Leon?"

The interrogator. "Yes."

Camarena. "Well, I think so sir. But I don't know how to find him."

Again the interrogator asked. "You don't know where he lives?"

(In the background on the tape is the sound of water dripping, perhaps into a sink or lavatory.)

And Kiki replied, anxiously. "If you take me to the office I will get you the information. Right?"

"You have it there?" Asked the interrogator.

In a weak voice Kiki said. "I imagine that it is written down there, but I don't remember now." (In the background there is the sound of running water or perhaps someone urinating) "Some house of his, where he might be, if only I could give you something, I'll rest a little and I'll give it to you, I'll tell you all you want to hear."

¿O Plata O Plomo?

Rafael Caro had two maternal uncles that were as important in the drug traffic as anyone could be. But they were very different in character.

Both were short in height but Juan Jose Quintero-Payan was stout running to fat while his younger brother, Emilio, was skinny as a rail and hyperactive. Juan Jose was vindictive, it's true, but Emilio was a mad dog, given to fits of murderous rage. Emilio Quintero was as evil as they come. He grew up in the Sinaloa mountains, participating in many bloody feuds between the trafficking families and was a full-fledged drug lord when he fell into the hands of the Mexican Federal Judicial Police in Nuevo Laredo, Mexico in 1978.

The "Operation Cashcrop" investigation into the illegal activities of Juan and Emilio Quintero in Houston revealed transactions totaling some nine million dollars that had been transported or transferred to Houston from Guadalajara by Juan Jose Quintero and his wife. The money was then transferred to an account opened by Carlos Behn, the young and aspiring manager of a branch of the Mexican Government bank, Banamex, located on Avenida Chapultepec. Carlos Behn then flew to the Cayman Islands and opened accounts in "dummy" shell corporations, depositing the money in those accounts, and then transferring the money to accounts in Houston in the names of the shell corporations.

When Carlos Behn moved the money from Houston to the Caymans and back to Houston he failed to mention the name of its true owner. When he learned that his presence was needed to answer questions about the origin of the money, he opted to stay in Guadalajara, Mexico, where he and his wife opened up an exclusive furniture store, the price of which should have been out of sight for a bank manager with his salary. His name was published in several Mexican newspapers, along with the news of his indictment in the money laundering scheme. His participation in the multi-million dollar criminal operation was not deemed important enough to warrant a Mexican government investigation, however, in spite of the fact that private bank accounts in U.S. dollars were forbidden in Mexico at the time. Eventually, the US government seized a luxury home on Lake Livingston and many millions of dollars in this investigation.

"Operation Cashcrop" was not our case but we contributed to its success, and the Guadalajara DEA office was mentioned in the court documents. That is the way the system works. It was a damn good case, with some brilliant investigative work by officers from several law enforcement agencies. We were glad to help.

There are several "Manolo's" restaurants in Guadalajara. It is a chain of eating establishments that specialize in the typical "parillada" while mariachi bands play for the customer. A man who had provided us information on the Mexicali rafficker, Rene Verdugo, was eating at a "Manolos" just off Lopez Mateos Avenue, the evening of September 30, 1984. "Luis Valiente" had just lifted a glass of brandy and Coca-Cola to take a drink when he recognized a man, Licenciado Cendejas-Cendejas, who stopped at his table and pulled a .45 semi-automatic pistol out of his shirt. "Luis" couldn't set his drink down before Cendejas starting firing, emptying the big pistol into the torso of the seated man. We heard about the incident the following day and Kiki visited "Luis" at the clinic where he had been taken by the "Cruz Roja". Shot-up as he was, he managed to grin and joke. He told Kiki that Cendejas worked for "Don Neto" and was sure the shooting was meant to discourage people from working with us.

His wounds were serious, several rounds had touched his spine and the doctors were having a hard time controlling infection, his father visited our office and expressed his fear that "Luis" wouldn't make it. The older man believed the doctors were purposely negligent in their treatment of his son. He had depleted his savings and mortgaged everything he owned, including his home in southern California, to pay for his son's treatment in Guadalajara. While the son's condition got worse, the father ran out of money. The father was a proud man, proud of his son and proud of his adopted country, it wasn't easy for him to come begging. If we could help him borrow some money, he would try to move "Luis" to the states, his condition was critical, the infection was spreading and the local doctors couldn't stop it.

DEA made us proud. Someone in headquarters directed me to a problem solver; he found a program and levied it for funds, then arranged for the doctor, the hospital, and the medevac flight, with a doctor on board. He did it all, competently, quickly and without asking for thanks, and without going through DEA's hierarchy, especially Mexico City. He even arranged to reimburse the father for much of what he had spent.

Kiki and I met the airplane when it arrived and saw him off, already hooked up to the oxygen, IV and heart monitor. He could hardly wave his hand, he was so ill. Two months in the hospital in Guadalajara had nearly done him in.

As much as he liked to traffic in dope, Rafael Caro liked women even more. He took a fancy to one of his follower's female acquaintants and, in January of 1985 he spirited her away from her family. A seventeen year old girl, named Sara Cosio-Martinez, won his heart with her fully mature figure and coquettish face which she kept half-hidden behind hair which she swept across one eye. She probably didn't know how far he would go to have her. After she didn't return home from a day out with her friends, her family learned the identity of the man who had taken her, not altogether against her will. Since her uncle was the head of the PRI, Mexico's ruling party, they contacted him to secure his aid in locating her and returning her to her home. The uncle contacted the government and the Director of the MFJP was ordered to track down the culprit, Rafael Caro. Manuel Ibarra ordered First Comandante Lorrabaquio to look for the pair in northern Mexico. The comandante's first stop was at the DEA office in Guadalajara, asking for any leads DEA could provide him on Rafael Caro's location. Kiki and Shaggy provided him the addresses of several of Rafael Caro's houses and ranches and Lorrabaquio began his search, which eventually took him into the states

James Kuykendall

of Sonora and Sinaloa. He didn't find the elusive Caro but the search accomplished its purpose as the girl was returned to her home. The parents refused to lodge charges against her alleged abductor, letting bygones be bygones.

CHAPTER 14
THE MILITANT

One of the names on the list of possible suspects in the kidnapping that the MFJP received from my hand was Javier Barba-Hernandez. He was a former leader of the politically powerful and very militant university group called the "FEG", ("Federation de Estudiantes de Guadalajara"). Javier Barba had associated himself with the traffickers, first with the younger men in Rafael Caro's following, then with Ernesto Fonseca and, finally, taking care not to appear too competitive, Barba was becoming a drug dealer in his own right. Smart and ruthless, he was a natural criminal.

There are at least two interrogators, one is calm and doesn't lose his temper but the voice on the end of the tape labeled "copia 2" and the beginning of the tape labeled "copia 4" is different.

Angry, cursing, threatening, his questions are about Javier Barba and when Kiki answers he snaps back. "What do you know about him? Who told you that?"

Kiki said. "Only that he is up and coming, that he is ambitious."

The other interrogator, the calm one, asked. "Where has your investigation led you to on him?'

And Kiki answered. "He lives next door to Comandante Espindola." And that Espindola lived on Paseo del Prado.

The new interrogator shouted, screamed. "That's not true!"

For several minutes the line of questioning continues along the same theme, about Javier Barba, with at least two separate questioners; the calm one leading, the angry one interrupting and sometimes cursing but apparently not in charge. When Kiki tried to explain that neither he nor anyone else in the office had driven by Javier Barba's house, that he only knew where the house was because he had been to see Comandante Espindola on one occasion, the interrogator reacted.

The angry inquisitor exclaimed. "Chingado, muertele al cabron". (Damn, kill the bastard).

In fact, the house Kiki was referring to was the house of Emilio Quintero-Payan, not Javier Barba. Obviously he was extremely tired and confused. Barba did not live next door to Espindola. The questioning goes on, and on, about Barba, and about Barba's brother, Jorge, who was killed in an altercation with a Guadalajara police officer on the highway to Puerto Vallarta in November of 1984. But always with the angry interrogator asking, how do you know? Who told you?

The angry interrogator knew too much. He asked the right questions and he was irate over Kiki's knowledge of Javier Barba's activities and just as angry when the information Kiki provides is incorrect. Was the voice that of Javier Barba himself? It certainly seems so.

The existence of the tapes was not public knowledge until the end of 1985.

Even leaks to the press didn't start until late summer.

The young man we called "Jesus Ramirez" was in danger. He had known it from the beginning. On May 13 he called and asked to meet, perhaps in a forested area west of the city, in an hour.

Bill Moeckler, one of the agents from DEA headquarters who had been assigned as an investigator in Operation Leyenda arrived that afternoon so I took him with me, to the small Eucalyptus forest southwest of Guadalajara, near Zapopan. "Jesus" was waiting for us, with an older brother, in a small white truck. He got out and we walked slowly down a trail. The brother followed us in the vehicle, watching for trouble.

"Jesus" stopped to talk. The previous day, he said, he had been visited by an acquaintance, someone he thought of as a friend, a man named Samuel Cortez who brought him a warning.

Cortez told "Jesus" that he had accompanied Javier Barba to a residence in Guadalajara on the day of the abduction of DEA Agent Camarena and witnessed the interrogation of the agent. Cortez said that Camarena was told to write information about DEA investigations and was physically abused by the interrogators when they felt his answers were misleading. Present at the house were Rafael Caro and Ernesto Fonseca, as well as Barba, but Camarena was not aware of this since he was blindfolded.

According to Cortez, agent Camarena talked of an informant named "Jesus Ramirez" and physically described the informant, convincing Barba-Hernandez that the man we knew as "Jesus" was a DEA informant. Cortez said that he was not convinced of that and decided, as a friend, to warn "Jesus" of the danger. "Jesus" had not been inquisitive, asking for the address of the house or other information because he was trying to convince Cortez that he had been correct that, in fact, "Jesus" was not an informant.

Cortez had also said that Captain Alfredo Zavala and two other men were being held captive along with agent Camarena. Again "Jesus" did not ask for the identities of the other two men, trying to appear indifferent.

"Jesus" explained that Samuel Cortez was a compadre (godparent relation) to Javier Barba and was employed on his "finca" or ranch, located near the village of Tonala.

Cortez had told "Jesus" that he and Javier Barba had departed the residence at the same time as Rafael Caro and Ernesto Fonseca. The two traffickers told their men to remain with Camarena, advising that they would return the following day.

Kiki answered. "It is this person I call Jesus Ramirez, who says that Javier Barba is one of those who is getting better, moving up."

The interrogator. "This Jesus Ramirez has passed a lot of information to you, but you say you've only seen him two times?"

Kiki said. "Yes, yes!"

Question. "You're not lying?"

James Kuykendall

"No, because see, sir, remember that I told you he worked with Roger, Roger Knapp and I saw him on two occasions, but I just go as a witness, to listen, right. But I've never worked him, I've never paid him a nickel." Was Kiki's reply.

When Kiki told the interrogators that "Jesus" had passed on information to him about "Samuel" the interrogators were confused and demanded an explanation. Kiki explained that there were two men, two informants, named "Jesus". He further told them that "Jesus" had said "Samuel" had an apartment on Cangrejo Street.

The interrogator said. "Yes, you already told me that."

But neither of the interrogation tapes contain prior conversation about that apartment, nor about "Samuel".

Samuel Ramirez-Razo was Ernesto Fonseca's constant companion. They reportedly drove around Guadalajara in Samuel's beat-up blue Mustang, visiting bars and cantinas, drinking and snorting cocaine all night. Then, after holing up in one of Fonseca's houses or apartments for a few hours with some girl (or girls) they had rented, they would start again the next day.

Samuel and his wife lived in a cheap apartment a block from Cangrejo St., behind the Suites Real, which are located on Ave. Lopez Mateos. But on neither of the tapes is their prior mention of Samuel or his apartment, just one more indication that the tapes, as delivered to the U.S. government, did not constitute all of the interrogation to which Kiki was subjected.

Javier Barba-Hernandez was killed in Mazatlan, Sinaloa, in December of 1986 during a shootout with federal authorities, along with two traffickers named Abelardo Fernandez and Eliseo Vasquez. The world was definitely better off with the demise of these three individuals, Fernandez and Vasquez had been part of the so-called security for Ernesto Fonseca.

Samuel Cortez was killed at Javier Barba's finca, sometime in 1987. The informant, "Jesus Ramirez", continued to live in Guadalajara but the

¿O Plata O Plomo?

traffickers eventually caught up with him. He was shot from a passing car in 1988.

CHAPTER 15
OPERATION PADRINO

The recording that the Mexican Government failed to turn over contained references to a high-ranking member of that government, which might explain why it was held back when the other tapes were turned over to Walter White. But it also held many clues to the reasons behind Kiki's abduction.

Throughout the transcript of the lost recording the interrogators asked Kiki about the activities of Miguel Angel Felix-Gallardo. Just as often they were not convinced when he told them how difficult it had been to work against Miguel Felix' group and that we had not been responsible for the large cocaine seizures from Felix-Gallardo's organization made in the United States.

The interrogator asked. "The whereabouts of Miguel Felix, where can we find him?"

Kiki answered. "I know that he goes often to the Suites Real, he has an apartment there and he has an office at . . ."

A question. "How do you know?"

And the answer. "Well, I've seen him there, right, I've passed by there and seen his car."

Questioning Kiki about the cocaine, the interrogator asked. "What problem does he have with you?"

Kiki responded, "Like I explained before, they seized some cocaine that was coming in by airplane."

" Where was it seized?" A question from the interrogator.

"In the state of Arizona, I don't recall exactly what town." Was the reply from Kiki.

Pushing for more information, the interrogator said. "The co-worker of yours, the one that just transferred from Laredo, did he participate in that, in the seizure of those drugs?"

And Kiki answered. "No, he had nothing to do with that, nor the other agent, it was the Phoenix office, well not exactly the Phoenix office, because someone saw the airplane land and called the sheriff's office and the sheriff's office went there and arrested some people."

If there had ever been doubts that the cocaine in the Arizona seizures had belonged to Miguel Felix-Gallardo and Juan Mata-Ballesteros, this interrogation transcript removed all that.

Jesse James surely did not commit every train robbery in Missouri but he was blamed for most of them. It seems that the DEA office in Guadalajara was believed by the traffickers to have been responsible for all their losses. Many Latin American traffickers had taken up full or part time residence in Spain, for many reasons, not the least of which was the common language. In 1983 the Spanish law enforcement authorities decided to do something about one of them.

A man, obviously from Hispanic America, had settled in Spain and, having enormous wealth, had acquired the BMW automobile dealership in Madrid. He had also purchased an expensive villa and was spending money freely. But many of his friends were from South America and, all too often, their names were found in DEA's data banks. After months of fruitless surveillance, the Spanish police obtained the necessary legal authority and established intercepts on the principal home and business telephones utilized by the foreigner. The man, using the name of Jose Lopez-Ruiz, was burning up the international telephone lines between Spain and Mexico, with many additional calls to Colombia, Los Angeles and Miami.

After listening for a while, it was apparent that Jose Lopez was associated with some powerful Mexican traffickers who were transporting drugs from South America through Mexico to the southwestern United States.

The Spanish authorities responsible for enforcing narcotics laws had excellent relations with the DEA representatives in Spain at the time and most of the information they received about the interesting Mr. Lopez was shared. DEA Madrid, in turn, passed this information on to DEA Mexico City.

It is an interesting fact that almost every new investigation will turn up old names. Some of the players in this organization were retreads. And some were previously unknown. DEA in Mexico City began to look into the activities of this big time operation.

Many of the calls from Madrid were made to a remote area in the state of Veracruz, Mexico. Some surveillance of the area and a few inquiries revealed the calls were being received at a farm on the outskirts of Nautla, Veracruz. The farm was in control of a notorious trafficker named Arturo Izquierdo-Ebrard, brother-in-law of the chief of police of Mexico City, Arturo "El Negro" Durazo. Arturo Izquierdo had been around as a trafficker for many moons. It was ascertained that the farm was endowed with an airstrip, an essential accessory for the type of operation being pursued by the Madrid automobile dealer and his associates. Other telephone calls were made to Mexico City, to a house utilized by another well-documented narcotics trafficker, Jorge Fabela-Escobosa. Fabela was even spotted meeting with "Don Jose" at his home in Madrid.

With their suspicions confirmed, the Spanish authorities listened more intently, telephone calls were going to several places in Colombia, as well as to the Los Angeles, California area and to Guadalajara, Mexico. It would take a while to identify the recipients of the calls in Colombia and the United States but the numbers in Guadalajara were well known and all were associated with Miguel Angel Felix-Gallardo.

Felix-Gallardo wasn't one of those traffickers who stayed out of the public eye. He openly owned two hotels in Guadalajara and several other businesses, all in the names of people he paid handsomely for the privilege of using their names for that purpose. He had been arrested at least twice for narcotics violations in Mexico and skated each time. He also kept at least two airplanes in a hangar at the Guadalajara airport. DEA had a long running investigation on him and he was mentioned prominently in many other cases.

In 1982, several million dollars in cashier's checks had shown up in South American banks, drawn on Miguel Felix's accounts at Banpacifico and Banco del Atlantico in Guadalajara through money held in the Bank of America in San Diego, California. The checks, in amounts of $40,000 and $50,000, were negotiated in Peru, Bolivia and Ecuador. Records at the Bank of America showed these transactions in one year alone totaled twenty million dollars. After DEA agents visited the bank in San Diego to look into the transfers, the account was closed.

Operation "Padrino" was initiated in Mexico City and centered on the activities of Jorge Fabela and others. The most important being Jose Lopez in Madrid, who had now been positively identified as Juan Ramon Mata-Ballesteros, a documented cocaine trafficker. Toward this end the MFJP in Mexico City put a wiretap in place in cooperation with the Mexico City DEA. In the meantime, the agents in Guadalajara were conducting their part of the investigation against Miguel Felix, already the subject of an open investigation in Mexico. With the information coming from Spain, augmented by information developed unilaterally, the Guadalajara agents located most of the homes and businesses utilized by Felix and his gang. As the size of the operation became more apparent, other DEA offices became involved as well. Information developed in the investigation revealed the traffickers were using single-side-band radios to communicate with each other and with their various aircraft. DEA begin to develop the ability to intercept these communications and the agents in Guadalajara found the house the Felix group was using as their base of communications. The wiretap in Mexico City was never very productive so, with some reluctance,

James Kuykendall

DEA Mexico City decided to relocate the wiretap to Guadalajara. It took some time to establish the telephone intercept in Guadalajara, one of the main obstacles being to find Mex-Feds who were not already compromised to operate the listening post. A site not far from one of Felix's hotels, Las Americas, was identified and the listening post was set up. In the beginning, at least, it appears the Mexican agents assigned to listen to the telephones did not compromise the operation. Tapes were forwarded to their superiors and DEA, providing valuable intelligence.

Telephone wiretaps work great when the targets have no idea they are under surveillance. An MFJP agent named Juan Gilberto Hernandez lived at the motor hotel Las Americas. His immediate supervisors knew this and accepted it and the MFJP in Mexico City knew this and accepted it. He was, among other things, the errand boy for the MFJP Comandante. When the comandante needed a visa for his wife or girlfriend, he would send Juan Gilberto over to see us and try to convince us to recommend the person for a visa to visit the US. We also had lunch and drinks with him from time to time, trying to pump information from him while he tried to pry information from us. In June of 1984, the wiretap picked up a call from someone named Cesar to Juan Gilberto Hernandez in room number 225 at the Las Americas. Cesar asked Juan Gilberto if he had a kilo, Juan Gilberto replied that he had 20, Cesar told him that was too many but he would stop by. Eventually we learned that "Cesar" was Cesar Fonseca, who was a cousin of Ernesto Fonseca but was closely associated with Miguel Felix and was a close friend of Juan Gilberto Hernandez. Juan Gilberto actually had a call sign on Felix's radio network of M8. On another occasion a call was received at the hotel from German Harper, the bank manager at Multibanco Comermex, who handled money for all the major traffickers, Harper asked the hotel receptionist for Juan Gilberto Hernandez and was connected to his room, Harper then asked Juan Gilberto if he knew Cesar Fonseca to which Juan Gilberto replied in the affirmative. Harper then advised Juan Gilberto that Cesar Fonseca had been to see him because Juan Gilberto owed him money and he wanted Harper to turn it over to him. Harper told Juan Gilberto that he had about 100 million pesos in his account, Juan Gilberto advised Harper that someone else owed the money to Cesar Fonseca, not him and not to give him any money from his account.

The DEA agents in Guadalajara were working on several cases but the Felix organization took up a lot of their time. In April of 1984, the office received information that one of Felix's aircraft, an Aerocommander with Mexican registration, was traveling to Laredo, Texas, with Felix's business manager, Tomas Valles, as a passenger. The agents found a vantage point, which allowed them to watch the hangar where the Aerocommander was stored and then observed the arrival of several automobiles. Some of the men in the cars exited and, toting automatic weapons, formed a security barrier around the hangar, remaining there until the airplane exited the hangar and taxied out to the runway. The DEA agents in Guadalajara forwarded this information to DEA in Laredo with a request to determine the reason for the visit. It was a Saturday but several agents took some time off from watching television to set up surveillance at the Laredo airport. The Aerocommander arrived and taxied to the U.S. Customs arrival area. The pilot declared the sum of $25,000 dollars to the Customs Inspector on duty. One of the passengers, Mardoqueo Alfaro-Margarino, declared $5,180,000.00 and signed the customs monetary declaration form, making it legal for him to enter the United States with the money. The pilot hung around the airport while Mardoqueo Alfaro and the other four passengers entered a waiting automobile, driven by the manager of the Tesoro Savings and Loan in Laredo. The driver headed for the residential area of the city known as Del Mar where he dropped off three of the passengers, the wife and two children of Tomas Valles, at a nice suburban home. The driver of the automobile then took Mardoqueo Alfaro and the remaining passenger, Tomas Valles, to the offices of Tesoro Savings and Loan where he counted and deposited the money into accounts following Alfaro's instructions. The

Savings and Loan was normally closed on Saturday but the bank officer opened it and accommodated his loaded clients from Guadalajara. Inquiries later disclosed that Tomas Valles' father-in-law and mother-in-law lived in the house in Laredo where his wife and children were dropped off.

Altogether, Mardoqueo Alfaro would bring in more than thirteen million dollars for the Miguel Felix organization through the airport in Laredo, most of which he deposited in Tesoro Savings and Loan. He deposited an additional six and a half million dollars in another bank in El Paso, Texas.

In June of 1984 the Guadalajara DEA office advised the Santa Ana, California office that some associates of Tomas Valles were at a hotel in Anaheim and might bear investigating. The agents jumped right on the information and, following their own investigation and surveillance, arrested two individuals in possession of $4,140,579 and two "Glory" money counting machines, along with $1,040.00 in counterfeit US currency. The men arrested were eventually released for lack of sufficient evidence to sustain prosecution. The hotel rooms occupied by the men were registered in the name of Mardoqueo Alfaro and the investigation led to the identification of yet another bank account in San Isidro with an additional $626,000 deposited in the name of Mardoqueo Alfaro. This incident also led to the discovery of the millions deposited in the El Paso bank. Tomas Valles' son was in one of the hotel rooms being cared for by a female associate. Valles and Mardoqueo Alfaro had left the child in the care of the woman while they went shopping. Out of fear of arrest, Valles refused to return to the hotel for his son. The woman and child were not detained.

Following the money seizures in Anaheim the IRS levied a $26,000,000 lien against Mardoqueo Alfaro, citing his known monetary transactions as justification and mailed a copy of the lien to his address in Guadalajara.

Unfortunately, the U.S. Government could not seize all the money. An upstanding member of the U.S. legal profession gave a little assistance to the traffickers by spiriting millions out of the savings and loan in Laredo to a bank in Panama, due to the Justice Department dragging its feet in freezing the funds. That same upstanding lawyer also defended Mardoqueo Alfaro's bid for return of the money frozen and seized from the bank in El Paso but the government's attorney in that case was more dedicated.

Miguel Felix knew we were watching him. On March 29, 1984, MFJP Comandante Manuel Espindola called Kiki at the office twice. Failing to contact him, he left his home telephone number. Kiki called him at that number late that evening and Espindola stated he needed to talk but was going to Mexico City the next day and would return on April 2, Kiki said he was leaving town on April 2 and would not return until April 6. Espindola said his need to talk was urgent so he and Kiki agreed to meet that very night in spite of the late hour. Kiki put in a call to me, advising me of the meeting at the Camino Real Hotel. He met with Espindola about 10:30 PM in the bar of the hotel.

Following some general conversation, Espindola told agent Camarena he had been visited in his office on March 28 by Miguel Angel Felix-Gallardo, requesting that Espindola repay a favor he owed him. Without explaining the favor, the Mexican officer told Kiki that he had agreed, Miguel Felix then asked Espindola to contact James Kuykendall, the head of the DEA office, and give him a message. Comandante Espindola told Felix-Gallardo he had met Mr. Kuykendall only once but was better acquainted with Enrique Camarena and would give the message to him. Miguel Felix told Espindola to tell DEA to "leave him alone as he was not doing anything." He said the person DEA should be looking at was Rafael Caro-Quintero. Kiki dutifully wrote a memorandum addressed to the Agent-in-Charge in Mexico City, reporting the gist of the conversation.

Espindola was contacted later by agents from the Guadalajara office and asked if he felt that Miguel Felix's message should be considered a warning. Comandante Espindola replied that there was no doubt it had been meant as a warning. He added that Felix had also said he knew we were watching him from the Plaza del Sol Hotel. Of course he really meant his organization and we had used a room at the Plaza del Sol to watch the activities at the Motor Hotel Las Americas, located right across the street.

For some, still unknown reason, Jose Lopez aka Juan Mata decided to move to Guadalajara in April of 1984.

DEA in Mexico City developed an informant who had an airplane pilot's license, which he had put to extensive use flying airplanes for any trafficker who asked him, for a substantial fee. Since this new CI had some information about traffickers in Guadalajara, they referred him up to me. He, rather fearlessly, came to the consulate to talk. He said he had flown airplanes loaded with marijuana into Arizona and California and he had flown airplanes loaded with Cocaine from South America to Mexico. He seemed to be rather proud of what he saw as his accomplishments and was not shy about relating his exploits. He said he had flown cocaine shipments for Miguel Felix Gallardo, picking up the drug in Colombia then flying into Central America for refueling. He continued to the Guadalajara area where he offloaded but he said he had never flown cocaine loads into the United States for Felix. On Felix's orders he had, on several occasions, landed at an airstrip in Costa Rica, right on the border with Nicaragua, to refuel before continuing on into Mexico. He said the airstrip was very busy, with camouflaged aircraft coming and going continuously and that he believed it was a, not so clandestine, CIA operation. He also said no one ever asked him what he was carrying or attempted to search his airplane. It turned out that I knew about this guy's past activities. He had been the pilot of the airplane when Ernesto Fonseca was arrested in Cuenca, Ecuador. It shook him when I asked about that. He said he wanted to work with us and would call to set up and other meeting. He didn't call back nor did Mexico City ever hear from him either.

Miguel Felix kept his airplanes in the hangar that was also the Cessna dealership at the airport in Guadalajara, which was actually just another

¿O Plata O Plomo?

front for his illegal activities and provided a little un-needed cover. The owner and manager, Hugo DeVere, maintained a semi-legitimate reputation and was able to travel to the United States to conduct business for Felix, such as acquiring aircraft and aircraft parts. He also recruited the pilots for Miguel's various airplanes.

One day Roger Knapp and an agent from Mexico City were driving around the area where Felix's motels and houses were located. They were checking out the information received from the wiretap, a blue car pulled them over to the side of the road and several tough-looking young men exited, flashing state judicial police credentials. They asked Roger who he and his companion were and what they were doing in the area. The two DEA agents gave them a story that only marginally satisfied their curiosity.

Our wiretap operation with the MFJP was cut off in July after only four months of listening. It had been productive, perhaps too much so. There were several reasons given for the halt but the main ones were lack of operational funds and lack of drug seizures. We knew Felix's organization was still very active so we requested some equipment to listen to their radio networks, the existence of which had been revealed during the wiretaps. The best we could get was a Radio Shack scanner with the frequencies of their local radios. We set the scanner up in Shaggy's office after he arrived and he overheard some interesting conversations.

The scanner was busy picking up conversations almost daily, most of which had no actionable value. The Felix organization had several mobile units, using call signs numbered M1 to M8. Miguel Felix himself was M1. On the 8th day of January 1985, at 11:35 AM, one of the mobile units, M5, advised Tomas Valles that "they" were being followed. Tomas Valles questioned the M5 unit about this and M5 responded that the people were getting into a taxi. Tomas Valles notified Miguel Felix that the people were in a taxi on Avenida Marino Otero leaving the Plaza del Sol area. Miguel Felix immediately joined Tomas Valles and several other mobile units in following the taxi. At 11:45 AM they forced the taxi to stop on a frontage road adjacent to the Lazaro Cardenas Boulevard. Miguel Felix ordered his henchmen to take the occupants of the taxi to a base station and to keep the passengers down and with their eyes covered by a shirt or jacket. We never learned what happened to those people.

On January 30, a transmission was received on the Guadalajara DEA radio frequencies, a whistle was heard, someone said "hello" in English, and then Mexican music was played over the frequency. None of the DEA employees had made the transmission and all radios were accounted for. On the same day, around noon one of Felix's mobile units was overheard on the scanner advising that he was under surveillance by individuals in a black Gran Marquis, with license plates from the state of Mexico. Miguel Felix ordered some other mobile units to conduct counter-surveillance on the black Gran Marquis, which was followed to a residence. Felix ordered the mobile units to note the address, the numbers on the license plates and to break off the surveillance. Still later that day, Miguel Felix was overheard on his radio frequency, conversing with an apparent radio technician.

It's strange how some things work out. From all the information we had gleaned and the wealth he displayed, it was obvious DEA had not been successful against Felix-Gallardo's trafficking organization in the past. But 1984 was turning out differently. While identifying assets and trafficking patterns might be a positive thing to an investigator, it didn't mean anything to the trafficker, if you weren't hitting him, you weren't hurting him. The money seizures in 1984 could be attributed to superior law enforcement activities on DEA's part but two other setbacks were just chance and good for us, bad for him. The radio intercepts, telephone taps, airplane bugs, etc. had just not been adequate enough to allow us to seize narcotics from the group. Then, in August of 1984, the Gila County Arizona Sheriff's officers seized 1,680 pounds of cocaine from the ground crew at a clandestine desert airstrip and one of Miguel Felix's Aerocommanders was identified as the airplane that had smuggled the load into the United States. Again, in

¿O Plata O Plomo?

November of 1984, a retired law enforcement officer and his wife found a deposit of 1,494 pounds of cocaine on another remote airstrip in Arizona. They contacted the authorities and four people were arrested. The airplane was not seen but the tire marks indicated it was probably an airplane of the type utilized by Felix's group. The day following the cocaine seizure an Aerocommander used by the group was located and seized in Wilmington, Delaware.

In December of 1984, a man named John Drummond was arrested in Arizona and charged with the murder of one of his drug associates. Drummond was a direct client of Felix as well as a provider of ground crews and was one of the men to whom the cocaine seized in Arizona was destined.

We eventually searched the residence where Juan Mata-Ballesteros aka Jose Lopez aka Fernando Garcia lived. We had known about the house at 231 Chimalpopoca for some time but had not searched it after Juan Ramon Mata fled Mexico. Leticia Corona told us a friend of Miguel Felix, named "Don Jose" Reyes was staying at the house and she said he had a Colombian wife named Nancy. Property records showed the properties at 229, 231 and 233 Chimalpopoca to be owned by Rosario Valenzuela-Diaz, either an alias used by Miguel Felix or a name loaned to him by another person. Because of other matters we considered more pressing at the time we just neglected to follow up on the address after Leticia was picked up. Finally, on July 8, 1985 DEA and MFJP agents entered the house at #231 Chimalpopoca. The home and grounds are actually comprised of two lots, #229 and #231. The home was a luxurious one story, three-bedroom residence, expensively furnished and there was a single-side-band radio antenna on the roof. In a large pantry off the kitchen were a maintenance manual and a wiring manual for a Gulfstream Commander 1000. There were also several personal flotation devices and a five man inflatable life raft. There was an air chart of central Mexico with a line drawn from Tampico to San Luis Potosi to Mazatlan. The closets contained men's and women's clothing and the bathrooms were well equipped with all necessities. In a front room, equipped as an office, was a single-side-band radio, which was connected to the antenna on the roof and was fully functional. Atop a bookcase was a, fully loaded, Thompson .45 caliber sub-machine gun, manufactured by Auto-Ordnance of Bridgeport, Conn. On the desk lay a Guadalajara newspaper, "El Jalisciense", dated February 9, 1985 and a Mexico City newspaper, "Excelsior", dated February 8, 1985,

In one bedroom an un-posted Christmas card dated December 13 was found. It was addressed to Carlos Lozano and family with no address. The handwriting seemed to be feminine and was signed inside "Ramon Mata, Sra y hijos". The caretaker was interviewed and stated he had worked there for about a year and believed Tomas Valles owned the house. He had obtained the job through an acquaintance at the motel Las Americas. The house had previously been occupied by two couples but they left in February and the house had remained empty since then, One of the couples he described fit the descriptions of Juan Ramon and Nancy Mata. A high block fence with a separate entrance enclosed the lot next door to the house, with the address of #233 Chimalpopoca. Inside the enclosure were three vehicles and a motorcycle. This property was listed on official records as being the property of Jorge Leon Keschner, Rafael Caro's purported business manager.

The transcript ends with the interrogators asking about the wiretap operation on Miguel Felix.

From the interrogator. "No problem you keep on."

And Kiki answered. "A man who has a ranch with an airstrip, in Veracruz."

Hugo DeVere was arrested by the MFJP and questioned under such duress that he was hospitalized for what was reported to be a heart attack but some of his statements rang true, based on what we had already learned. He said he had been introduced to Miguel Felix by Tomas Valles. Felix wanted him to buy airplanes and recruit pilots for his drug transporting operation. In the beginning they used Colombian pilots to fly the loaded planes from Colombia to the airstrip at Nautla, Veracruz, then the Mexican pilots from Guadalajara would fly the drugs into the United States, make the drops and return to Guadalajara. The Colombian pilots would make their way separately to Guadalajara to meet the planes on their return and fly them back to Colombia. Each flight carried approximately 600 kilograms of cocaine.

One of Miguel Felix's pilots was interviewed by DEA agents on February 12 and gave insight into some of the group's activities. Miguel Walls-Plasencia said he went to work flying an Aerocommander 1000 on July 1, 1984 after answering a newspaper ad for pilots, posted by Hugo DeVere. His first trip was to a dirt strip near Guerrero Negro, Baja California with one armed passenger. They were met by a tall, corpulent, man who arrived in a pickup truck with a camper. This man transferred ten cardboard boxes from the camper to the airplane, each box about one cubic foot in size and wrapped in cloth. Walls stated he did not see the contents of the boxes but was sure they contained money because of the attention of the armed men who accompanied him on the trips and when Miguel Felix met him upon his return to Guadalajara. Walls said he made an additional three trips to Guerrero Negro, each time returning with similar boxes under the same circumstances.

Miguel Felix had a first cousin named who was born in California and lived in the Los Angeles area. During the Padrino wiretap operation his name surfaced several times and he was identified as a guest at the motel Las Americas on several occasions. He testified in Federal court in Los Angeles in the trial which included Juan Matta. He had spent some time in Sinaloa, Mexico in his youth and enjoyed being with his cousin so he took a trip to visit him in Guayaquil. He found his childhood friend always in the company of bodyguards and personal assistants and obviously living high. Miguel and Juan insisted that he get involved in the drug trade to make some real money. He was gainfully employed in California but the lure of the big bucks was too much so he agreed. His first foray into the traffic was as an unsuccessful cocaine vendor. When that soured he became a money courier and facilitator for the distribution of the cocaine that Felix and Matta were sending to Los Angeles. He would meet the airplanes at clandestine strips in Arizona and southern California and help to offload the cocaine and bring the drugs to safe houses in Lake Elsinore and Santa Monica from where it was eventually distributed. The loads usually weighed about 600 kilos. He said he couldn't remember how many loads there were. Then he bought a motor home, stashed a large sum of drug money in it and drove it to Guadalajara. When the money was counted he was told it was short by one hundred and fifty thousand dollars. Miguel and Juan Ramon were very angry but agreed to give him another chance instead of punishing him. He testified he made about twenty more trips, never carrying less than five million dollars each trip. He estimated he transported approximately one hundred fifty million dollars between 1982 and 1989. In 1983 and 1984 we had placed lookouts with US customs for him to be searched at the ports of entry but he was only searched on his northbound journeys, southbound lookouts were not in vogue at the time.

CHAPTER 16
BLACK, WHITE and GRAY
DFS, DEA and the CIA

So, what the hell was the DEA doing in Guadalajara, Mexico, anyway? In the beginning the Federal Bureau of Narcotics, then a branch of the Treasury Department, was created to enforce the few laws then existent against illegal drug trafficking, eventually enforcing the more rigid laws passed through the years.

The FBN, as it was popularly called, was a very small organization within the U.S. Treasury Department with a very strict mission, arrest traffickers in illicit drugs. Drug abuse was a serious problem in the United States after the turn of the century, with housewives addicted to heroin and cocaine being touted as a cure-all. The Harrison Act was passed to regulate the dispersal of drugs and someone had to enforce the law.

The FBN was still a small organization when it opened its first office in the U.S. Embassy in Mexico City in the middle sixties. The traffic in marijuana from Mexico had increased and its use had spread to other than poor Mexican migratory workers. Actors and musicians in the United States were turning on with Mexican pot and Mexican heroin had been introduced into markets as far from the border as Chicago.

As the problem with Mexican drugs grew, the FBN opened its second Mexico office, in Guadalajara, Jalisco, in 1969. That office continued in operation throughout the various name changes and reorganizations of the drug law enforcement agencies within the U.S. government.

In February 1985 the offices of the United States Drug Enforcement Administration were located inside the U.S. Consulate General on Progreso Street. At the time the office had an authorized strength of five agents and three secretaries, more than ever before. There were, however, only four of those agents' positions filled. Enrique Camarena, who was known universally by his nickname of "Kiki", was a naturalized U.S. citizen, born in Mexicali, Mexico, and raised in Calexico, California. He had previously been employed by the city of Calexico, California as a police officer and was an ex-marine who missed service in Vietnam because he joined after the conflict ended. But he had lost a brother in that war. He had joined DEA in Calexico, worked for a while in Fresno, California and transferred to Guadalajara in the summer of 1980. Kiki was married to his high school sweetheart and they had three very young sons. Kiki was quiet and intense but had a ready smile for friends. He had relatives in Guadalajara including his grandmother. He was also a tenacious and intelligent investigator.

Victor "Shaggy" Wallace had been in Guadalajara since September of the previous year and was picking up the pace well. An ex-Imperial County deputy sheriff, he and Kiki had worked together before becoming federal officers. Shaggy had been looking forward to fighting the traffickers on their home turf alongside his old friend. A big man with a great sense of humor, Shaggy had the mane of hair that had earned him his nickname and the unique courage some men have which enable them to work undercover in narcotics cases, and work them well.

Alan Bachelier had arrived only a couple of months before from his prior duty station in Laredo, Texas, and was still feeling his way. His family was living in a hotel until housing was located.

Yours truly arrived in Guadalajara on February 15, 1982 from Houston, looking forward to spending a few years chasing drug traffickers. From previous tours of duty on the U.S./Mexican border, I had picked up the nickname of "Jaime" and much experience with the narcotics traffic in Mexico.

Back in 1982 we realized there was something missing; much of what had happened in the past six years had not been noticed and that which had been was not properly recorded. So it was that an information void existed which we began to try to fill, and in the filling encountered corruption and official collusion on a scale too large to readily believe. Corruption is not new to any government and certainly not Latin American ones. Mexico is famous for its "mordida" system, but what was revealed almost daily was too much, even for our jaded consciences. It was also embarrassing to realize that our colleagues and management had done such a miserable job of intelligence gathering, reporting and analyzing.

Narcotics traffic was rampant in the Aztec nation and nobody knew it. The few who tried to sound the alarm were quickly made aware that Mexico was considered the model country in the U.S. foreign narcotics control program. As such the U.S. authorities did not want to hear any criticism of the Mexican government's so-called "permanent campaign" against the traffic.

An unholy alliance existed between the major Mexican narcotics traffickers and the Mexican Government. Nowhere was this as blatant as it was with an organization called "Direccíon Federal de Seguridad" (DFS), the so-called federal security police whose official duty was the internal reporting on opposing political parties, a not so innocent duty to begin with. What this agency had evolved into was the private army of the narcotics traffickers and their direct link with the government. The agency, if it can be called that, was formed in the seventies to consist of a few well-placed agents in political trouble spots. Answering as it did to the Secretary of Government, second only to the military in influence, the DFS was an all-powerful and untouchable organization. Almost immediately that power was misused. Traffickers were provided credentials as agents of the DFS and local commandants received enormous amounts of money to protect the traffickers and their activities.

Almost without exception the houses and buildings occupied by the DFS as its offices and places of billeting in Guadalajara and surrounding areas were provided by traffickers. Automobiles were either trafficker provided or stolen, usually from the United States. Communications networks were trafficker provided and completely compatible with those of the traffickers. So-called safe houses were trafficker owned and used for the billeting of DFS agents and sometimes for hideouts when the DFS kidnapped someone and held him, either for ransom or to delve into his politics.

There was almost a revolving door policy in those days between the DFS and the Mexican Federal Judicial Police. When each presidential administration was replaced the Judicial Police were purged of agents who went to DFS looking for work. When a subsequent administration took office, the agents returned to the Federal Judicial Police, if they hadn't by then become important enough in the DFS that the move would be an economic setback. The DFS created positions called Zone Coordinators, and split the country, and therefore the riches, into zones of responsibility for these coordinators. The Zone Coordinators were all major narcotics traffickers in their own right, and wielded tremendous influence over everyone but the military within their zones. In those days displaying credentials from the DFS struck fear in the hearts of some very tough hombres.

In the early eighties these omnipotent men, who answered only to the Director of the DFS and his boss, the Secretary of Government, were; Daniel Acuña for the northwest zone with his headquarters in Tijuana; Rafael Aguilar for the northeast zone with his headquarters in Juarez; Rafael Chao-Lopez for the east central zone with his headquarters in Monterrey and Tomas Morlett for the south zone with his headquarters in Oaxaca.

Daniel Acuña was an ex-Federal Judicial police agent, Rafael Aguilar was a renowned drug trafficker, Rafael Chao was an ex-Federal Judicial police agent who had once been indicted in California and Tomas Morlett was an ex-petty thief who had been deported from the United States for car theft. Rafael Aguilar-Guajardo was just a drug trafficker and hadn't ever been anything else until he was given the position of coordinator for DFS.

Federico Castel del Oro was appointed to be the Coordinator for the west central zone, with headquarters in Guadalajara, in 1982, replacing Rogelio Munoz-Rios, who, after quadruple bypass surgery in Houston, Texas, obtained a great retirement job as head of security for several major traffickers, as long as he retained his DFS credentials and standing.

Castel del Oro immediately occupied a house on Avila Camacho in Guadalajara provided to him by the gambling kingpin, Antonio Alcaraz. A drive by that house on any given day would give you a glimpse of half a dozen motorcycles, either stolen or smuggled illegally into the country. He later moved to yet another house belonging to Alcaraz, located at the corner of Avenida Mexico and Hernan Cortez, which had been the residence of Antonio Alcaraz's mother.

The building occupied by DFS as office space was provided by Miguel Angel Felix-Gallardo, as influential as any crime lord who ever existed anywhere. Manuel Salcido alias "Cochiloco" (the crazy pig), who was Castel del Oro's compadre, was an almost daily visitor to the DFS office in Guadalajara, always bringing with him some goodies for Castel del Oro's nose.

The story goes that when Castel del Oro was a Federal Judicial police agent in Culiacan some years previously, he ingratiated himself by delivering five members of a rival gang, that of Braulio Aguirre, to Cochiloco to extract vengeance against Braulio, who had killed some of Cochiloco's men in a drug feud between the two men. After Cochiloco tortured and murdered the five men, he drove a bulldozer back and forth across their bodies. Some said that the men were not yet dead when he crushed them with the tractor. Cochiloco was reported to be completely unpredictable and homicidal.

Another particularly disturbing fact was the association of the U.S. Central Intelligence Agency with the DFS. In their zeal to maintain a close vigil over the activities of the Russians and the Cubans in Mexico, they developed a close relationship with the DFS and trained many of its agents thus providing the DFS with sophisticated electronic surveillance capabilities and advanced training. They also established several of the higher-ranking agents as informants. This relationship was made very public when the U.S.

James Kuykendall

Attorney for the Southern District of California, William Kennedy, indicted the, then, Director of the DFS, Miguel Nazar-Haro, in 1982 for being the intellectual head of a major car theft and smuggling ring responsible for stealing luxury cars worth millions of dollars in California and smuggling the cars to Mexico where the car thieves' DFS credentials guaranteed them safe passage to the interior behind the wheels of Mercedes Benz, BMW, Porsche and other high dollar cars.

The possession of any such luxury car was strictly prohibited in Mexico and there was no provision, under the law, for an exception to this prohibition. Nevertheless drug traffickers and politicians alike, not to mention Mr. Nazar-Haro himself, were wheeling these pretty cars around Mexico City and Guadalajara. Once the cars were in the country, fake importation papers were created and signed by the head of the Federal Directorate of Automobiles at the time, a man named Tomas Morlett.

Mr. Kennedy was a man of high principals but that indictment cost him his job. He was fired from his position of U.S. Attorney by then President Reagan for the actions of his office. Elaine Shannon, in her excellent book "Desperados", reported that the members of the car theft ring were saddled with one thousand, an amount recommended by the Justice Department in Washington. That was just the right amount, as Nassar made his bond without difficulty and skipped the U.S. and U.S. justice.

Forced to resign from the position of head of DFS because of the public scandal, Nazar was replaced by Jose Antonio Zorilla-Perez. Zorilla moved into Nazar's position in every sense of the word, including his liaison with the CIA.

The respected Mexican magazine "Proceso" reported in 1989 that an investigation by their reporters had disclosed some gifts from Rafael Caro-Quintero to Zorilla-Perez. Apparently Rafael Caro knew just what it took to win his way into the hearts of the men in Mexico City. Several reports were received in 1984 that he had given an Arabian horse to General Juan Arrevalo-Gardoqui, the Mexican Secretary of Defense. The horse had been purchased on the African continent and flown to Mexico for just that purpose. There was the suggestion that someone in Israel had arranged the purchase.

Zorilla had a few experienced lawmen employed as comandantes in the country and he picked up a few more. But their real experience was in intimidation and how that intimidation could be made to pay off, in millions, and millions, of dollars.

Rafael Chao-Lopez was an ex-Federal Judicial Police Comandante with intimate knowledge of the narcotic traffic. He was a large man, despite his Chinese ancestry, and sadistic. When he was the comandante of the DFS for the north central area, operating out of Monterrey, he kept a Bengal tiger in a room in the house, which served as the headquarters of the DFS in Monterrey. The tiger was expensive to feed but more than paid for his keep by serving as a very visible threat to anyone who was stupid enough to believe that he could withstand any torture the DFS agents could devise to extract information or money. The big cat was very effective but jittery neighbors in the up-scale neighborhood eventually were able to exert enough influence to force the DFS Comandante to move his tiger.

Rafael Aguilar-Guajardo was very influential in the open, cattle country of his region. He loved fast horses, cocaine and power. His influence was felt hundreds of miles away from Juarez, Chihuahua though. Traffickers with DFS credentials under his signature turned up everywhere, especially those associated with Rafael Caro and Ernesto Fonseca. Two of these were Javier Barba-Hernandez and a friend, David Garcia-Madrid, both ex-student activists in Guadalajara who had turned traffickers for the wealth and power.

Pete Hernandez and Kiki introduced me to some very unusual characters one night at Arthur's Pub. The Pub was the only place in town with beautiful waitresses clad in scanty Playboy Club type costumes. The decor was supposed to be reminiscent of an expensive and exclusive English Pub. It was close enough, the steaks were good, the drinks were strong and the clientele were people with money. Traffickers have money, so, I learned, did DFS agents.

There were three of them, two sitting on stools at the bar drinking and talking with the bartender. The third was sitting in a booth across from the bar and enjoying himself with a luscious brunette who was obviously taken with his evil good looks. Pete and Kiki knew one of the men at the bar and introduced him to me as Juan Manuel Castro. They told me he was with DFS and he introduced me to his two companions. The man in the booth didn't waste much time acknowledging the introduction before returning to his verbal seduction of the brunette. The acquaintance of Pete and Kiki was friendly enough, in an insolent kind of way. He was a smooth-talking individual wearing cowboy boots and hat and sporting a Colt.45 semi-automatic. We talked for a while with him before the fellow from the booth came to join us for a few words.

Now this guy was something else, about five feet ten inches tall, a solid two hundred pounds and he looked like he had never had an excess pound of fat on him since the day he was born. Dressed in Levi's, cowboy boots and wearing the ever-present .45 caliber pistol, he looked ready for war. There was gold everywhere, on his pistol grips, his Rolex President watch, his diamond studded bracelet and the four or five chains around his neck, which were displayed prominently due to his shirtfront, open almost to his midriff. He was drunk, obnoxious, mean and armed. He looked like one of Errol Flynn's pirates, but if this guy had been a pirate, Errol Flynn would have taken up another line of work. He was definitely not one thing though, in spite of his credentials, he was no policeman.

He tried to provoke us, and it was obvious that he wanted a response. We didn't step back, we were in Mexico where we had no authority but we couldn't afford to show timidity either. No problem though, the girl was too tempting to leave alone and he abandoned us for her more earthly delights. I remember thinking to myself; "This scum bag was no more than a common criminal but he had all the airs of a spoiled millionaire with a license to kill." We were in for big trouble.

A year before I arrived in Guadalajara, Pete and Kiki had tried to tell the Agent in Charge in Mexico City their concerns about the relationship between the traffickers and the DFS. The Agent in Charge, whose only association with the DFS was at official functions in Mexico City, advised the two agents from the field that DFS provided the security for the U.S. Ambassador and that the agency provided valuable assistance to the CIA. He said. "If we can't trust them, who can we trust?" The experienced field agents, armed with facts from trusted sources of information, answered in unison. "Nobody!"

You were considered a well-informed member of the U.S. administration if you promoted the theory that communist backed terrorists financed their operations through their involvement in the narcotics traffic. But their goal is terrorism, to tear down the system, to maim and kill, then run and hide under their rocks. They strive to remain anonymous so they can squirm out after dark and maim and kill again. They live austere; secret lives because they believe in some selfish, shadowy quest. Their cause is promoted and their filthy crimes publicized but the terrorists themselves must always hide, for to be in the public eye is certain death.

Narcotics traffickers are not idealists; their goals differ greatly. Dope dealers are not trying to tear down the system. They love it. They do not hide. Rather, they flaunt their riches in defiance of the law, they bring attention to themselves through their life styles but they do not promote any cause. Drug dealers are in it for the money, and even the quiet ones spend it, on farms, ranches or businesses, homes equipped with different wives.

The point is that traffickers and terrorists really share only one thing, their disregard for human life. Narcotics traffickers receive enormous sums of money for their product, and they spend it, usually on the hedonistic things in life and usually on themselves.

James Kuykendall

What Miami dope dealer doesn't want to have a lifetime reservation for the best table in the house at the Copa Club? What Colombian coke smuggler doesn't dream of having his own mansion overlooking the blue Caribbean waters on the north coast of Colombia? And these people want to have those things under the system, as they know it. They don't want to replace any governments with some rebel band of reformers. They wouldn't mind buying a few government officials to keep the heat down so they could go partying on the town without worrying about too much law enforcement, or so they could plant their crops in areas a little more accessible without worrying about helicopters or fumigators.

The Mexican drug kings had no desire to cause problems for the government. They liked things the way they were. They had found out how to prevent crop failure. The biggest item on their list of overhead expenses was crop failure prevention, commonly called "mordida", but results were guaranteed, more or less.

There was one problem, and only one, DEA. The traffickers were told, "We don't control DEA and they have some good informants. If they find your fields we'll have to destroy them. If they discover your warehouses we'll have to raid them." In practice those raids were always delayed enough to allow people and drugs to disappear. But without the urging of the DEA agents, arrests and seizures were few and far between.

The U.S. government was languishing and content, fully believing that Mexico was still under the constraints brought about by Operation Intercept, Operation Trizo and the cultivation detection programs of the early seventies. This apathetic attitude and the resultant lack of real intelligence about narcotics activity in the country left the gate wide open for the excesses of the eighties.

By 1980 DEA and the United States government were caught with their pants down, as far as narcotics intelligence was concerned.

¿O Plata O Plomo?

A tour in Mexico was considered a peaceful assignment with plenty of sightseeing opportunities and rumors of delightfully liberal American and Canadian beach bunnies to be found at the beautiful Mexican beach resorts.

Certainly there were dedicated agents who served in Mexico during that period and there were even some who saw what was happening and tried to bring it to the attention of their superiors. They were met with derision or apathy. Mexico was the showpiece for the State Department's eradication program and any disparaging words about the program were treated as if it were an attack on the flag. DEA, worldwide, was a second-class citizen in the United States Embassies in those days and even DEA bosses of strong character didn't have much luck trying to convince Ambassadors to get tough on narcotics. So the Ambassadors were echoing Washington's policies, so? Mexico was where it was happening and nobody knew it, or wanted to know.

During the month of May 1982, the consulate was buzzing with the news that the ambassador would be visiting Guadalajara and the consulate. Everyone, the women especially, could hardly contain their impatience for the opportunity to see and meet the handsome ex-movie star.

The Consul General had a reception at his residence and everyone from the consulate was invited to attend. I believe everyone in town showed up. The place was packed, with every public official in the city attending along with the wealthy and powerful. As expected, the women were barely able to control themselves as they took turns being photographed with the Ambassador. When we five DEA agents were introduced to Ambassador John Gavin he told us that narcotics control was one of the bright spots in U.S./Mexico relations and that he would tell our boss, Mac Tanner, what a fine job we were doing. Then he quickly dismissed us.

We were deflated, not only was he misinformed about the narcotics trafficking situation but he didn't even know who we worked for. Mac Tanner was the head of the State Department's narcotic's assistance unit in

James Kuykendall

Mexico City. The ambassador was an impressive looking man and very articulate but he definitely needed some education about the dope problem in Mexico.

In July of 1982 a tragic incident occurred that would cause some reflection in the future about what lengths the Mexicans were willing to go to defuse an embarrassing situation.

An American college professor, Dr. Nicolas Schrock, disappeared while driving through the State of Sinaloa en route from the University of Colorado to Guadalajara to teach for the summer at the Universidad Autonoma.

Since Ambassador John Gavin was an acquaintance of close friends Dr. Schrock, the disappearance was treated with more urgency than the average disappearance of a U.S. citizen in Mexico. The U.S. Embassy put a lot of pressure on the Mexican government to find Dr. Schrock, or his body.

Dr. Schrock's Japanese made pickup truck was reportedly found abandoned on a back road and the last witness to have seen him was a young service station attendant in the village of San Ygnacio, Sinaloa.

The pressure increased as the U.S. media started filing stories on the missing professor. This just couldn't be another of the hundreds of unsolved crimes against U.S. citizens in Mexico.

The pressure helped. The Mexican government arrested seven local policemen and announced that these men had robbed Dr. Schrock, killed him and buried his body. When federal investigators had arrived in San Ygnacio, they had encountered the mayor of the village driving Dr. Schrock's truck. The mayor reported that the chief of police had found it and turned it over to him. Not knowing where the owner of the vehicle was, the mayor had decided to put it to official use.

Where, the Embassy demanded to know, was the body? In furtherance of its investigation the Mexican government agents convinced the local policemen to confess to the crime and lead them to the body. The trail led to a pauper's grave in the local cemetery where the unfortunate man had been buried after the policemen forced the resident gravedigger to help them.

The embassy thanked and congratulated the government for its help and excellent investigative work. The body was exhumed and returned to Dr. Schrock's family for proper burial. Prior to burial a routine examination of the remains was performed to insure there would be no future legal problems. The body was not that of Dr. Nicolas Schrock, absolutely not, definitely not. The body was that of a Mexican man at least ten years senior to Dr. Schrock who had suffered from periodontal disease and was uncircumcised. The seven policemen were eventually charged with robbery and released for lack of evidence, their torture extracted confessions no longer acceptable.

Dr. Schrock's greatly decomposed remains were discovered, quite by accident, in 1987, not far from where his vehicle had been located in 1982. So what happened? Who killed Dr. Schrock? The Mexican government doesn't really solve many murders, or many other crimes, either, especially those against U.S. citizens. In this case they were reacting to pressure from the U.S. Government and they came up with a solution, not the correct one, but so what? A few sacrificial lambs thrown to the wolves never bothered the GOM.

Sometime in mid-1982, we had become aware that Miguel Felix had direct dealings with one bank, and then two. A man, identified as Tomas Valles-Corral, was handling financial matters in Banpacifico and Banco del Atlantico for Felix and we thought he was a bank officer with those collateral duties. A small bank in Hermosillo named El Ganadero y Agricola de Sonora had been absorbed by Banpacifico and then enlarged. The owners then opened another bank catering to the traffickers, called Banco del Atlantico. Tomas Valles would eventually by joined by German Harper to handle the vast sums of money being generated by Miguel Felix's narcotics trafficking.

James Kuykendall

As one Mexican journalist would eventually put it, the "gomeros" and the "marijuaneros" came out of the mountains with their bales of money and bought tractors and necessities with cash. For convenience they went to the banks for help with transactions. The banks went from merely helping with purchases to encouraging investments. When the bankers met the traffickers, the cartels were born. The bankers applied Tide and Fabuloso to the money; when the detergent dried, the money went into the economy, all nice and clean, and their hands were too, they thought. Mexico boomed.

CHAPTER 17
THE AFTERMATH

The Mexican government, through its judges, meted out some heavy sentences for the major traffickers arrested and convicted for their part in the kidnapping and murder, and for trafficking in narcotics. Rafael Caro-Quintero initially received a sentence of 136 years in prison for his part in the crimes and Ernesto Fonseca-Carrillo was sentenced to 109 years. The sentences were watered down somewhat afterward.

Miguel Felix-Gallardo fell into the hands of the Mexican Judicial system in 1989. He denied any part in the murder of Kiki Camarena.

Several traffickers who had figured prominently in the narcotics traffic and the murder investigation died at the hands of the Mexican police. In addition to Javier Barba and Cesar Fonseca, Miguel Vielma, the ex-DFS Comandante in Zacatecas, was killed in a shootout in Acapulco in the company of another well-known trafficker.

A few made it into the U.S. courts.

Los Angeles DEA agents made good use of the information furnished by Rafael Caro's associate, Rodolfo Lepes-Montes. When he was "interrogated" that night, Lepes-Montes had told Comandante Ventura about a major trafficker and Caro associate in California nicknamed "el cachas" and even remembered his telephone number. The DEA agents in Mexico made sure this information reached their brother agents in the States. DEA in Costa Rica learned that a man named Jesus Felix-Gutierrez had purchased Rafael Caro's finca. They turned out to be one in the same. Jesus Diaz De Leon aka Jesus Felix-Gutierrez was finally located in California and arrested. DEA had a strong case against him and he pled guilty to narcotic trafficking.

One of the Jalisco State Police officers arrested by Ventura's group in their sweep of Guadalajara's police forces was a man named Raul Lopez-Alvarez. Lopez-Alvarez was allegedly charged with drug violations but didn't spend too much time in Mexican jails before being released. He eventually found his way to California and started bragging about his role in the abduction and murder of Enrique Camarena and offering his services as an assassin. An informant introduced him to a DEA undercover agent who convinced Lopez that he was looking for a hit man. During the lengthy undercover conversations, Lopez told a convincing, and gruesome, story of the torture and murder of the DEA agent. The negotiations were halted and Lopez was arrested for his part in the murder for hire sting.

Barely audible, on one of the interrogation tapes Kiki murmured the name "Verdugo" and he told the interrogators that was the name of man in Mexicali who was smuggling marijuana into the United States. One of the Sanchez brothers stated that he had given a ride to a man he knew as Rene Verdugo when he left the house at 881 Lope de Vega on February 8, 1985. He had carried Verdugo and a Comandante Nieblas to the Hyatt Regency hotel. Hotel records indicated that Verdugo had registered into the hotel on February 7 and checked out on February 9. One of the calls from the house at 881 Lope de Vega on February 8 had been to a real estate company in San Luis Rio Colorado belonging to Rene Verdugo. Deputy U.S. marshals put together a plan to have Rene Verdugo answer to charges in the United States. Mexican police officers were convinced, for some monetary consideration, to help him on his way. He was picked up near the Sea of Cortez and driven to the border quickly, then shoved, unceremoniously, through a hole in the fence and into the waiting arms of the U.S. Border Patrol. Verdugo was taken into custody and charged with narcotics trafficking.

James Kuykendall

A federal grand jury indicted Raul Lopez-Alvarez, Jesus Felix-Gutierrez and Rene Martin Verdugo-Urquidez for implication in the murder of DEA agent Enrique Camarena. A sensational, and lengthy, trial was held in Los Angeles, California. The jury sat stone-faced as the clerk of court read the guilty verdicts to the courtroom. The judge came prepared and passed sentence in the same session.

Rene Verdugo received 240 years to serve, along with life in prison. Raul Lopez, who had recanted his claim to having been present during the interrogation and murder of Kiki, received 240 years and life in prison. Jesus Felix was convicted of complicity for his role in aiding Rafael Caro to escape from Mexico and received 10 years in prison, to be served consecutive to the 15 years he had already received from his narcotics conviction.

Mexican citizen Jose Ruben Zuno-Arce was stopped when he entered the United States by commercial airline from Mexico at the airport in San Antonio, Texas, where he had maintained a residence since 1978 when he fled Mexico after killing, or assisting his chauffeur to kill, two Mexican Federal Judicial Police officers. Ruben Zuno was the son of an ex-governor of Jalisco and the brother-in-law of an ex-president of Mexico but, apparently, his family's influence wasn't strong enough to prevent revenge from being visited upon him so he bought a house in San Antonio and lived there, returning to Mexico occasionally but almost always to the small town of Mascota, Jalisco, where he felt more secure. It seems he was prone to violence and, being one of the younger members of the Zuno family, probably lorded his position and wealth over others while growing up and never displayed any humility.

The inspector at the airport in San Antonio, because of increased efficiency of the computer system, more access to either Customs or DEA files, or perhaps just zealousness, learned that Ruben Zuno was in government data banks as a suspect in the 1985 kidnapping of Kiki Camarena so he advised his superior who detained Zuno for a period while he contacted people trying to find the specific details. Zuno had entered the

United States at San Antonio dozens of times, his name had been duly entered into the computers many times and this had never occurred before.

The word reached "Operation Leyenda", now based in Los Angeles. The agents in the group had never heard of Ruben Zuno but they looked in DEA's computer system, found some references to the fact that he was a suspect, in 1985, in the kidnapping and told the immigration in San Antonio to arrest him and hold him as a material witness while they gathered the material necessary to charge him. A warrant was issued and he was transferred to Los Angeles.

Another grand jury indictment was obtained, charging four more men with complicity in the crime. The second trial was set against Jose Ruben Zuno, the Honduran trafficker Juan Matta, an ex-Mexican police officer named Juan Jose Bernabe-Ramirez and a reputed killer named Javier Vasquez-Velasco. Bernabe had been among the group of thugs arrested by Mexican police in Puerto Vallarta along with Ernesto Fonseca and Vasquez was one of three brothers who made their living killing people for the traffickers.

As each group of collaborators of the United States Government helped to bring one of the Leyenda targets into the hands of the U.S. system of Justice, they also became fugitives, in Mexico.

In Mexico these men, and a few women, were regarded as kidnappers by their government because the men they had abducted or caused to be spirited to the United States were not charged with any crime in Mexico which would not have extradited them in any case. Mexican policy and law had precluded that possibility, frowning on the extradition of Mexican citizens with the promise of prosecuting the violator in Mexico for offenses committed extra-territorially, a promise seldom kept.

When Rene Verdugo-Martin was pushed through the fence near Calexico, the Mexican officers doing the pushing, and those who had helped push him into the car earlier, climbed through the hole in the fence also and requested asylum in the U.S. Their families, both close and extended, joined them soon afterward. And many other Mexican citizens who provided information to the U.S. government or testified in one of the trials were granted limited residency in the country, usually joined in time by family members. A few of the parolees worked as informants and some found gainful employment.

Juan Ramon Mata-Ballesteros was a Honduran citizen, not a country with a U.S. border and the people who picked him up and expelled him were Honduran military, their actions sanctioned by that government. Therefore no one needed fear prosecution in Honduras for his return to the United States.

A DEA agent named Victor Cortez was picked up by Jalisco State Police in Guadalajara in August of 1986 and brutally tortured. The prompt actions of an honest citizen of that city and the equally prompt response by the agent-in-charge, kept him alive. He was quickly moved to the United States to recuperate while the two governments traded accusations. The state police officers had picked up Cortez in the company of a man named Antonio Garate-Bustamante. Garate-Bustamante had been a police officer in Guadalajara and had put his expertise in electronics to work for the major traffickers, helping them by conducting illegal wiretaps and installing communications systems. Garate used this knowledge to help DEA and the MFJP make some impressive cocaine seizures after he turned against his old friends and became an informant. Garate was relocated also, to prevent retaliation. Among Garate's old friends were to be found some of the most unsavory characters in Guadalajara. To insure that DEA not grow tired of his presence, he began to recruit some of them to help out in the Leyenda investigation.

Reaching back into his past, he brought up some men who had been Jalisco police officers, working for him. One of these men was Hector Cervantes-Santos. Cervantes-Santos swore that he had worked for the student activist turned attorney turned trafficker, Javier Barba, on his farm just outside of Guadalajara, as some kind of handyman or butler, a job that allowed him to listen in on all the important meetings Javier Barba held with the major traffickers and corrupt Mexican officials. The list of officials attending the alleged meetings staggers the imagination. Cervantes stated that the Minister of Defense, Juan Arevalo-Gardoqui, was in attendance as well as the Secretary of Government, Manuel Bartlett-Diaz. According to Cervantes the main topic of the meetings he overheard was the kidnapping of a DEA agent. The meetings allegedly took place in the fall of 1984. Two other attendees at the meetings were Juan Matta and Jose Ruben Zuno. Hector Cervantes became the government's star witness at the second trial and his testimony was what really sank Ruben Zuno. Basically this was the government's case against Zuno, that and the fact that he had once owned the house where the torture and interrogations allegedly took place, a difficult thing to prove since there was supportive evidence that he really had sold the house a month before the kidnapping, as he claimed.

Even as the second trial was in process, another suspect in DEA's crosshairs was being reeled in.

Not everyone that Garate summoned would testify, some had such nefarious reputations they were totally unreliable but they had friends that could help. A woman named Ester Camberos was welcomed into the fold. The same "La Comanche" who controlled almost all of the houses of prostitution in Guadalajara, who had employed murderers and traffickers as security in her clubs, was allowed to live in the U.S. if she could provide information about some of her former associates.

Someone thought the scenario was reminiscent of a movie about a group of mercenaries sent to rescue an African civil rights activist imprisoned by rivals, so the operation was informally called "Operation Wild Goose", after a Richard Burton movie of the same name. But this was not a rescue and the man to be brought out was not much on civil rights.

James Kuykendall

As early as 1986 DEA investigators were aware that a Guadalajara doctor, Humberto Alvarez-Machain, had been at the house on Lope de Vega on February 7th and 8th of 1985. But Guadalajara is a long way from the U.S. border. Some of Garate's associates thought they could spirit the Guadalajara gynecologist to the United States. It's confidence bolstered by the successful convictions of four people charged in the conspiracy to kidnap agent Camarena and the favorable publicity, DEA gave the go ahead and offered a substantial reward for the successful completion of the objective, bringing Humberto Alvarez to the U.S. side of the international border.

One of the girls who had worked for Ester Camberos, "La Comanche", made an appointment to be seen by the rotund gynecologist in his office, even though the appointment was outside of regular business hours. Perhaps the good doctor expected an unorthodox method of payment for his services! When she gained admittance to the high-rise office, she let the men in, they were all large and armed and their leader was a former police officer. They quickly subdued Alvarez-Machain, he didn't resist much, rushed him downstairs and into a waiting vehicle. A fast drive to the neighboring state of Guanajuato, where a rented Lear Jet was waiting at the airport, followed. The pilot didn't realize he was transporting a prisoner and flew the craft toward Juarez, Chihuahua. Just before arriving he was told to change his destination and land in El Paso, Texas. The frightened pilot protested, stating that he did not have clearance to land in the United States and must stop in Juarez first, to clear Mexican customs. One of his passengers, brandishing a firearm, told him the clearance was already arranged in El Paso and instructed him to contact the tower in El Paso to confirm this. A radio check with the airport authorities in El Paso confirmed that someone was waiting for his aircraft and the pilot, convinced it was the thing to do by his passengers, crossed the international boundary and landed his plane at the El Paso International Airport on April 2, 1990.

Further surprises awaited him. The group of men on the aircraft were met by another group of men, among them an old associate of

¿O Plata O Plomo?

Humberto Alvarez-Machain, from the good old days when the traffickers ruled the roost in Guadalajara. Antonio Garate, once the confidante and close associate of Ernesto Fonseca, approached Alvarez and welcomed him into the fold. Alvarez told the agents that he was glad, at last, to be able to get the weight of his participation in the kidnapping of the American agent off his conscience.

After consulting with an attorney, he changed his story, saying he had merely accompanied Guillermo Sanchez to the house on Lope de Vega and never saw Kiki, but he gave the name of another doctor in Guadalajara and said that medical person had been the one who might have ministered to the injuries of Kiki and, it is assumed, Capitan Zavala and whoever else might have been imprisoned with them.

The routine processing of the Guadalajara doctor included taking his fingerprints and submitting them to the FBI for comparison and archiving. But his fingerprints received more than routine attention from the agency once they arrived. Comparisons were made with all the prints and partial prints that had been lifted during the technician's visits to the sites and vehicles that had surfaced in the Guadalajara investigation and a couple of those prints proved a positive match. The plastic cleaner's bag which had been deposited into the FBI agent's evidence sack while he scoured the house at 881 Lope de Vega in 1985 had been processed for latent fingerprints and fingerprints were found which matched those of Humberto Alvarez.

The U.S. lawyers defending the doctor railed at the government's actions in kidnapping and bringing him before the courts to answer for his alleged role in the sordid events and demanded he be returned to his comfortable home in Mexico. The U.S. government's position was that he had given medications to Kiki to keep him alive for his interrogators. Alvarez-Machain got assistance for his plight from an unexpected source. The president of Mexico, Carlos Salinas de Gortari, went through the ceiling, denouncing the United States and issuing an edict that anyone helping to kidnap a Mexican citizen and spirit that citizen to a foreign country would be considered a traitor and tried for treason. According to Mexican newspaper accounts, he also suggested that Mexico might want to reconsider the benefits of joining the North American Free Trade Agreement.

The federal judge in Los Angeles decided the U.S. government had overstepped itself in arranging the kidnapping of the doctor and his subsequent involuntary travel to the northern side of the border and ordered him released because it violated the terms of an extradition treaty between Mexico and the United States. The United States Attorney's office appealed the decision to the Ninth Circuit Court of Appeals. The Ninth Circuit sided with the judge and an emergency appeal was made to the ultimate authority, the Supreme Court of the United States. As fate would have it, the United States Government had recently invaded Panama to deal with a dictator who defied the President of the United States by refusing to abdicate and leave Panama. Manuel Noriega had been detained in Panama and flown to Florida, involuntarily, to face charges of aiding the drug traffic. The court confirmed its previous ruling that the manner in which an individual is brought before a court does not deny the court it's right to try that individual for a crime, if the court has the authority to hear evidence in that crime.

Before most of the legal wrangling over Alvarez's abduction ended, the Jury in the case against Matta, Zuno, Bernabe and Vasquez made its statement. The four men were convicted of the multiple charges brought against them. Federal District Judge Edward Rafeedie continued his practice of lengthy sentencing as seen in the first trial while showing respect for Juan Matta-Ballesteros' reputation as a successful escapee. The multi-millionaire drug trafficker was remanded to the maximum-security prison in Marion, Indiana to serve out his life, several times over.

Ruben Zuno's lawyers contended that a reversible error had been made by one of the assistant U.S. attorneys during his closing arguments, an inappropriate comment about their client. The appeals court agreed and granted a new trial, a trial that would include the recently arrived Guadalajara gynecologist. The government prepared its case against Humberto Alvarez-Machain and Jose Ruben Zuno-Arce.

Opening arguments, evidence, testimony, and the trial was proceeding along as planned, with the heinous details of the kidnapping and murders obviously swaying the jurors, just as had happened in the first two trials.

The star witness in the second trial, Hector Cervantes-Santos, would not testify. His character was so shaky and his motive so financially transparent that he had lost the confidence of the government's attorneys. Two new miscreants from the Guadalajara underworld surfaced as witnesses for the prosecution, testifying that they also had been witness to the meetings at Javier Barba's finca. The government had the fingerprint expert and an unwavering witness to prove Alvarez-Machain had been at the house on Lope de Vega. The prosecution felt that a guilty verdict was almost assured.

The judge surprised everyone by stopping the trial, declaring the government's case against the doctor was based on hunches and the wildest speculation and acquitted the defendant, directing the government to return him to Mexico, immediately. The world's fastest deportation took place with Alvarez-Machain being placed on a flight to Guadalajara before an appeal could be made. His arrival in Guadalajara was greeted with wild enthusiasm by many Mexicans who were elated that he had beaten the gringos.

Three days later, Mexican President Carlos Salinas de Gortari, U.S. President George H W Bush, and Canadian Prime Minister Brian Mulroney individually signed the first documents needed to initiate the North American Free Trade Agreement.

Jose Zuno was still on trial and the U.S. Attorney's office pursued its prosecution against the remaining defendant. The jury quickly convicted the brother-in-law of former Mexican President Luis Echevarria and the judge slapped him with two life sentences and twenty years.

Not everyone from that tragic era fared badly, Enrique Alvarez del Castillo, the governor of Jalisco who failed to return Consul General Morefield's calls, became the Mexican Attorney General, perhaps to reward him for stonewalling things as long as he could. Colonel Pablo Aleman-Diaz, the head of the Jalisco anti-riot police, who was the first person in the government to possess the interrogation tapes, became the director of the MFJP, perhaps to reward him for his cautious handling of the interrogation recordings.

Credibility is always a problem when dealing with someone who has spent his life on the wrong side of the law. Criminals are accomplished liars, along with other unique character traits peculiar to them. Some of the witnesses recruited to testify in the trials in Los Angeles were criminals, or ex-criminals.

Some of them had a big problem with the truth.

Two other informants claimed they had pertinent information concerning the fate of the four missing Jehovah's witnesses, the young people who disappeared in December of 1984 in Guadalajara. Before that information would be made available however, the two men must be awarded immunity against prosecution for their participation in the disappearances. The Leyenda group really wanted to sink Zuno-Arce and Alvarez-Machain and to be credited with clearing up the case of the four missing Americans. This took care of all that with one fell swoop.

The two men got their promise of immunity, and then proceeded to state they had been present when the four missionaries were kidnapped, tortured and murdered. No matter that their stories were full of holes, there was no one to dispute them.

The testimony of the two men was never used in court however, as the judge ruled that he would allow no evidence or testimony concerning any crime other than the murder of DEA agent Enrique Camarena to be introduced during the trial of Jose Ruben Zuno-Arce and Humberto Alvarez-Machain. The two recent recruits got their immunity and didn't have to face the grueling cross-examination of the defense lawyers. And they didn't get to present their controversial testimony to the jury.

But what to do with these two dudes? They were on the government payroll and their very presence in the United States had proved embarrassing, they must be made to produce something. One allegedly stated that he knew where the four people were buried, in Primavera Park, just outside Guadalajara!

Once again the families of the missing couples were forced to contemplate their government's actions as the search for the bodies of the missing Americans took place in the fall of 1993.

Armed with the directions provided by the witness in the United States, now reluctant to return to his homeland, DEA and MFJP agents watched as backhoe operators dug holes in the wilderness area named Primavera Park, the same park where the bodies of John Walker and Albert Radelat had been disinterred.

After 10 days of digging, the pressure on DEA was pretty intense. The operation was stopped and evaluated. Some hard words were spoken to a man in California. Perhaps he was threatened with deportation or expulsion. No matter, CYA was in order so the so-called witness was flown to Guadalajara with promises by the Mexican authorities that he wouldn't be molested and the digging resumed, now with the witness on site.

The digging didn't continue too long this time. It was obvious the man had no idea where to look. It had been too long, things had changed, he just couldn't remember!

He was returned to the U.S., to enjoy his work permit and his immunity. The families of the Mascarena and Carlson couples had to endure one more tragic episode in the black comedy the U.S. officials had subjected them to.

James Kuykendall

Two American citizen couples, missing now for almost twenty-one years, the only clues those furnished by the residents of that quiet street in Guadalajara. More than one hundred narcotics traffickers, corrupt police officers and their associates were picked up and tortured without mercy, without even a hint of where to begin to look for their bodies. When Dennis Carlson's father tried to investigate, he was treated with distain by the Mexican authorities and sent to talk to the DFS, which should have had no authority in the matter. If the Mexican military was involved, the MFJP lacked the clout to pursue an investigation, even if inclined to do so. Suggestions that the retired general be interviewed were turned down as ludicrous. The military is all but untouchable in Mexico.

An ex-MFJP agent needed some money and had some information to sell; he surfaced in Tijuana and San Diego, offering to tell what everyone already knew, the names of the major Mexican drug traffickers and their associates. He found a U.S. government agency eager to listen to him, even though his information was very dated. DEA learned of his presence and pushed for access. The other agency balked, only relenting when DEA agreed to its conditions. The would-be informant was hooked up to a polygraph machine and asked a series of questions. Juan Gilberto Hernandez failed the polygraph examination in the most visible manner possible. He suffered a partial stroke caused by the stress.

Since Juan Gilberto had been a frequent visitor to the Guadalajara DEA offIce, he knew Kiki well enough to have been allowed to take his picture and he had every opportunity to give the picture to Miguel Felix, since he lived in his hotel. DEA agent Joe Gonzalez had already quizzed Juan Gilberto and he helped me get a chance to do the same. I was anxious to talk to this double or triple agent because there had always been the big question as to why the traffickers took Kiki. It was illogical that they would have picked him up just because he was a DEA agent.

Juan Gilberto confirmed that he had been involved in the drug traffic while he was in Guadalajara working as a MFJP agent. He said he had some marijuana cultivations and one of those fields had been seized because of Kiki's actions. He also said that another MFJP agent, a group supervisor, had told Miguel Felix that Kiki was taking money as a payoff. Juan Gilberto adamantly stated that he had never told anyone that Kiki was taking money. He also said he had not taken the photo that was found in Miguel Felix's home but he did admit that he knew both Miguel Felix and Rafael Caro very well and had spoken to both of them after the kidnapping and murder but they did not discuss those events. He said that he had lost his job with the MFJP after he was no longer able to pay his supervisor, Comandante Nicolas Flores-Almazan, mordida for the employment because of the loss of his marijuana plantations and a great amount of money he had in the bank in Guadalajara, which was seized by Mexican officials. During the interview I had with him he was noticeably nervous. An arrest warrant was eventually secured for him but he mysteriously crossed into Tijuana in a taxi just hours before the DEA agents attempted to serve it. He was never seen again.

    Kiki's kidnapping angered many U.S. law enforcement agents and they intensified their efforts against the Mexican traffickers and corrupt Mexican police officers. If they couldn't cross the border to arrest them, they could, at least, find and seize some of the millions of dollars deposited in U.S. banks as a result of their illegal activities.

    In March of 1985, U.S. Customs Investigators in San Isidro, California began an investigation into the activities of Ramiro Mireles-Felix and his brother, Pedro. Ramiro, of course, was the owner of the "Rancho El Caminero" in Zacatecas which we had raided along with Comandante Aldana and his men and where the marijuana was discovered in the undercover silo. Pedro Mireles and another man had deposited $400,000 into an account in a San Isidro bank, then had the money wired to the account of another trafficker named Raul Guzman in San Antonio, Texas. When Pedro Mireles attempted to return to Mexico that same day, he was stopped and arrested after failing to declare an additional $300,000 that he was transporting in the car he was driving. A safe deposit box at the bank, rented in his name, was subsequently searched and another $162,000 was encountered. U.S. Customs seized the $300,000 that Pedro had in his possession and the money found in the bank. The information concerning the money wired to San Antonio was furnished to customs agents in that city, who located the account and froze the funds that were in it, which totaled $426,000. The investigation in San Antonio revealed that Raul Guzman also owned a home in San Antonio, which was utilized by his wife and children several times during shopping trips. A little more digging led the agents to discover that Guzman had purchased an airplane in Laredo, Texas, so the agents seized that too.

Subsequent interviews with people associated with these traffickers revealed that Pedro Mireles had exchanged more than two million dollars in U.S. currency in Tijuana between January and March of 1985. The manager of the money exchange said he had been doing business with Pedro since August of 1984 but record keeping was not legally required and he did not remember how much money he had exchanged during that time.

Not to be outdone, DEA agents in Monterrey, Mexico, and McAllen, Texas, found and seized more than $4,700,000 from bank accounts in the name of ex- Mexican Federal Judicial Police Comandante Rodolfo Moises-Calvo, named by Rafael Caro-Quintero as a protector of his marijuana cultivations.

A Mexico City attorney named Francisco Alatorre was relieved of his ill-gotten gains by DEA agents in San Diego, California. Alatorre was visiting Rafael Caro-Quintero while he was imprisoned in Mexico City and was employed by Caro as a business administrator during his imprisonment. Information developed by the agents indicated that Alatorre could not have amassed a great amount of money legitimately but he had purchased two expensive residences and had deposited a large amount of money in several U.S. banks. They also had information that some of the money would be used to bribe judges in Mexico to suppress, or find illegal, some of the evidence used against Rafael Caro and Ernesto Fonseca in the Mexican government's case against them. The DEA agents seized more than one and a half million dollars from bank accounts and over $300,000 in a bank safe deposit box. Inside the bank deposit box they found a .45 caliber semi-automatic pistol with a diamond embedded gold handle. The pistol was engraved "R 1", which had been Rafael Caro's call sign on his radio network in Guadalajara. Its value was estimated at $10,000. Mr. Alatorre also lost his expensive Chula Vista house as well as a condominium in Villa Serena. It was revealed during the investigation that a Mexican Supreme Court Justice, Luis Fernandez-Doblado, had visited with Francisco Alatorre in Southern California. The noted jurist claimed he had done nothing wrong and the Mexican government again accused the United States of meddling in its internal affairs.

As the U.S. agents delved into the affairs of the traffickers they learned that Rafael Caro's two teenage sisters had attended a Catholic high school in Tucson, Arizona. The girls had been taken out of the school in March of 1985. With the girls gone, there was not much reason to look into the matter of their student visas.

He faced off murderous drug traffickers armed with automatic weapons. He was privy to the Mexican government's darkest secrets. Under government orders, he had helped eliminate political dissenters. He became immensely wealthy while earning a meager salary as a federal police officer. Known as much for his loyalty to the government as for his ruthlessness and cruelty, First Comandante Florentino Ventura seemed an unlikely candidate for a suicidal conscience. But, after a night on the town, boozing and snorting cocaine, the fearless Mexican officer reportedly shot his mistress and then her girlfriend before turning his pistol on himself. But he did not shoot the girlfriend's companion, who had accompanied them on their night of revelry. The companion, who had spent several years in prison for kidnapping a wealthy Mexican industrialist, said Ventura apparently was depressed over a fight with his girlfriend and the cocaine heightened the anxiety, causing him to commit the murders and suicide. Since there was an eyewitness to the crimes, the investigation was over almost before it began.

In the wee hours of the morning on August 9, 2013, Rafael Caro walked out of a Mexican prison after 28 years of incarceration. A tribunal, meeting in secrecy, ruled that he had been incorrectly imprisoned by a federal court for a state crime, that of murder, and that the time he had already served satisfied the required sentence for his past drug crimes. He disappeared into the mountains of Sinaloa. The US government cried foul and filed a formal protest and petition for extradition with the Mexican government. A warrant for his arrest was issued in answer to the extradition request. If he is ever re-arrested, a legal battle will decide his fate.

On July 28, 2016, Ernesto Fonseca was released from Puente Grande prison after serving 31 years for drug crimes and his involvement in Kiki's kidnapping and murder. He will allegedly remain under house arrest for the remaining 9 years of his sentence. A federal judge ordered the release due to "Don Neto's" advanced age and medical issues. His new residence will be in a gated subdivision of luxury homes with values in excess of five hundred thousand dollars US.

Miguel Felix was picked up by military officials in 1988, along with one of his nephews. The nephew was tortured to death, either to extract information or to demonstrate to Miguel what could happen to him if he didn't cooperate. He was released after reaching an agreement with the arresting officials. DEA didn't know about the "arrest" until after he was released. In April of 1989, the four month old, Mexican government of Carlos Salinas made a big splash in the press when they announced the arrest of Miguel Angel Felix Gallardo in Guadalajara. He was subsequently given the same 40 year sentence for his part in the murder and related crimes.

I had taken a photo of Kiki in the marijuana fields in San Luis Potosi in 1982. Kiki had it made into a poster, which he placed on the wall in his tiny cubicle of an office. When everything was over it was taken down and framed, along with a bronze plaque, it was all we had left. We asked Mr. Morefield if he would consider hanging it in the consulate. It was an unnecessary question. For several years, that large photo of Enrique Camarena greeted everyone who visited the second floor of the U.S. Consulate in Guadalajara. Pete Hernandez put the inscription on the plaque to his "compadre".

"Por tus pasos nadie caminara" (No one will walk in your footsteps.) It has been more than thirty years and, so far, Pete's been right.

James Kuykendall

INDEX

Aceves-Fernandez, Carlos, 31,41-43,57,78
Acuña, Daniel, 82,83,269
Aguilar-Guajardo, Rafael 159-161,213,269,272
Aguirre, Braulio, 270
Alatorre, Francisco, 295,296
Alba-Leyva, Samuel, 197,198,237
Alcaraz-Ascencio, Antonio, 31,32,41,77,270
Aldana-Ibarra, Miguel, 15,116,161,225-232,294
Aleman-Diaz, Pablo, 13,133,291
Alfaro-Margarina, Mardoqueo, 70,256,-258
Alvarez-Machain, Humberto, 147,162,194,195,287,288,290-292
Alvarez Del Castillo, Enrique, 40,180,291
Alvarez, "El Chango", 181
Alvarez, Jose Refugio, 181
Alvin, Albert J., 68,84
Arteaga, Alberto, 41,42,50,57,119,128
Arrellano-Felix brothers, 82
Arrevalo de Gardoqui, Juan, 15,271
Arroyo, Ralph, 140,143,144
Aviles-Perez, Pedro, 23,30
Ayala, Tony, 72,73,77,98,99
Bachelier, Alan, 40,41,43,45,55,67,98,108,117,267
Bannister, Joan, 186
Barba-Hernandez, Javier, 15,146,181,246-249,272,281,285,286
Bartlett-Diaz, Manuel, 286
Bazan-Padilla, Jose Albino, 121,125-127
Behn-Fregoso, Carlos, 242
Beltran-Alvarez, Jose Luis, 121,143
Bentsen, Lloyd, 180

Bernabe-Ramirez, Jose, 284,289
Bernal, Cesar, 238
Bravo-Cervantes, Manuel, 97,98,101,102
Bravo-Segura, Hugo 99
Bravo-Segura, Manuel, 99
Bravo-Segura, Rigoberto, 101
Briseño, Nicolas, 213
Brito, Juan Antonio, 5,17,153,157-166,185,213
Brown, John, 59
Brusolo, Silvio, 58,118,119,140-144
Burnet, David, 197,237
Bush, George H. W., 290
Camarena, Enrique Kiki",11,12,13,14,16,19,37,39,40,52,53,60,63,64,68,72-74,91,92,97,100,104,108,109,110,112,115,126,134,139,140,143,145,153,156,158,163,165,167,171,174,175,181,209,241,248,258,267,281-283,287,291,298
Camberos-Gomez, Maria Ester "La Comanche", 32,33,286,287
Camberos, Adan, 116
Camberos, Jesus, 150
"Camelot" Restaurant, 38,52,54,55
Campero-Villanueva, Juan Carlos, 122
Cardenas, Cuauhtemoc, 100
Carlson, Dennis, 167,168,164,292,293
Carlson, Rose, 167,168
Carlson, Norman, 170,174
Casillas-Zavala, Luis Ernesto, 74
Castel Del Oro, Federico, 159,269,270
Castillo, Bobby, 104,123,165,181,
Castillo-Beas, Julio Cesar74
Castro, Fidel, 145
Castro-Prada, Juan Manuel, 163,273

Carrasco, Fred, 23

Carlos-Ochoa, Jose Maria, 78

Caro-Lerma, Rafael "El Charel", 235

Caro-Quintero, Rafael "Rafa", 15,55,62,71,75,114,120,122,123,125,132,134-136,139,143,148,157,160,161,164,165,178,181,186,209,211,216,217,229,-235,237,239,238,239,240,241,242,244,246,248,263,271,272,281,283,294-296

Castaños, Carlos Manuel, 48,49

Cepeda-Arrellano, Ramon, 144

Cervantes-Santos, Hector, 285,285,290

"Champion", 159

Chao-Lopez, Rafael, 82,83,269,272

Chavez, Manuel, 209-213,214-216,218-224,226-229,231

Coonce, Bill, 11-14

Contreras-Subias, Jose Leonardo, 122,130,131

Corona-Santander, Leticia, 67-69,262

Cosio-Martinez, Sara, 75,120-123,244

Cortez, Samuel, 247-249

Cortez, Victor, 285

Cueva-Cerpa, Mario Alberto, 57,197,198,201,225,229

Devere, Hugo, 260,263,264

Donalson, Henry, 68,69,74

Drummond, John, 262

De La Madrid, Miguel, 220

Del Valle-Lopez, Eduardo Fabian, 85-87,94

Diaz-De Leon, Jesus "El Cachas" 125,126,281

Echeverria, Luis, 24,28,31,144,145

"El Mareño Ranch", 98,100,101,184

España de Walls-Sanchez, Martha, 72

Esparragosa-Moreno, Juan "El Azul", 15,77,186,190,229

Espindola, Manuel, 191-193,246,247,258
Elenes-Payan, Jose "Kennor", 148,161,165
Elenes de Fonseca, Doris, 162
Esquivel, Juan Manuel, 102
Estrella, Alberto, 159
Estrada, Violeta, 122
Fabela-Escobosa, Jorge, 253,254
Felix-Gallardo, Miguel, 15,16,30,42,58,59,63,67,69,70,71,72,7374,78,79,-82,94,120,235,246,1498,154,160,180,181,186,191,214,228,229,236,251,253-256,258-265,270,278,281,283,293,294,297
Fernandez, Abelardo, 249
Fernandez, Sylvia, 240
Fernandez, Eduardo "Lalo" "El Profesor", 240
Fernandez-Doblado, Luis, 296
Figueroa, Eduardo Alfonso, 105
Flores-Almazan, Nicolas, 294
Fonseca, Gilberto, 240
Fonseca, Cesar "El Cheshire", 117,118,220,255,256,281
Fonseca-Carrillo, Rafael Ernesto "Don Neto", 8,13,29,30,41,69,74,76,78,-82,117,118,119,120,127,132,134,135,139,146,147,153,163,181,186,191,215,235,236,240,255,259,272,281,284,288,296,297
Fonseca-Solares, Juan Antonio "El Doc", 161
Fonseca, Tomas, 117
Gallo-Ortega, Luis Rodolfo Dr., 109
Garate-Bustamante, Antonio, 285-287
Garcia, Fernando, 95,262
Garcia, Sergio, 13
Garcia-Garcia, Manuel, 74
Garcia-Madrid, David, 272
Garcia-Torres, Licenciado, 229,230
Garcia, Juan "C.I.Juan", 15,156,209-213,216-218,220-224

¿O Plata O Plomo?

Gastelum-Ruiz, Sotero, 74
Gavin, John, 90, 114,180,276,277
Gerenger, 167,168
Gomez-Barajas, Juvenal, 30
Gomez-España, Jorge, 147, 148
Gonzalez, Joe, 85,104,165,293
Gonzalez-Aguilar, Enrique, 92
Gonzalez-Gonzalez, Gabriel, 117,177
Grant, Mervin, 70
"Guillen", 97
Gutierrez-Felix, Jesus, 281, see Diaz-de Leon, Jesus
Gutierrez-Martin, Galo, 220,236,232
Guzman, Raul, 294,295
Harper, German, 68,69,256,278
Heath, Edward "Ed",
13,14,40,4,44,45,56,57,62,63,98,104,107,109,110,123,124,128-130,153,156,157,165,181
Hernandez, Bobby, 100
Hernandez, Pete, 192,209,272,298
Hernandez, Saul, 93
Hernandez, Juan Gilberto, 73,,255,293
Hernandez-Ochoa, Juan Francisco, 116,120
Herrera-Perez, Tomas Alejandro Dr., 108
Holquin-Manzano, Esteban, 74
Ibarra-Herrera, Manuel, 41,42,57,58,68,72,90,95,116,244
Izquierdo-Hebrand, Arturo, 149, 253
Jimenez-Lopez, Juan Manuel, 74
Kennedy, William, 93, 271
Knapp, Roger, 12,13,53,126,214,225,233,237,238,239,249,260
Kuykendall, James "Jaime", 76, 258,267

Labra, Jesus, 82
Lawn, John "Jack", 12, 13, 44,115,153,156,1202
"La Primavera Park", 182,184,292
Leon-Keschner, Jorge, 85,122,241,263
Lepes-Montes, Rodolfo, 125,126,281
Levy-Gallardo, Rogelio, 43,51
Locheo, Benjamin, 78,116
Lope de Vega 881, 141-143,146-151,180-182,282,287,288,290
Lopez-Alvarez, Raul, 282,283
Lopez-Portillo, Jose Luis, 30,31
Lopez-Razon, Victor Manuel, 43, 51
Lorrabaquio, 42, 229,230,244
Lotz, Werner, 123
Luna-Vega, Miguel Angel, 121
Lucero, Daniel, 213,224
Mascarena, Ben, 167,168,172,192
Mascarena, Paula, 167
Martinez, Carlos, 181
Martinez-Hernandez, Jose, 144
Mata-Ballesteros, Juan Ramon "Juan Jose", 94,95,96,135,136,137,149-
,193,252,254,259,262,263,285
Maxwell, Kenneth, 132
Medina, Filemon "Chombi", 209,224
Meese, Ed, 240
Mendez, Jaime, 127
Mendoza, Oscar, 46,47
Mera-Cruz, Luis, 170
Miller, Frank, 77
Mireles-Felix, Pedro, 294,295
Mireles-Felix, Ramiro, 160,212,213,214,217,218,222,228,229,294
Moeckler, Bill, 247

Moises-Calvo, Rodolfo, 127,128,295
Monastero, Frank, 44,45
Montoya, Bob, 93
Morefield, Bill, 51
Morefield, Richard, 40,41,42,51,88,291,298
Morlett-Borquez, Tomas, 84,85,87,91,92,93,93,291,298
Mullins, Francis "Bud", 89,95,115
Muñoz-Alcaraz, Octavio, 80,81
Muñoz, Rafael, 77-80
Muñoz-Rios, Rogelio, 60,61,62,159,269
Murillo de Felix, Maria Elvia, 71,72,74
Nazar-Haro, Miguel Angel, 93, 174,175,194,271
Navarro-Rodriguez, Antonio, 103,104
Navidad de Quintero, Irene, 193,194
Nieblas, Arnulfo, 148,282
Nixon, Richard, 24,25,28
Nuncio, Aparicio "Ñoño", 160
Nuñez-Rodriguez, Ramiro, 144
Padilla, Jesus, 126
Pavon-Reyes, Armando, 59,60,61,62,63,68,72,73,76,87,95,97,98,-99,101,104,116
Peña-Quiroz, Saul, 74
Perez-Contreras, Astolfo, 74
Perez-Parra, Antonio, 189-192,196,197,202,231,232,223
Quintero-Payan, Emilio, 76,126,191-194,236,242,247
Quintero-Payan, Juan Jose, 9, 242
Radelat, Albert, 172,177,179,184,185,292
Radelat, Felipe Dr., 173-177,183
Rafeedie, Edward, 289
Ramirez, Jesus, 11,12, 235,237,239,247,248,249

Ramirez-Gil, Jaime, 177
Ramirez-Ortiz, Eduardo, 92
Ramirez-Razo, Samuel, 134,181,249
Rios-Valenzuela, Marco Antonio, 121
Rivera, Julio, 224
Rizzivuto, Tony, 186
Rocha, Colonel, 224,226
Rodolfo, "El Feo", 190,231
"Rodriguez", 8,9, 33
Rodriguez, Art, 88
Romero de Velasco, Flavio, 33
Rouselon, Mauricio, 30
Saavedra, Sergio, 57,58,60,61,129,130
Salazar, Jorge, see Salazar-Ortegon, Jose Salazar-Ortegon, see Jose "El Paton", 78,92,133,161,164
Salcido, Manuel "El Cochiloco", 77,80,82 270
Salinas de Gortari, Carlos, 288,290,297
Salgado-Salinas, Luis, 108
"Samuel", "Sammy", 131,181,249, see Ramirez, Samuel
Sam-Lopez, Jesus, 88, 218,219
Sanchez, Fidel, 40
Sanchez, Guillermo "Willie", 141,277
Sanchez, "MIguel", 110,180,188,204,224
Sanchez, Pedro, 62
Sanchez-Barba, Ruben, 144,146,147
Sanchez-Celis, Leopoldo, 78
Sanchez-Duarte, Rodolfo, 78
Santos-Santos, Francisco, 69
Sauceda-Lopez, Martin, 142
Schrock, Nicholas, 277,278
Sears, "Butch", 73,186,204,208,212,2125,228,233

Segura de Bravo, Celia, 101
Shannon, Elaine, 271
Sicilio-Falcon, Alberto, 119
Solana-Macias, Carlos, 171
Soto-Martinez, Eliseo, 133
Spencer, Jerry, 110,111
Tanner, Mac, 276
Tejeda-Jaramillo, Francisco "Paco", 82,83,249,180,181,182
Torres-Sanchez, Luis Alberto, 46-47,48
Trott, Stephen "Steve", 13, 153
Valencia-Baez, Jose Guadalupe, 30, 134
Valencia-Baez, Rosa Ester, 30
Valenzuela-Diaz, Rosario, 79,121,262
Valdez, Francisco, 76
Valdez, Roberto, 73
"Valiente, Luis", 115,243
Valles-Corral, Tomas, 40,41,65,67,68,72,269
Varenhorst, Harvey, 110,225,231
Vasquez, Eliseo, 249
Vasquez, Nancy Marlene, 135
Vasquez-Velasco, Javier, 284,289
Vega de Torres, Maricela, 45,46,49
Velasco-Trigueros, Rafael Ruiz, 133,284
Velasquez, Alfonso, 101,102
Ventura, Florentino, 114,115,116,119,123,124,125,126,127,128,-139,169,175,176,181,182,183,281,282,296
Verdugo-Orquidez, Rene Martin, 30,148,149,243,282,283,284
Vielma-Heras, Miguel Angel "El Negro", 159,160,161,217,218,220,221,281
Villanueva-Moreno, Gilberto, 51,87
Von Raab, William, 90

Walker, Eve, 174
Walker, John, 172-177,179,183-185
Wallace, Victor "Shaggy", 7,37,40,42,53,54,55,64,100,109,244,260,267
Wallace, Yolanda, 40,67
Walls-Palencia, Miguel, 74,264
Wayne-Collins, William, 83,84
White, Walter, 11,12,16,39,40,42,44,95,96,218,220,224,226,228,251
Zavala-Avelar, Alfredo "Capitan", "Capi", 43,44,45,46,47,48,49,63,77,100,-103,104,109,110,111,113,118,120,126,130,143,174,181,185,214,217,227,-248,288
Zorrilla-Perez, Jose Antonio, 271,272
Zuno, Guadalupe, 143
Zuno-Arce, Alvarado, 144
Zuno-Arce, Jose Ruben, 144,145,146,147,182,283,284,286,289,290,,291,292

Printed in Great Britain
by Amazon